The challenges facing emergi[ng market economies resemble]
those confronting the issuers o[f major international currencies, nowhere]
more evident than in Latin America. This volume provides a broad overview of the
principal issues facing the region's monetary authorities, together with detailed consideration of the impact of spillover effects, and an examination of these issues' implications for their policy frameworks. It is an excellent and timely contribution to a highly relevant policy debate.

—**John Lipsky**
Johns Hopkins University School of Advanced International Studies
Former First Deputy Managing Director, International Monetary Fund

Latin American economies have made substantial progress in monetary policy. Independent central banks with a firm handle on inflation and flexible exchange rates were key to successfully weathering the global financial crisis. This book is an excellent contribution toward helping us understand the challenges facing central banks in the new economic landscape, and analyzes prescient issues such as the autonomy of monetary policy in the context of spillovers and the role of macroprudential policies in addressing financial stability challenges. There is a lot to learn from this book.

—**José De Gregorio**
University of Chile
Former President, Central Bank of Chile

Having tamed inflation, Latin American central banks face a new challenge: Whether and how to move on from inflation targeting, without losing their dearly acquired credibility? If you want to know where they stand, on monetary versus macroprudential policy, on the handling of capital flows, etc., you cannot do better than to read this extremely interesting and well-informed book.

—**Olivier Blanchard**
Peterson Institute for International Economics
Former Chief Economic Counsellor, International Monetary Fund

Future monetary historians will divide the history of central banking into before and after the global financial crisis of 2008–09. Before, central banks would quietly steer the monetary ship through low-inflation waters without worrying about much else. After, a perfect storm forced central banks to desperately try to prevent the ship from sinking by resorting to new, untested, and controversial monetary navigation methods. Did they go too far? Did the new "unconventional" instruments work? Was hard-earned autonomy lost in the process? This fascinating volume offers a first look at these critical issues through the lenses of five major Latin American central banks. After reading this book, it is hard to escape the feeling that perhaps a century of trials and tribulations in the region has helped central bankers to navigate these uncharted waters with more aplomb, ingenuity, and resourcefulness than many of our neighbors to the north. In this new era, learning has become a two-way street.

—**Carlos A. Végh**
Fred H. Sanderson Professor of International Economics
Johns Hopkins University

Challenges for Central Banking
Perspectives from Latin America

Editors
Yan Carrière-Swallow
Hamid Faruqee
Luis Jácome
Krishna Srinivasan

INTERNATIONAL MONETARY FUND

© 2016 International Monetary Fund

Cataloging-in-Publication Data
Joint Bank-Fund Library

Names: Carrière-Swallow, Yan. | Faruqee, Hamid. | Jácome, Luis Ignacio. | Srinivasan, Krishna, 1965- | International Monetary Fund.
Title: Challenges for central banking : perspectives from Latin America / editors: Yan Carrière-Swallow, Hamid Faruqee, Luis Jacome, Krishna Srinivasan.
Description: Washington, DC : International Monetary Fund, 2016. | Includes bibliographical references.
Identifiers: ISBN 9781515391766 (paper)
Subjects: LCSH: Banks and banking, Central – Latin America.
Classification: LCC HG2710.5.A7C46 2016

978-1-51359-176-6 (paper)
978-1-47553-682-9 (PDF)
978-1-47553-681-2 (ePub)
978-1-47553-684-3 (Mobipocket)

The views expressed in this book are those of the authors and do not necessarily represent the views of the IMF, its Executive Board, or IMF management.

Please send orders to
International Monetary Fund, Publication Services
P.O. Box 92780, Washington, DC 20090, U.S.A.
Tel.: (202) 623-7430 Fax: (202) 623-7201
E-mail: publications@imf.org
Internet: www.elibrary.imf.org
www.imfbookstore.org

Table of Contents

Foreword v

Acknowledgments vii

Contributors ix

1   Introduction: Latin America's Central Banking Challenges—Past, Present, and Future 1
    Hamid Faruqee and Krishna Srinivasan

PART I   PROGRESS AND CHALLENGES

2   A Historical Perspective on Central Banking in Latin America 11
    Luis I. Jácome H.

3   Central Banking in Latin America: The Way Forward 41
    Yan Carrière-Swallow, Luis Jácome, Nicolás Magud, and Alejandro Werner

PART II   MONETARY INDEPENDENCE IN AN INTEGRATED WORLD

4   Implications of Global Financial Integration for Monetary Policy in Latin America 83
    Yan Carrière-Swallow and Bertrand Gruss

5   The Impact of the U.S. Term Premium on Emerging Markets 109
    Alberto Naudon and Andrés Yany

6   Forward Guidance and Prudence in Conducting Monetary Policy 131
    Julián Andrés Parra Polanía

PART III   MACROPRUDENTIAL POLICIES AND MONETARY FRAMEWORKS

7   Financial Stability Objectives: Drivers of Gains from Coordinating Monetary and Macroprudential Policies 145
    Jessica Roldán-Peña, Mauricio Torres-Ferro, and Alberto Torres

8   A Brazilian Perspective on Macroprudential and Monetary Policy Interaction 173
    Fabia A. de Carvalho and Marcos R. de Castro

9   De-dollarization of Credit in Peru: The Role of Conditional Reserve Requirements 219
    Paul Castillo, Hugo Vega, Enrique Serrano, and Carlos Burga

Index 251

Foreword

Since the global financial crisis, central banking has been undergoing a massive renovation. The crisis brought to light fundamental challenges for central bankers in terms of our purpose, our instruments, and what we hope to achieve. From the lessons learned, we have made progress in rewriting the central banking handbook, as it were, but that handbook is still a work in progress. Innovations such as quantitative easing, macroprudential policies, and the postcrisis capital framework for banks are still in their infancy, and public debate about the appropriate objectives and role of central banks is ongoing in many parts of the world.

That debate about central banking is no less important for emerging markets, including in Latin America. This is both because there are lessons to be learned from others' experience and because today's world is so interconnected. An overarching theme that connects us in both advanced and emerging market economies alike is that of setting monetary policies in an increasingly financially integrated world and addressing the underlying challenges that this presents.

At the IMF–World Bank Annual Meetings in Lima in October 2015, I had the pleasure of moderating a panel discussion on central banking challenges in Latin America from the perspectives of the central bank governors from five major economies: Brazil, Chile, Colombia, Mexico, and Peru. There was a strong consensus that central bank independence has been a great accomplishment in Latin America that should not be jeopardized. It has helped deliver low and stable inflation after a long history of countries' struggling to achieve price stability and, in some cases, experiencing episodes of hyperinflation. Looking forward, concerns have shifted to the challenges of price stability in a world of globally integrated capital markets. A common theme is the volatility of capital flows and the lack of synchronization of cycles in the United States and many Latin American economies. For some, this poses challenges in terms of the independence of monetary policy.

Some challenges are more specific to Latin America. The region has greater exchange rate flexibility than other emerging market regions, so vulnerability to large exchange rate depreciations associated with negative terms-of-trade shocks is to some degree driving a rise in inflation above that observed in the other emerging market regions. Countries dependent on commodities have also had greater vulnerability to terms-of-trade shocks that then spilled over into balance of payments and fiscal challenges.

This volume is timely and important in many respects. As evident from the discussions in Lima with the five governors, Latin America's central banks have to contend with new challenges in pursuing their policy mandates. They are doing so at a time when many of the traditional paradigms associated with central banking are in flux. The identification of those new challenges suggests a new agenda for research and policymaking, especially in terms of maintaining financial stability and containing international spillovers.

For the inflation-targeting central banks in Latin America, this volume brings together a discussion of core challenges such as monetary autonomy and spillovers with highly integrated financial markets, including issues such as exchange rate pass-through, managing market expectations, and the use of forward guidance.

From a financial stability perspective, how and when to use macroprudential policies and how to best coordinate with a flexible inflation-targeting framework are as much of an issue in Latin America as in the United Kingdom. But there are some differences in the challenges facing central banks in Latin America, such as the role of foreign capital flows with shallower domestic markets and the impact of a high degree of dollarization on their financial systems.

This book also addresses the link between macroprudential and monetary policy—a subject that is much debated in both advanced and emerging market policy circles. Macroprudential policies are increasingly seen as a first line of defense (along with microprudential supervision) to address concerns about financial stability, but experience with these tools is still nascent, and we have not accumulated enough evidence through a credit cycle to make definitive judgments about optimal policy. In that sense, this book makes a contribution to the discussion of a topic on which views are not yet conclusive, and from the distinct perspective of regional policymakers and researchers.

Finally, producing an authoritative volume such as this requires considerable analytical work and coordination (much of it behind the scenes), particularly by the staff of the IMF's Monetary and Capital Markets Department and Western Hemisphere Department. In addition, the joint work between the staffs of the IMF and of the five central banks that contributed to this volume reflects a broader, conscientious effort to build a closer intellectual partnership between the Fund and its members in Latin America—an effort that I observed during my time as a Deputy Managing Director. In a way, this collaboration represents a deeper type of engagement—not one of the IMF giving policy advice, but rather of building a shared understanding of the issues as a stepping stone to developing policy strategies together. It is a good example of the IMF's seeking to become more agile, integrated, and member-focused to better engage and serve its membership in pursuit of its global mandate.

Minouche Shafik
Deputy Governor
Bank of England

Acknowledgments

The editors are grateful to Alejandro Werner and José Viñals for their unwavering support of research on central banking issues in Latin America and of this project in particular. This collaboration would not have been possible without the support of central bank governors Agustín Carstens (Mexico), Ilan Goldfajn and Alexandre Tombini (Brazil), José Darío Uribe (Colombia), Julio Velarde (Peru), and Rodrigo Vergara (Chile). Under their leadership, senior staff members across the various central banks have been able to dedicate valuable time to study the critical questions that make up this volume. Indeed, the governors themselves participated in a seminar on the topic of this book during the 2015 Annual Meetings of the International Monetary Fund in Lima, Peru, which was moderated by Minouche Shafik, Deputy Governor of the Bank of England.

The editors gratefully thank Maria Gutierrez and Andrea Herrera for their dedication and graceful assistance throughout the process; Rocio Arevalo and Modupeh Williams for helping organize the seminar in Lima; and Zohair Alam, Steve Brito, and Genevieve Lindow for excellent research assistance. Michael Harrup, Joanne Johnson, and Patricio Loo of the IMF Communications Department provided invaluable inputs to the editorial process and production of the book.

Contributors

Carlos Burga is an Economist in the Monetary Programming Department of the Central Reserve Bank of Peru.

Yan Carrière-Swallow is an Economist in the Western Hemisphere Department of the International Monetary Fund.

Paul Castillo is Deputy Manager for Monetary Policy at the Central Reserve Bank of Peru.

Fabia Aparecida de Carvalho is an Advisor in the Research Department at the Central Bank of Brazil.

Marcos Ribeiro de Castro is an Advisor in the Research Department at the Central Bank of Brazil.

Hamid Faruqee is a Division Chief in the Western Hemisphere Department of the International Monetary Fund.

Bertrand Gruss is an Economist in the Research Department of the International Monetary Fund.

Luis I. Jácome H. is a Deputy Division Chief in the Monetary and Capital Markets Department of the International Monetary Fund.

Nicolás Magud is a Senior Economist in the Western Hemisphere Department at the International Monetary Fund.

Alberto Naudon is the Chief Economist at the Central Bank of Chile.

Julián Andrés Parra Polanía is a Senior Researcher in the Research Unit of the Central Bank of Colombia.

Jessica Roldán-Peña is Manager of Monetary Research at the Central Bank of Mexico.

Enrique Serrano is a Senior Economist in the Monetary Programming Department at the Central Reserve Bank of Peru.

Krishna Srinavasan is a Deputy Director in the Western Hemisphere Department of the International Monetary Fund.

Alberto Torres is Head of Public Credit at the Ministry of Finance of Mexico. At the time of writing, he was Chief Economist at the Central Bank of Mexico.

Mauricio Torres-Ferro is an Economist in the Research Department of the Central Bank of Mexico.

Hugo Vega is Head of Monetary Programming at the Central Reserve Bank of Peru.

Alejandro Werner is the Director of the Western Hemisphere Department of the International Monetary Fund.

Andrés Yany is a graduate student in the Economics Department at Stanford University. At the time of writing, he was an Economist in the Macroeconomic Analysis Department at the Central Bank of Chile.

CHAPTER 1

Introduction: Latin America's Central Banking Challenges—Past, Present, and Future

Hamid Faruqee and Krishna Srinivasan, International Monetary Fund

In the wake of the 2008–09 global financial crisis, central banking and monetary policy in many corners of the world—mainly, in advanced economies—came under intense pressure and entered unchartered waters. Two overarching aspects encapsulate well the serious challenges that major central banks faced during the crisis and its aftermath.

First, the breadth and scale of central bank operations were modified or expanded in unprecedented and even unimaginable ways given the circumstances. Specifically, unconventional policy measures and communications strategies were vigorously pursued initially to prevent a financial sector meltdown, and subsequently to support economic activity given a disappointing recovery and stubbornly high unemployment.

Second, as lessons from the crisis were being drawn, a fundamental rethinking of central banking and its policy frameworks has been taking place.[1] Notably, this has included the consideration of new objectives and instruments surrounding financial stability. Moreover, the experience with the crisis led some to ask whether the exceptional monetary measures deployed should remain part of the "normal" policy toolkit. Beyond this, there has been a wide-ranging discussion of institutional arrangements and whether central banks should be tasked with regulating and supervising financial institutions—banks and nonbanks—or if such responsibility should be assigned elsewhere.

In response to the crisis, central banks lowered policy rates to essentially zero given the sharp fall in output below trend but stable inflation. Conventional policy space was quickly exhausted in major advanced economies. To support and strengthen a fragile recovery (a burden that largely fell on monetary policy),

---

The authors thank Alejandro Werner, Luis Jácome, and Yan Carrière-Swallow for their help and comments in guiding and coordinating the efforts behind this volume, as well as our central bank colleagues for their important contributions on the key central banking challenges facing the region.

[1] See Blanchard and others (2012) and Akerlof and others (2014) for a discussion.

central banks thus had to improvise and resort to a range of unconventional policies, ranging from quantitative easing to negative interest rates.[2] Many of the measures undertaken were new and their efficacy not well understood, and some blurred the lines between monetary and fiscal policy. This posed longer-term risks (e.g., quasi-fiscal costs) that might ultimately hurt central bank independence. Nevertheless, the risks of policy inaction were perceived to be simply too high. With policy rates near zero, there were unusual challenges in terms of policy communications as well. Several central banks experimented with forward guidance to help shape the market's expectations of future policy accommodation to further stimulate domestic demand given persistent weakness in private spending.

Alongside these policy challenges, the central banking paradigm itself has been reevaluated in the wake of the crisis. Specifically, inflation targeting—relying essentially on one objective and one instrument—came into question. In retrospect, price and output stability were insufficient to ensure financial stability. Many asked if multiple objectives with multiple instruments were needed, albeit with less agreement on which ones constitute the right combinations (Akerlof and others 2014). Four main lines of questioning have emerged:

1. Should policies be more proactive in addressing asset-price developments and safeguarding financial stability (i.e., "lean against the wind")?
2. If so, should the central bank do this (with an expanded mandate) or does the task need to be assigned elsewhere?
3. How should such policies be carried out, and, more specifically, what choice of instruments is most effective?
4. How should macroprudential and monetary policies, given their interactions, be coordinated?[3]

Furthermore, given that exceptional monetary accommodation remains in place globally, concerns persist about moral hazard (i.e., excessive risk-taking), begging the question of how current policies (including interest rates) should be calibrated to mitigate financial stability risks given a still-fragile economic recovery and potential trade-offs between supporting growth and managing risk. Finally, against this backdrop, there have been emerging voices calling for greater coordination and "rules of the game" for monetary policy given international spillovers from the major central banks—notably, through capital flows and exchange rates.

In emerging markets, a fundamental rethinking of central banking, its evolving challenges, and its policy frameworks has received relatively less attention since the global financial crisis. Part of the reason is that these economies were not

---

[2] See, for example, Blanchard and others (2012).

[3] Some have argued that microprudential policies—that is, regulation and oversight of individual financial institutions—may also be pursued too narrowly and should be part of broader coordination efforts with other policies given the existence of systemically important firms, interaction among financial firms, and interactions between the financial and real sectors. See Akerlof and others (2014).

at the epicenter of the crisis that ensued following the collapse of the U.S. investment bank Lehman Brothers in September 2008.[4] Moreover, in Latin America, central banks underwent a successful transformation in the 1990s in transitioning to formal inflation-targeting frameworks and delivering price stability for their economies. The focus has remained on preserving these gains. That said, two fundamental issues strongly suggest that many of the same central banking concerns that have arisen in the context of the global financial crisis are no less important in emerging markets, including in Latin America, requiring some rethinking.

First, *spillovers and interdependence* in monetary policy were evident during the crisis and the subsequent "taper tantrum" episode. This has raised issues about the extent of local monetary autonomy in an increasingly integrated global financial system (Rey critique).[5] Indeed, one can argue that some of the recent monetary policy decisions in Latin America were taken more in response to changing external conditions than domestic exigencies. As mentioned above, some have argued in this context that unintended consequences across borders from unconventional policies in major central banks may exceed their domestic benefits, and that this calls for stronger rules of the game for monetary policy (Rajan critique).[6]

Second, issues on how best to *safeguard financial stability* similarly arise in Latin America given the prevalence of inflation targeting in the region and the importance of domestic and external financial developments. Specifically, Latin America has been striving for larger, deeper, and more inclusive financial systems, which can raise financial stability concerns. At the same time, emerging markets have been coping with volatile capital flows against a backdrop of exceptional monetary accommodation in advanced economies, with risks of boom-bust cycles and financial instability. This has led to rethinking about the appropriate use of capital flow management measures in this policy domain, but more so than in the other areas.[7] For these reasons, more attention is needed in a postcrisis world on managing the evolving policy challenges facing emerging market central banks in key dimensions.

This volume reflects a multilateral effort to help close the gap in our knowledge in meeting these challenges. It provides perspectives on critical challenges confronting central banks in Latin America from major players in the region as

---

[4]In the immediate aftermath of the Lehman event, the U.S. Federal Reserve was at the forefront of policy responses, introducing multiple liquidity facilities (i.e., credit easing) to support dislocated financial markets. Other central banks, including in emerging markets, also faced challenges in the early days of the crisis. For example, dollar swap lines with the Federal Reserve were introduced to address the shortage of dollar liquidity and disruptions in several funding markets.

[5]See Rey (2013).

[6]Rajan and Mishra (2016) question the ability of central banks in advanced economies to effectively boost internal demand at this stage and whether continued stimulus risks doing more harm than good through beggar-thy-neighbor implications. In this context, they argue for needed "rules of the game" across central banks.

[7]See Ostry and others (2011) and Ostry and others (2015).

well as from IMF staff. The project started in the fall of 2014 when IMF staff reached out to chief economists from five major central banks in the region—Brazil, Chile, Colombia, Mexico, and Peru—and invited analytical contributions from their staff for this volume. This culminated with the five governors participating in a seminar on central banking challenges for the region at the IMF–World Bank Annual Meetings in Lima, Peru in October 2015.

ROADMAP

This volume is divided into three sections. The first section provides a panoramic overview of the policy progress made to date and the challenges that lie ahead for central banks in Latin America. Specifically, this section lays down the historical context of how central banking has evolved over the past century in the region and outlines the policy challenges for monetary authorities going forward in a more financially integrated global economy. The related issue of spillovers and monetary independence is taken up more fully in the next section with three chapters by staff from the IMF and from central banks in the region. The final section presents chapters by staff from three central banks that reexamine macroprudential and monetary policies and policy frameworks from their perspective. Key themes from each of these three sections are summarized below.

Past Progress and Future Challenges

To understand the future challenges facing Latin American central banks, one needs to first understand the historical context and policy progress made by these institutions over the years. How did we get here? In the second chapter, Luis Jácome provides a historical narrative on the evolving nature of the institutional arrangements and performance of these central banks since their inception in the 1920s. Notably, it took about 80 years for Latin America to achieve low and stable inflation. Along this long and winding road, central banks were assigned different mandates and governments influenced monetary policy to varying degrees. As a result, many countries went through periods of high inflation or hyperinflation. The 1990s, however, marked a turning point for the region as central banks were increasingly granted political and operational autonomy to focus primarily—and even exclusively—on inflation. Following this institutional reform and subsequent introduction of forward-looking monetary policy aimed primarily at fighting inflation, a number of central banks achieved price stability.

Latin American central banks later contributed decisively to successfully weathering the global financial crisis. Having said that, the consequences of the crisis may usher in a new era of central banking in the region—something already happening in many advanced economies where central banks are being called upon to provide extraordinary support to economic activity by expanding both their balance sheets and their role in safeguarding financial stability. The challenge for Latin America is to avoid new institutional and policy frameworks that might undermine central bank autonomy and accountability and, in turn, the hard-won credibility the central banks earned in fighting inflation.

With this historical context in mind, Alejandro Werner, Luis Jácome, Yan Carrière-Swallow, and Nicolás Magud outline in Chapter 3 the main challenges going forward for central banks in Latin America in order to build on the important progress made in achieving price stability. These policymakers will need to confront emerging challenges following the global financial crisis, when the roles and tools of central banks are being expanded. The chapter covers operational and communication issues that are instrumental for strengthening the inflation-targeting regime as the nominal anchor and revisits the role of the exchange rate and central bank intervention in currency markets for these five major economies in the region.

Spillovers and Monetary Independence

With the continued reliance on exceptional monetary accommodation in the wake of the crisis and subsequent episodes of market volatility such as the U.S. taper tantrum episode, issues of financial spillovers and local monetary policy autonomy remain on the radar screen for many emerging markets.[8] For example, Rey (2013) challenged the conventional wisdom of an "impossible trinity"—between monetary independence, capital mobility, and fixed exchange rates—in favor of a "policy dilemma" where central banks essentially must choose between monetary independence and an open capital account. Behind this view, a global financial cycle acts as an important driver of local monetary and financial conditions for more financially integrated economies, complicating if not undermining domestic monetary policy efforts.

In Chapter 4, Yan Carrière-Swallow and Bertrand Gruss reexamine the issue of monetary policy autonomy in Latin America. Over the past few decades, the region has embarked on a process of removing restrictions on the movement of international capital, moved from fixed to more flexible exchange rate regimes, and adopted inflation targeting as the nominal anchor. By better anchoring inflation expectations, the new frameworks have led to greater monetary autonomy and declining exchange rate pass-through (with second-round effects from currency depreciations not perceivable in many countries). Consistent with this, the chapter finds that a large degree of correlation in interest rates across countries does not necessarily reflect a lack of monetary autonomy, but rather is largely a consequence of co-movement in business cycles. This does not imply that financial spillovers are irrelevant for the region—spillovers to domestic long-term interest rates from changes in the U.S. term premium, for instance, can be large. Moreover, some Latin American economies do not enjoy full autonomy in pursuit of domestic price and output stability objectives and are, to a certain extent, forced to follow external signals given the extent of financial dollarization and

---

[8] See Sahay and others (2014) on the cross-border effects and policy responses in emerging markets during the taper tantrum episode.

credibility of their nominal anchor. However, with careful design and implementation of their policy frameworks, central banks in Latin America can enjoy substantial monetary independence to achieve their domestic objectives even in the face of shifting global financial conditions.

In Chapter 5, Alberto Naudon and Andrés Yany study the macroeconomic effects of the global financial cycle on small and open economies and their monetary policy implications. To tackle this issue, they examine long-term interest rates in nine small and open economies and the United States, decomposing these rates into two components—the expected path of short-term rates and the term premium. The former is related closely to the future path of monetary policy and the latter is influenced inter alia by financial factors, including through spillovers. The analysis suggests a clear "pass-through" to local financial conditions with a rise in U.S. long-term interest rates and term premiums. These effects may be stronger in Latin America than in other emerging markets. From a general perspective, the global financial cycle can have significant effects on small and open emerging market economies that might pose financial stability trade-offs for the central bank. This issue will be crucial going forward as U.S. monetary policy continues to gradually normalize.

In Chapter 6, Julián Parra Polanía looks at central bank communications, exploring the role of forward guidance (i.e., committing to future policy rates), and monetary policymaking under uncertainty. He argues that unconditional forward guidance—that is, one that is time-based—improves welfare only in the most severe zero lower bound cases and should likely be reserved only for these exceptional circumstances. With regard to dealing with uncertainty, a prudent central bank may change its policy rate more or less aggressively to a demand shock, depending on the clarity of the signal (e.g., volatility of measurement errors), the extent to which markets are forward looking, and the central bank's degree of risk aversion.

Macroprudential and Monetary Policy Frameworks

A central lesson from the global financial crisis is that a price stability mandate (e.g., inflation targeting) is not sufficient by itself to guarantee macroeconomic and financial stability. This applies to Latin America as well, where domestic financial deepening and foreign capital flows can raise stability risks in local financial markets. Thus, greater attention to macroprudential frameworks and instruments is needed to help safeguard stability. How do monetary and macroprudential policies interact, and how can they be integrated in Latin America to meet these dual objectives of price and financial stability?

In Chapter 7, Jessica Roldán-Peña, Mauricio Torres-Ferro, and Alberto Torres examine potential trade-offs between the pursuit of inflation targeting and financial stability. First, they show in a simplified framework for Mexico that when monetary policy "leans against the wind" to reduce the volatility of financial variables, this typically implies greater volatility for both inflation and output. That is, there may be a trade-off using a single policy instrument (especially when financial shocks are more prevalent). The degree of the trade-off depends on the strength of the credit channel of monetary policy—for example, the impact of changes in credit and spreads on macroeconomic variables. This opens the door for macroprudential policy as a second instrument and for coordination among policy instruments, but the gains from coordination need not be large. The larger the impact of macroprudential policy on credit spreads, the greater the gains from coordination. The results highlight the importance of further research on at least two fronts: the behavior of banks and profit margins in understanding credit dynamics, and the characteristics of the financial system in shaping the amplification and persistence of financial shocks to the real economy, as well as how the effectiveness of macroprudential instruments can be enhanced.

In Chapter 8, Fabia de Carvalho and Marcos de Castro note that Brazil's credit cycle appears to be significantly influenced by financial deepening, foreign capital flows, and fiscal policy. These factors can create domestic financial vulnerabilities and pose challenges for central bank policies in dealing with them. Financial deepening resulted from greater financial inclusion following technological improvements, income distribution policies, and credit origination policies of public banks (which adds a fiscal dimension). In terms of financial vulnerabilities, household indebtedness increased substantially and credit accelerated. On a number of occasions, key policy instruments (e.g., reserve requirements) were used for macroprudential purposes in Brazil, and some were used countercyclically. However, when related policy announcements were out of sync with monetary policy, the anchoring of inflation expectations was challenged. This stresses the importance of improving the communication of the central bank's policy intentions. Examining different combinations of macroprudential and monetary policy rules that react to the financial cycle, the chapter also finds that simpler rules that are easier to implement—such as reserve requirements, risk-weight factors, and monetary policy—can nonetheless achieve results close to those that involve a more comprehensive set of policy instruments.

In the last chapter of this volume, Paul Castillo, Hugo Vega, Enrique Serrano, and Carlos Burga examine the interaction between monetary and macroprudential policy in the context of financial dollarization in Peru. In economies affected by significant financial dollarization, a large depreciation of the exchange rate can lead to higher default rates among firms and affect the balance sheets of borrowers. In a sense, the existence of a currency mismatch on the balance sheet of some domestic agents generates an externality for the financial system as a whole. In contrast with other inflation-targeting central banks, Peru's monetary policy regime thus needs to consider the implications of dollarization on monetary transmission and financial stability. In particular, liquidity and credit risks induced by exchange rate fluctuations or foreign currency liquidity shocks are highly relevant for domestic stability. Important instruments include higher reserve requirements on foreign currency liabilities, holdings of international reserves, and exchange rate intervention in spot and forward markets. The chapter evaluates the use of such unconventional monetary policy tools to reduce credit dollarization. The empirics show that high reserve requirements, used countercyclically since 2010, and the de-dollarization program put in place by the central bank since 2013, have had beneficial effects in Peru. Furthermore, measures aimed at reducing vulnerabilities such as credit dollarization have enhanced financial stability, thereby creating space for monetary policy to fulfill its traditional role.

REFERENCES

Akerlof, G., O. Blanchard, D. Romer, and J. Stiglitz. 2014. *What Have We Learned?* Cambridge, Massachusetts: MIT Press.

Blanchard, O., D. Romer, M. Spence, and J. Stiglitz. 2012. *In the Wake of the Crisis.* Cambridge, Massachusetts: MIT Press.

Ostry, J. D., A. R. Ghosh, M. Chamon, and M. S. Qureshi. 2015. *Capital Controls.* London: Edward Elgar.

Ostry, J. D., A. R. Ghosh, K. Habermeier, L. Laeven, M. Chamon, M. S. Qureshi, and A. Kokenyne. 2011. "Managing Capital Inflows: What Tools to Use?" IMF Staff Discussion Note 11/6, International Monetary Fund, Washington, DC.

Rajan, R., and P. Mishra. 2016. "Rules of the Monetary Game." Reserve Bank of India. Unpublished.

Rey, H. 2013. "Dilemma Not Trilemma: The Global Financial Cycle and Monetary Policy Independence." In *Proceedings from the 2013 Federal Reserve Bank of Kansas City Economic Policy Symposium*, Jackson Hole, Wyoming, August 22–24.

Sahay, R., V. Arora, T. Arvanitis, H. Faruqee, P. N'Diaye, and T. Mancini-Griffoli. 2014. "Emerging Market Volatility: Lessons from the Taper Tantrum." IMF Staff Discussion Note 14/9, International Monetary Fund, Washington, DC.

PART I

Progress and Challenges

CHAPTER 2

A Historical Perspective on Central Banking in Latin America

LUIS I. JÁCOME H., INTERNATIONAL MONETARY FUND

The primary goal of this chapter is to analyze the historical evolution of central banking in Latin America that will serve as the backdrop for the rest of the book. The chapter describes the evolving institutional arrangements and policy frameworks since the foundation of Latin American central banks in the 1920s as the key drivers of monetary policy. It highlights the fact that monetary policy did not render good results in terms of inflation until the 2000s, when central banks had a clear policy mandate and were granted political autonomy.

Following Jácome (2015), this historical journey distinguishes three main periods: (1) the early years, which span from the 1920s, when countries in the region endorsed the gold standard, up to the end of the Second World War; (2) the developmental phase, which spans from the postwar period to the early 1990s, when central banks turned into development banks under the aegis of the government; and (3) the golden years, covering the last 20 years, when central banks enjoyed political autonomy and achieved price stability.

The chapter also identifies transitory stages that emerged between these three periods. First, the collapse of the gold standard in the early 1930s left monetary policy in an interregnum, as the convertibility of domestic currencies was abolished. This transitory period lasted until the Bretton Woods system reestablished the convertibility of currencies in the mid-1940s, this time vis-à-vis the U.S. dollar—and through this to gold. A second interim period emerged following the breakdown of Bretton Woods in the early 1970s, as the convertibility of the U.S. dollar to gold was abandoned and countries were free to choose any exchange rate regime. This transitory phase was replaced by a new paradigm in the 1990s, when central banks were granted political autonomy to focus on fighting inflation in an environment of exchange rate flexibility and open capital accounts.

Central banks in Latin America may enter into a new transition, one that is already in progress in advanced economies in the wake of the global financial crisis. The new central bank blueprint stresses an enhanced role for central banks

---

Previous versions of this chapter benefited from comments by Ana Corbacho, Nicolás Magud, Miguel Savastano, Krishna Srinivasan, and seminar participants at the 2015 Meetings of the Latin American and Caribbean Economics Association.

in preserving systemic financial stability and fostering economic activity.[1] As in the past, central banks in Latin America are likely to follow this trend. Several central banks in the region also face the challenge of preserving monetary policy independence in a world of highly volatile capital flows.

The next section of this chapter provides a historical perspective of the changes in the institutional foundations of monetary policy in Latin America. That is followed by a description of the evolving monetary policy framework throughout the three periods considered. The chapter then maps the institutional and policy changes of central banking to the historical performance of inflation in Latin America, before offering some concluding remarks.

THE EVOLVING INSTITUTIONAL FOUNDATIONS OF MONETARY POLICY

The first central banks in Latin America were founded in the 1920s. The institutional basis for monetary policy reflected the rules of the gold standard prevailing at that time,[2] and the political economy behind the creation of central banks with the monopoly of currency issue (Box 2.1). From then on, central banks' institutional underpinnings varied over time, mainly in response to domestic factors but also due to the influence of international academic trends. This section analyzes how monetary policy in Latin America has changed historically in response to the evolving mandates and governing arrangements of central banks over the years.

Mandate

The mandate of central banks in Latin America changed significantly over time (Figure 2.1). In most countries, central banks were initially assigned multiple functions with a view of fulfilling three main goals: (1) maintain monetary stability; (3) finance the government on a limited basis; and (3) help preserve a sound banking system (Appendix 2.1). Monetary stability would result from an orderly currency issuance associated with the rules of the gold standard, which would also

---

[1]The crisis ignited a debate about a new role of monetary policy beyond its primary responsibility of preserving price stability. The general perception is that in the run-up to the crisis, financial vulnerabilities grew unchecked. Central banks were blamed for failing to act to prevent the crisis, which was attributed to their narrow mandate that assigned them limited duties for preserving systemic financial stability. In the aftermath of the financial crisis, there was a sense of dissatisfaction with the tepid recovery that still prevails in many advanced economies. One of the alternatives considered has been to expand the focus of monetary policy to include growth.

[2]The term "gold standard" is used throughout this chapter, but it was really the "gold exchange standard" that most Latin American countries actually endorsed. The latter allowed countries to convert domestic bank notes into bills of exchange denominated in a foreign currency that was convertible into gold at a fixed exchange rate.

> **Box 2.1. The Origins of Central Banking in Latin America**
>
> The first central banks in Latin America were established at the time when a worldwide consensus had been reached about the need for all countries to have a central bank. The first central bank was the Reserve Bank of Peru, founded in 1922, followed by the Bank of the Republic of Colombia created in 1923. Chile and Mexico established their central banks in 1925, followed by Guatemala, Ecuador, and Bolivia in 1926, 1927, and 1929, respectively. Important sources of impetus for the creation of central banks were the Brussels International Financial Conference in 1920 and the Genoa Conference in 1922, which recommended that countries endorse the gold standard. Since these central banks adhered to the gold standard, they committed to maintaining the convertibility of their currencies.
>
> There had been several failed attempts to create central banks in Latin America before external experts were brought to the scene to provide informed advice. This is not surprising, since giving the central bank the monopoly of currency issue affected vested economic interests associated with the power to legally issue bank notes, which in turn granted banks' shareholders strong political influence. To overcome this gridlock, foreign experts were often called in to provide their knowledge and credibility to the reform process involving the creation of central banks. The various Kemmerer missions during the 1920s and early 1930s played this role in Colombia, Chile, Ecuador, Bolivia, Guatemala, and in Peru to reform the existing central bank.[1] The recommendations were the same for all countries, namely the creation of a central bank with the monopoly of currency issue, endorsement of the gold standard in order to stabilize the value of local currencies, introduction of bank legislation to regulate and supervise banks by a separate agency, and reform of public finances to make them consistent with the goal of preserving the stability of the currency.
>
> ---
>
> [1] Edwin W. Kemmerer was an economics professor at Princeton University who led missions of experts to seven Latin American countries between 1917 and 1930 to advise on monetary and financial sector issues.

secure a stable exchange rate and, ultimately, an environment of low inflation.[3] Central bank financing to the government, although allowed, was constrained by legislation in order to avoid previous episodes of generous—often forced—financing to the government by private banks that enjoyed the privilege of issuing local currency. In turn, by requiring commercial banks to be on a sound financial footing as a condition to benefit from rediscount operations, central banks contributed to maintaining financial stability.[4] With the same purpose, central banks were assigned functions as lender of last resort. When commercial banks faced

---

[3] Countries defined their exchange rate based on the rules associated with the gold standard. Given that the value of each currency was measured in terms of the amount of fine gold it contained, and because such value tended to differ across countries, it was possible to establish bilateral exchange rates. For example, because the sucre in Ecuador contained 0.300933 grams of fine gold in 1927 and the U.S. dollar contained 1.504665 grams, the exchange rate was 5 sucres per U.S. dollar (Carbo 1978). Similarly, since the Chilean peso contained 0.183057 grams of fine gold, the exchange rate was about 8 pesos per U.S. dollar (Carrasco 2009).

[4] Central banks could also discount paper to the general public (Chile, Colombia, Ecuador, Mexico, and Peru until 1932) although, in practice, these transactions were small.

Figure 2.1. The Evolving Mandate of Central Banks in Latin America

Early years	Developmental phase	Golden years
-Regulate money -Secure financial stability -Finance the government	Promote currency stability, financial system development, employment, growth, orderly economic development	Preserve monetary or price stability
Gold standard collapse	Bretton Woods breakdown	Financial crisis
Interregnum	Interim period	Transition phase

1920   1930   1940   1950   1960   1970   1980   1990   2000   2010

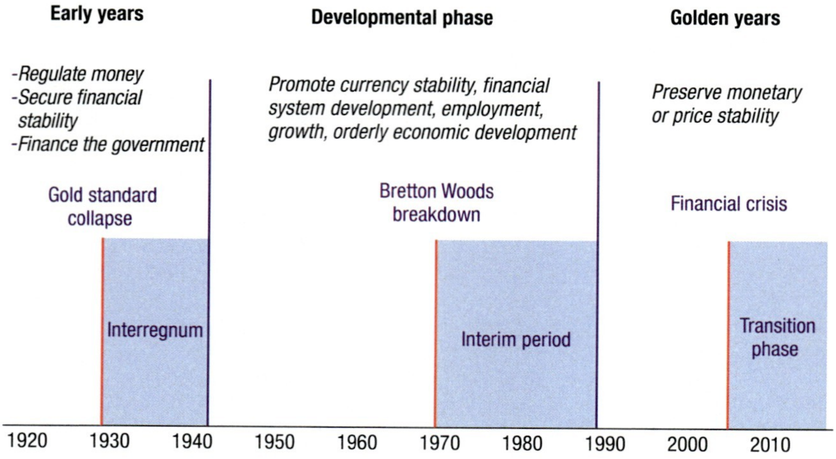

Source: Prepared by the author.

liquidity shortages, central banks were empowered to supply liquidity, provided the impaired bank was solvent according to the banking authority. Banking regulation and supervision was assigned to a different agency, as central banks were primarily given monetary policy responsibilities—the "Pacific model" as described in Jácome, Nier, and Imam (2012)—with only limited regulatory powers.

Following the collapse of the gold standard in the early 1930s, central banks in Latin America—like in the rest of the world—were no longer committed to maintain the convertibility of domestic currencies. During these years, a second group of central banks was established, including banks in El Salvador (1934), Argentina (1935), and Venezuela (1939).[5] Central bank legislation was adjusted to the new conditions that followed the collapse of the gold standard. Without having to maintain the convertibility of the currency, the Central Bank of the Republic of Argentina had more leeway to issue money and, therefore, had the mandate to regulate the amount of money and credit (Appendix 2.1). The Central Reserve Bank of El Salvador featured a similar mandate. The Central Bank of the Republic of Argentina was also required to build up international reserves to cushion the impact of adverse external shocks, and was a pioneer in having a mandate to preserve the value of the currency. In addition, it was the first central bank charged with banking regulation and supervision on top of its monetary responsibilities. Other countries in the region subsequently established

---

[5]As before, the creation of these central banks was influenced by external experts. Sir Otto Niemeyer and Frederick Powell from the Bank of England visited Argentina and El Salvador, respectively, and Hermann Max from the Central Bank of Chile advised Venezuela.

similar organizational setups (Brazil, Paraguay, and Uruguay) referred to as the "Atlantic model" in Jácome, Nier, and Imam (2012).

A new period of central banking started with the end of the Second World War and the establishment of the Bretton Woods accord. The new international monetary system was based on the convertibility of the U.S. dollar into gold at a fixed value. In a broader context, Keynesian ideas were quite influential at that time, leading to greater government participation in the economy. Government intervention also reached into monetary policy, which was used to finance fiscal expenditure and support import-substitution industrialization, the development strategy adopted by several Latin American countries.

New central banks were created and a wave of central bank reforms took place during this period. New central banks included those in Cuba and the Dominican Republic in the 1940s, and Costa Rica, Honduras, Nicaragua, and Paraguay in the 1950s. In the 1960s, the Central Bank of Brazil and the Central Bank of Uruguay finally became stand-alone central banks.[6] They were typically assigned the responsibility of formulating monetary, credit, and exchange rate policy, with the aim of supporting economic activity and also preventing inflation. In turn, central bank reforms reflected a general sense that previous legislation imposed constraints on the new economic strategy by limiting governments' influence on monetary policy.[7] Like before, some of these reforms followed recommendations made by external experts. In particular, Robert Triffin, from the U.S. Federal Reserve, influenced the reform adopted in Guatemala in the mid-1940s and later in Ecuador, and the creation of central banks in the Dominican Republic, Honduras, and Paraguay.[8] Triffin was opposed to the passive character of monetary policy embedded in the previous laws, which had worked as an amplifier of external shocks. Instead, he proposed legislation to support economic development and to allow central banks adopt countercyclical policies to mitigate a volatile external environment.

In practice, central banks became, to a great extent, development institutions focused on promoting economic activity and financing the government at the expense of being more tolerant about inflation. While some of the new laws also made references to inflation (for example, requiring central banks to "prevent inflationary and deflationary trends"), the overriding policy objective of monetary policy was, in general, to promote economic development. Such was the case, for example, in Chile, Colombia, and Peru. In Argentina, the central bank mandate shifted to preserving a high level of employment and the purchasing power of the

---

[6]Until then, state-owned banks—the Banco do Brasil and Banco Republica Oriental del Uruguay—conducted both commercial bank and central bank responsibilities.

[7]In some cases, the new legislation was necessary because the term for the existence of the central bank set in the initial laws had expired. Argentina, Bolivia, Ecuador, and Guatemala changed central bank legislation in the mid- to late 1940s, whereas Chile and Colombia made those changes in the 1950s. In turn, El Salvador, Peru, and Venezuela changed their central bank law in the 1960s.

[8]The Triffin missions were followed later by the Grove mission, also from the U.S. Federal Reserve, which provided similar recommendations to reform the Bank of the Republic of Colombia.

currency. For its part, the Bank of Mexico was required to formulate monetary, credit, and exchange rate policies with the triple objective of promoting the stability of the purchasing power of money, financial system development, and sound economic growth (Appendix 2.2).

The temporary suspension of the Bretton Woods monetary system in 1971 marked the beginning of an era when countries were allowed to choose their exchange rate regime. A new transitory period started. In some countries in Latin America—in particular in the Southern Cone—governments implemented populist macroeconomic policies with the support of accommodative monetary policies.[9] For example, in Argentina, the government introduced a far-reaching reform that included the nationalization of the banking system and a new central bank law that put monetary policy under complete government control. The central bank provided credit to the private sector under specific government guidance with the view of "increasing production and securing the highest standard of living and collective happiness."[10] In Chile, following the demise of the socialist government in 1973, a new central bank law was enacted that put monetary policy under government control—although not with a populist character. While macroeconomic instability spread to most countries in the region during the 1980s, no major changes in the central banks' mandate took place in that decade.

The 1990s marked a turning point for monetary policy in Latin America. After more than 50 years during which central banks were tasked with multiple mandates and governments had influence in their policy decisions, central banks were granted political and operational autonomy to focus primarily—and even exclusively—on abating inflation (Appendix 2.3). Thus, central banks were no longer directly responsible for output growth. Instead, monetary policy would aim at securing low and stable inflation—to reduce uncertainty in consumers' and investors' decisions—as a precondition to achieving sustainable economic growth. Fiscal policy helped in this endeavor. Breaking with the past, governments started to keep public sector deficits in check, without resorting to central bank financing—the main historical source of inflation. Furthermore, the structural reforms implemented from the second half of the 1980s helped to improve resource allocation and contributed to reducing inflation.[11]

---

[9]Dornbusch and Edwards (1990) defined economic populism as those policies that emphasize growth and income distribution and deemphasize inflation and deficit finance, external constraints, and the reaction of economic agents to aggressive nonmarket policies.

[10]See Central Bank of Argentina, *Annual Report*, 1973.

[11]See Lora (2001) for an analysis of the achievements of Latin America's structural reforms and Jácome and Vázquez (2008) for empirical evidence on the positive impact of structural reforms on reducing inflation.

TABLE 2.1

Central Bank Ownership and Board Membership in the Developmental Phase, Selected Countries

	Government Ownership	Government/Private Ownership	Private Sector Ownership
Mostly government representation	Argentina, Costa Rica, Dominican Republic, Guatemala	Venezuela	Colombia
Government and private representation	Peru	Chile, Ecuador, Mexico	El Salvador

Sources: Argentina: Law 25.120 (1949); Chile: Law 11151 (1953); Colombia: Decree 756 DE (1951), Law 21 (1963), and Decree 2206 DE (1963); Costa Rica: Law 1130 (1950); Dominican Republic: Law 1529 (1947); Ecuador: Law of the Monetary Regime (1948); El Salvador: Decree 64 (1952); Guatemala: Law 215 (1945); Mexico: Organic Law of the Bank of Mexico (1985); Peru: Organic Law 13958 (1962); Venezuela: Banco Central de Venezuela Law (1960).

Governing Structure

As the mandate of central banks changed over time, so did their governing structure. During their early years, central banks were run by a manager who executed policies approved by the board of directors, which typically included representatives of the government and private banks (Appendix 2.1). In some countries like Chile and Ecuador, business associations and labor organizations were also represented on the central bank board, while in Colombia one board member represented private citizens. In those central banks founded in the 1930s, the boards had a similar composition. The Board of the Central Bank of the Republic of Argentina had broad representation that included the executive branch, state-owned banks (national and provincial), private banks (domestic and foreign), and business associations. This wide representation was linked to the ownership of central banks, which in most cases included the government, the banking system, and the general public.

The shift in the mandate of central banks during the developmental phase was not accompanied by a change in their governing arrangement, except in a few countries. In most cases, the central bank's board remained comprised of government and private sector representatives (Appendix 2.2). Argentina and, in particular, Colombia were exceptions. In Argentina, while the private sector remained on the board of the central bank, its representatives were appointed by the executive. A Monetary Board was set up in Colombia, chaired by the Minister of Finance and composed of the cabinet members in charge of economic issues, as well as the governor of the Bank of the Republic. Interestingly enough, the board membership did not mirror the ownership of central banks, which in some cases became exclusively government-owned. Central banks featured various combinations of board membership and ownership (Table 2.1). Preserving private sector representation on the central bank board—from commercial banks and business associations— was associated during the developmental phase with central banks' policy of allocating credit across banks and economic activities. By the 1970s, all central banks in the region were already government owned.

The 1990s reform of central bank legislation in Latin America introduced a drastic change in their governing arrangements. In the vast majority of countries, central banks became governed by a board of directors that excluded government and private sector representatives (Appendix 2.3) and consisted instead of technocrats appointed for tenures ranging from 4 to 10 years—sometimes in a staggered fashion—and devoted full time to their job.[12] Thus, central banks were empowered to formulate monetary policy with a long-term perspective that exceeded electoral calendars. Often, the new laws called for the central bank's board of directors to not respond to the government. Moreover, in most cases, the reform established restrictions on the removal of the members of the board, except through procedures whereby the legislative or judicial branch approved dismissal on grounds strictly codified in law.

Independence

While central banks were not initially created as politically independent institutions, they enjoyed de facto operational independence. With a diversified membership of central bank boards, lawmakers tried to establish checks and balances by preventing any single party, public or private, from controlling central bank policy decisions. Moreover, while monetary policy was part of the government's broad economic policy, the issuance of currency was restricted by the rules associated with the endorsement of the gold standard, as explained later in this chapter. In addition, government and commercial banks were subject to specific operational restrictions when receiving credit from the central bank in order to protect its balance sheet.[13]

This operational independence was undermined when countries abandoned the gold standard. Restrictions to issue money were increasingly relaxed, and central bank credit to the government started to increase in several countries. While it was initially necessary to expand central bank balance sheets to bring the Latin American economies back from the brink of collapse during the Great Depression, governments became addicted to central bank financing, thus undermining central banks' independence.

During the developmental phase, central banks lost any vestige of independence. Since the new legislation modified the governing structure of some central banks, and because the banks' policy goals had changed, representatives of the government and state-owned financial institutions populated central bank boards. Moreover, the executive branch became directly involved in monetary

---

[12]Board members started to be appointed in a two-step process, nominated by the executive branch and appointed by the parliament.

[13]For instance, in Chile, central bank loans to the government—including local governments and public institutions—could not exceed 20 percent of its capital, although this limit could increase to 30 percent if approved by 8 of the 10 members of the central bank board (Carrasco 2009). In Colombia, this limit was initially 30 percent of central bank capital and increased to 45 percent in 1930 (Bank of the Republic website). On the other hand, the amount of rediscounts could not exceed 10 percent of the central bank's capital in Mexico.

policy formulation and decisions.[14] As a result, central banks extended credit through the banking system to priority sectors selected by the government and deepened the financing of government expenditure.

Governments' control of central banks deepened in some countries following the demise of the Bretton Woods system in the early 1970s, and continued until the late 1980s. Fiscal dominance became stronger in the 1970s, in particular in the Southern Cone countries, where central banks were put at the service of populist governments. In Chile, financing the fiscal deficit reached 30 percent of GDP by 1973 (Corbo and Hernandez 2005), and in Argentina central bank credit to the government increased almost 130 percent in 1973—well above the inflation rate of about 60 percent in the same year.[15] In the 1980s, "financial dominance" gained strength as governments decided to use central bank money on a large scale to cope with systemic financial crises.

In the 1990s, after more than 50 years of burdening Latin American central banks with multiple objectives, governments granted them political and operational independence to focus primarily—and sometimes exclusively—on containing inflation. Countries accepted that the main contribution of monetary policy to economic growth was to achieve and preserve low and stable inflation. In a region battered by decades of high inflation, a comprehensive monetary reform was necessary. Thus, all Latin American countries except Brazil approved new central bank laws—starting with Chile in 1989—throughout the 1990s and early 2000s.[16] Central bank independence was the backbone of this reform, serving as a way to avoid the inflationary bias stemming from political influences on monetary policy.[17]

Although the scope of the new central bank legislation varied across countries, it had four common elements. First, central banks were assigned as a single or primary objective to preserve price stability.[18] Second, they were granted political independence to formulate monetary policy with the aim of delinking monetary policymaking from electoral calendars; the new laws called for the central bank's board of directors to be independent of the government (and the private sector) and established restrictions on the removal of its members. Third, central banks

---

[14]For instance, in Argentina, the National Economic Council was assigned a direct role from 1947 onward in formulating credit regulations, leaving to the central bank the operational responsibility to implement those decisions. Moreover, the 1949 reform to the central bank law made the Minister of Finance the president of the board of the central bank. Similarly, in Chile, starting in 1953, changes in reserve requirements were approved by the Minister of Finance and, in some cases, by the President of the Republic.

[15]See Central Bank of Argentina, *Annual Report,* 1973.

[16]El Salvador approved new central bank legislation in 1991; Argentina, Colombia, Ecuador, Nicaragua, and Venezuela in 1992; Peru and Mexico in 1993; Bolivia, Costa Rica, Uruguay, and Paraguay in 1995; Honduras in 1996; and Guatemala and the Dominican Republic in 2002.

[17]The pioneering papers of Kydland and Prescott (1977), Barro and Gordon (1983), and Rogoff (1985) provided the theoretical basis for central bank independence.

[18]To minimize the chances that a future change in the law would dilute the focus on price stability, countries like Chile, Colombia, Mexico, and Peru enshrined the new mandate in the constitutions.

were granted operational independence to implement monetary policy, allowing them to increase or reduce their short-term interest rate to tighten or loosen monetary policy without government interference. The new legislation also restricted and even prohibited central banks from financing government expenditure—the chronic source of inflation. Fourth, central banks were held accountable with respect to their policy objective.[19]

The changes introduced by the new legislation implied a broad enhancement of central bank independence as measured by a modified Cukierman index of central bank independence (Figure 2.2, panel 1) (Cukierman, Webb, and Neyapti 1992).[20] As a result, Latin American central banks rank today among the most independent worldwide.[21] Unlike in advanced economies, central banks not only enjoy instrument independence (freedom to use monetary policy instruments without any political interference), but also goal independence (which allows them to set the inflation target without the need for government approval). Nonetheless, this trend has already been reversed in some countries like Argentina, Bolivia, and Venezuela, with the main objective of authorizing the central bank to finance the fiscal deficit. These countries either reformed central bank legislation or included relevant provisions in the yearly budget laws to bypass the restrictions included in the central bank laws. Panel 2 of Figure 2.2 offers a historical perspective of the reversal of central bank independence in Argentina.

POLICY FRAMEWORK

The historical evolution of monetary policy in Latin America can be tracked through the lens of the trilemma hypothesis.[22] This theory contends that small open economies can only simultaneously achieve two of the following three policy goals: (1) exchange rate stability; (2) financial integration with the rest of the world; and (3) monetary policy independence from global capital flows (Figure 2.3). In each of the three historical periods identified in this chapter, central banks in Latin America opted for different combinations of two of these three goals. The same analytical framework is also valid to discuss some of the constraints facing many central banks in the region in the aftermath of the global financial crisis.

Early Years

As countries in Latin America endorsed the gold standard in the 1920s (left corner in the triangle in Figure 2.3), central banks committed to preserve the

---

[19] For a comprehensive analysis of central bank reform in Latin America, see Carstens and Jácome (2005).

[20] See an explanation of the index used in the calculations in Jácome and Vazquez (2008).

[21] See Laurens, Arnone, and Segalotto (2009), Canales-Kriljenko, Jácome, Alichi, and Oliveira Lima (2010), and Dincer and Eichengreen (2014).

[22] This analytical framework, also known as the "impossible trinity," was pioneered by Fleming (1962) and Mundell (1963).

Figure 2.2. Central Bank Independence in Latin America

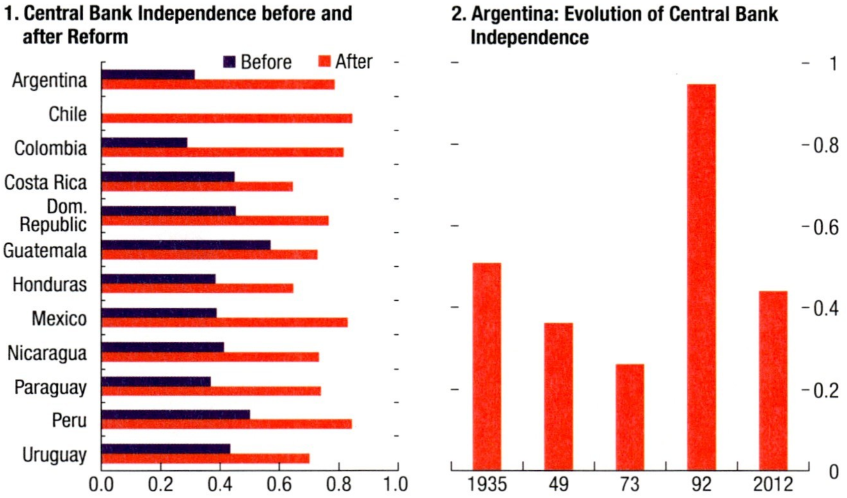

1. Central Bank Independence before and after Reform

■ Before ■ After

Argentina, Chile, Colombia, Costa Rica, Dom. Republic, Guatemala, Honduras, Mexico, Nicaragua, Paraguay, Peru, Uruguay

0.0　0.2　0.4　0.6　0.8　1.0

2. Argentina: Evolution of Central Bank Independence

1935, 49, 73, 92, 2012

0, 0.2, 0.4, 0.6, 0.8, 1

Source: Jácome and Vázquez (2008) for Panel 1 and author's calculations for panel 2.
Note: The index of central bank independence is measured on the *x* axis in panel 1 and the *y* axis in panel 2. The index of central bank independence in panel 1 is explained in Jácome and Vázquez (2008). The index used in panel 2 has been simplified to ensure comparability over such a long time period.

convertibility of their currencies at a fixed exchange rate and keep the capital account open. This monetary system imposed an automatic adjustment mechanism for balance of payment disequilibria, making monetary policy endogenous. Central banks could only issue bank notes if they were backed with international reserves, mostly gold and foreign currency convertible into gold. Thus, when international reserves declined, money supply also contracted. Interest rates then increased, attracting capital inflows and thus restoring international reserves and the money supply, although at the cost of restricting aggregate demand.

The main monetary policy instrument used was the discount rate. However, this rate could vary across economic agents and activities—like the industrial and agricultural sectors that paid lower rates.[23] The discount rate also varied depending on the amount of the loan and the likelihood of its recovery.[24]

---

[23]In Chile, for example, the central bank charged 1 percent less for commercial banks than for the general public. See Central Bank of Chile, *Annual Report* (1935).

[24]For instance, starting in 1926, the Bank of Mexico charged multiple rates in operations with the general public, ranging from 8 to 12 percent. See Bank of Mexico, *Informe a la Asamblea General Ordinaria de Accionistas,* 1926.

Figure 2.3. Central Banking in Latin America and the Trilemma Triangle

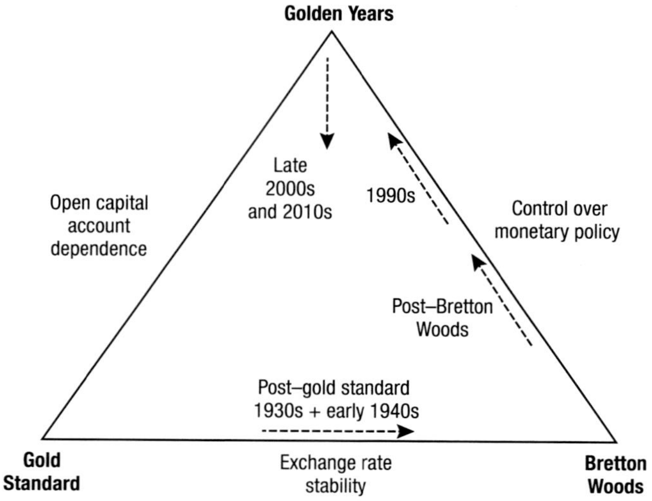

```
                        Golden Years
                             △
                            ╱│╲
                           ╱ ▼ ╲
                          ╱ Late ╲
                         ╱  2000s  ╲
          Open capital  ╱and 2010s  ╲  Control over
            account   ╱     1990s    ╲ monetary policy
          dependence ╱                 ╲
                    ╱         Post–Bretton╲
                   ╱            Woods      ╲
                  ╱                          ╲
                 ╱    Post–gold standard      ╲
                ╱     1930s + early 1940s      ╲
               ╱      ------------→             ╲
              ─────────────────────────────────────
              Gold          Exchange rate       Bretton
            Standard          stability         Woods
```

Source: Prepared by the author.

Endorsing the gold standard in the midst of the Great Depression became an insurmountable restriction. Thus, Chile, Colombia, Ecuador, Mexico, and Peru suspended the convertibility of their currencies and, later on, officially exited the gold standard during 1931 and 1932. As a result, central banks were no longer restricted to issue money and extend credit, and could potentially adjust the exchange rate as needed. In practice, central banks preserved exchange rate stability as they introduced capital restrictions that, in addition, allowed them to gradually gain control over monetary policy (lower side of the triangle in Figure 2.3). In addition, central banks were potentially able to implement countercyclical policies.

As monetary policy became exogenous, countries started to enhance their policy toolkit. Changes in discount rates gradually lost popularity and, as an alternative, central banks began to use other instruments. Pioneered by Mexico, changes in reserve requirements started to gain popularity as a policy instrument.[25] The central bank in Argentina issued Certificates of Participation and used Treasury Certificates in 1935 and 1936 for liquidity management purposes. During the early 1940s, several countries started to impose quantitative restrictions on central bank credit to avoid increasing the interest rates.

---

[25] The Bank of Mexico changed the reserve requirement rate within the range of 3 and 15 percent from 1936 onward, and by between 15 and 20 percent from 1941 onward. Argentina also changed reserve requirements in 1936, as well as Venezuela in 1940, Nicaragua in 1941, and Costa Rica in 1943, among other countries.

Figure 2.4 Central Bank Assets in Chile and Peru

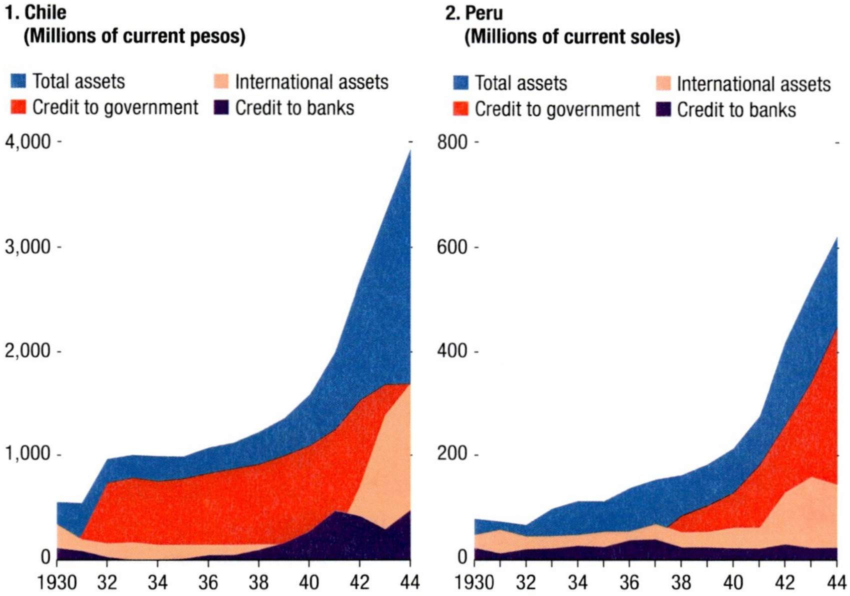

1. Chile
(Millions of current pesos)

2. Peru
(Millions of current soles)

Sources: Central Bank of Chile, Annual Reports; and Central Reserve Bank of Peru, Annual Reports.

Central banks' balance sheets expanded following the gold standard years, as financing to the government increased. In Chile, the surge in government financing was aimed at taming the economic contraction stemming from the Great Depression in the early 1930s, which was followed by the extension of credit lines to other public sector institutions. Later, in the early 1940s, the expansion was mostly driven by the increase in foreign exchange reserves. In Peru, credit to the government increased more than threefold between 1933 and 1938, and rose another 300 percent by 1944 (Figure 2.4). In Mexico, central bank credit to the government exceeded its loans to the banking system by more than five times and represented close to 45 percent of the Bank of Mexico's total assets by 1940.[26] Argentina was different, since the rise in international reserves was the main driver of the increase in the central bank's balance sheet.[27]

---

[26] The Bank of Mexico initially set restrictions on lending to the government at 10 percent of its capital. This restriction was relaxed in 1937 (Bank of Mexico, *Informe de la Asamblea General Ordinaria de Accionistas*, 1937 and 1940).

[27] Article 44 of the Law No. 12.155 authorized credit operations to the government of up to 10 percent of the previous fiscal year's revenues, with the aim of smoothing out the stream of such revenues. In turn, credit to financial institutions was provided by Banco Nación—a state-owned institution.

Developmental Phase

Monetary policy during most of the developmental phase was conditioned by the restrictions imposed by the Bretton Woods system established in 1945. The new international monetary system required countries to maintain fixed, although adjustable, exchange rates and to commit to the convertibility of their currencies against the U.S. dollar, which was chosen as the new reserve asset—instead of gold like in the gold standard years. The Bretton Woods Agreement provided rules to restore exchange rate stability and avoid competitive devaluations. While countries were required to state a par value against the U.S. dollar—or against gold—and to maintain it fixed within a 1 percent range above and below such value, countries were also entitled to change the par value by up to 10 percent. Countries also expanded their array of capital controls, which allowed central banks to fully enjoy an independent monetary policy (right corner in the triangle in Figure 2.3).

Against this backdrop, monetary policy became broadly aligned with governments' policies, albeit restricted by the rules of the Bretton Woods system. Central banks extended credit through the banking system to priority sectors selected by the government—typically to the agricultural and industrial sectors—with the aim of supporting its development strategy. Furthermore, central banks became the most important source of government financing, thus leading to increasing macroeconomic instability.

Because countries maintained a fixed exchange rate, expansionary monetary policy resulted in current account deficits that had to be financed with international reserves. The Bretton Woods system linked monetary imbalances with changes in international reserves, as the capital account was relatively closed. Thus, central banks' credit to both the private sector and the government had to be kept in check to avoid a drain of international reserves. This policy framework was the so-called "monetary approach to the balance of payments" popularized by the International Monetary Fund, as it was embedded in the economic programs negotiated with its member countries to eliminate balance of payments disequilibrium.[28]

Under this policy framework, financing economic development proved to be inconsistent with maintaining a fixed parity. Lax monetary policies resulted in current account deficits, which drained international reserves and led to currency crises and a rise in inflation. Inflation also contributed to the increase in money supply in order to preserve real money balances, thus creating mutually reinforcing feedback. The close co-movements of inflation and money supply in Brazil and Chile during 1946–70 illustrate this point (Figure 2.5).

Following the demise of the Bretton Woods system in the early 1970s, central banks could more freely adjust the exchange rate. Since the convertibility of the U.S. dollar into gold at a fixed value was no longer in effect, exchange rates in several countries were devalued frequently in response to the inflation associated with the loose monetary policies in place. In particular, in the Southern Cone

---

[28]The approach was formalized by Polak (1957) and extended by Frenkel and Johnson (1976).

Figure 2.5. Money Growth and Inflation in Brazil and Chile, 1946–70
(Percentage rate year over year)

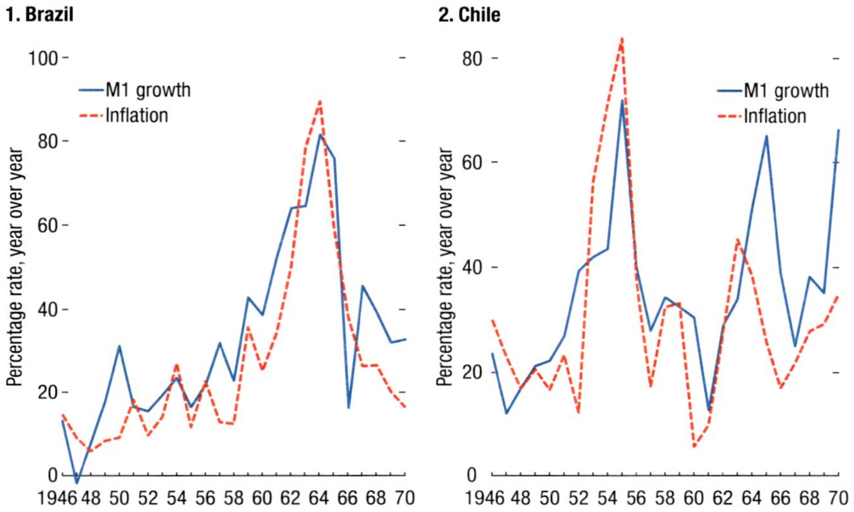

Sources: Brazil: Central Bank of Brazil and IGP-DI, FGV for inflation; Chile: Braun-Llona and others (2000).

countries, left-wing governments implemented expansionary fiscal and monetary policies that ended up fueling broad macroeconomic instability. As inflation soared, these countries turned to stabilization policies, implementing for the first time some sort of forward-looking monetary policy, the so-called "tablita" arrangements.[29] Other countries, in turn, received fresh capital inflows, which mostly translated into dollar credits and thus led to increased dollarization of the economies and to sizable fiscal and external disequilibrium.[30]

By the early 1980s, capital inflows reversed in response to the surge in interest rates in advanced economies. Most Latin American countries had by that time accumulated large external obligations to finance fiscal and external imbalances. Capital outflows generated large devaluations, which hit the dollarized balance sheets of firms, banks, and the government, thus leading to a triple crisis—currency, banking, and sovereign—that pushed inflation through the roof. Central

---

[29]The new policy regime was aimed at breaking inflation inertia by using the exchange rate to anchor inflation expectations. It consisted in pre-announcing a crawling peg, specifying a daily decreasing pace of devaluation. Despite some initial success, the tablita program was ultimately not sustainable. Neither inflation nor interest rates declined at the same pace as the pre-announced rate of devaluation. As a result, the domestic currency became increasingly appreciated and, ultimately, large depreciations took place. For a comprehensive analysis of the tablita experiments see Corbo (1985) on Chile and Fernandez (1985) on Argentina.

[30]International liquidity had increased as the so-called "petro-dollars" were recycled from the oil-exporting countries that had benefited from the surge in world oil prices.

banks were at the center of the policy response to cope with financial crises, providing exceptional monetary support to assist ailing banks, restructure the financial system, and support borrowers.[31] In turn, governments implemented income policy and price controls with a view toward tackling inflation inertia, considered the main factor driving inflation, as well as fiscal adjustment.[32] However, fiscal tightening faltered in most cases and, therefore, the exchange rate plunged and inflation—which initially had declined—eventually rebounded at even higher levels.

Golden Years

Protracted macroeconomic instability took a high toll on the Latin American economies. The 1980s became the "lost decade" for the region. As economic and social costs associated with persistent high inflation became insurmountable, countries decided to grant central banks political autonomy and assigned them the task of defeating inflation. The autonomy granted to central banks implied giving them independence to formulate monetary policy and increase or reduce their short-term interest rate to tighten or loosen monetary policy as needed without government interference. A handful of countries also introduced exchange rate flexibility, and most of them completely opened the capital account (upper corner in the triangle in Figure 2.3). Other countries used the exchange rate to reduce inflation (Brazil, Chile, Colombia, Ecuador). Thus, by the mid-1990s, inflation started to decline.

However, a new wave of banking crises hit Latin America from the mid-1990s to the early 2000s, which fueled bouts of inflation in some countries. Foreign capital had returned to Latin America in the early 1990s following the restructuring of external debts and attracted by the financial liberalization recently introduced. Capital inflows appreciated real exchange rates and boosted banks' credit, whereas financial and capital account liberalization encouraged new and often risky financial transactions. Yet, prudential standards did not keep the pace of financial innovations and the heightened risks incurred by banks, and thus financial vulnerabilities grew unchecked. The combination of financial and capital account liberalization and weak prudential regulation and supervision sowed the seeds of systemic banking crises that materialized starting in the mid-1990s in Venezuela and Mexico. In several crises, the lack of exchange rate flexibility played an amplifier role as central banks had to abandon the fixed or quasi-fixed parity. This turned into foreign exchange overshooting that hit back at the banking system (Jácome 2008). In the absence of appropriate crisis management instruments in most countries, central banks were once again required to monetize the crises, which inevitably led to simultaneous currency and, in some cases,

---

[31]See an expanded description of these measures in Jácome (2015).

[32]For a description and analysis of the so-called "heterodox" economic programs, see Bruno and others (1988) and Bruno and others (1991).

sovereign, crises. As a result, inflation accelerated once again (Jácome, Saadi-Sedik, and Townsend 2012).

As financial crises subsided and inflation declined again, several countries in the region introduced inflation targeting as their new monetary policy regime. Brazil, Chile, Colombia, Mexico, and Peru (the LA5) pioneered the adoption of inflation targeting in Latin America in the late 1990s and early 2000s, but other countries have followed.[33] The credibility of the LA5 inflation-targeting regimes increased over time as central banks fulfilled their promise, and inflation generally remained within the target range.[34] Compared to other emerging market inflation targeters, most LA5 central banks performed well, as the deviations of inflation with respect to the target were smaller (Figure 2.6).[35] Building up credibility had a reinforcing effect on the effectiveness of monetary policy, as market participants tend to align inflation expectations with central bank targets, thereby creating a virtuous circle. A key factor in this success has been a policy of clear central bank communication. Reversing a history of secrecy, central banks in Latin America increasingly started to disseminate information to the public. In particular, central banks issued press releases following their policy meetings—in which the central bank board decided about the policy rate—with the aim of explaining decisions and guiding inflation expectations in order to enhance the effectiveness of monetary policy.

Operationally, central banks moved to an intensive use of a short-term interest rate as their key monetary policy instrument, leaving behind the frequent use of reserve requirements and quantity-targeted open-market operations. Changes in the policy rate were aimed at affecting the real sector of the economy—output and inflation—and at signaling the stance of monetary policy in order to guide inflation expectations. The policy rate transmitted monetary impulses to the real sector via the financial system. Behind the scenes, central banks started to manage systemic liquidity and use open-market operations to keep the short-term interbank rate close to the policy rate. Central banks also introduced standing deposit and Lombard facilities, below and above the policy rate, to offer overnight liquidity absorption and provision.

The global financial crisis of 2008 tested the preparedness of Latin American central banks to manage large real and financial shocks. Based on macro-financial fundamentals that were stronger than in the past and on buffer mechanisms put in place over several years, the Latin American economies, and specifically the LA5, successfully handled large real and financial shocks stemming from the global financial crisis. Supported by their solid institutional underpinnings, central banks weathered the reversal of capital inflows well and contributed decisively

---

[33]These countries include Guatemala and, more recently, Costa Rica, the Dominican Republic, and Paraguay.

[34]While the Central Bank of Brazil does not enjoy *de jure* independence, in practice, governments have most of time refrained from influencing monetary policy decisions.

[35]A similar result is obtained when deviations are calculated with respect to the target range.

Figure 2.6. Inflation Deviation from Target in Inflation-Targeting Emerging Market Economies
(Percentage points, absolute value)

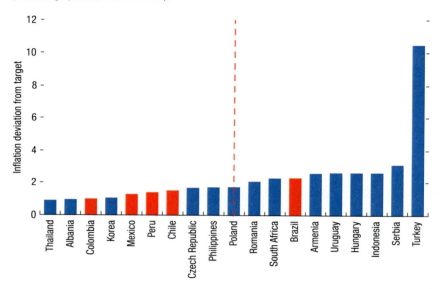

Sources: Central banks; Haver Analytics; and author's calculations.
Note: Average absolute value deviation of inflation from target since the adoption of inflation targeting until 2015:Q2. Most countries target the Consumer Price Index (CPI), with the exception of Thailand (Core CPI), Korea (Core CPI in 2000–06), and South Africa (CPIX until end-2008).

to stem subsequent deflationary pressures. The credibility already gained by central banks was critical for this achievement. The relatively modest impact of the financial crisis on the LA5 countries constituted a stark contrast to previous crisis episodes.

As the advanced economies lowered policy rates to the zero lower bound, capitals migrated once again to the financially integrated Latin American countries. To prevent excessive exchange rate appreciation and/or the buildup of financial vulnerabilities, the central banks in Brazil, Colombia, and Peru stepped up intervention in the foreign exchange market, and introduced or tightened capital flow management measures and/or macroprudential policies to discourage speculative capital inflows.[36] By using these measures and tools, the Latin American countries departed from the trilemma hypothesis (moved to the center of the triangle in Figure 2.3). While useful, maintaining a flexible

---

[36]Brazil used a wide range of policy measures, such as increases in the tax rate on financial operations for some foreign exchange transactions, higher reserve requirements, higher risk weights for some sector loans, and lower loan-to-value ratios in the housing market. Colombia and Peru mostly tightened reserve requirements.

Figure 2.7. Brazil, Chile, Colombia, and Peru: 100 Years of Inflation
(1 + inflation, logs, year over year)

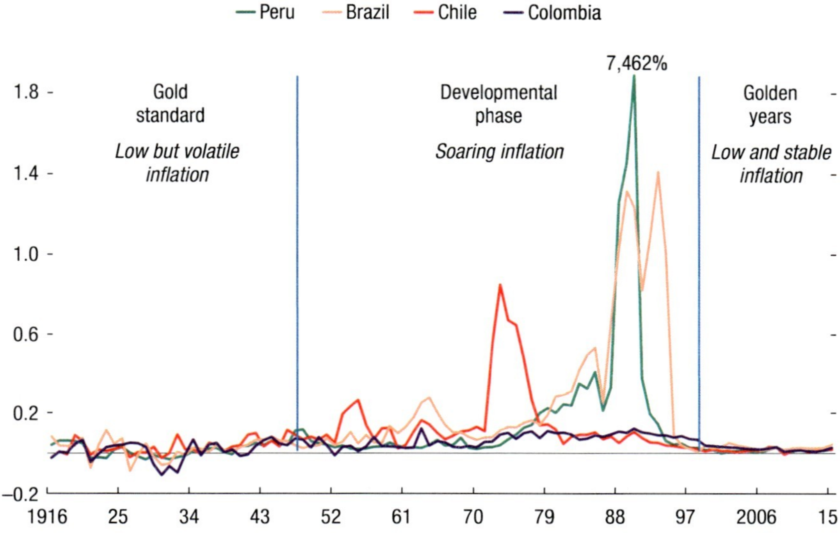

Sources: Peru: Central Reserve Bank of Peru; Chile: Diaz, Lüders, and Wagner (2010); Colombia: Grupo de Estudios de Crecimiento Económico (2001); Brazil: 1901–08: Suzigan and Villela (2001); 1909–47: Haddad (1978); 1948–2013: Instituto Brasileiro de Geografia e Estatística.
Note: Chile, Colombia, and Peru: annual inflation rate. Brazil: annual implicit deflator; from 1981 onward, Consumer Price Index.

exchange rate proved to be insufficient to keep full control over monetary policy while, at the same time, avoiding large exchange rate volatility and preventing financial vulnerabilities—that could eventually challenge the objective of price stability—in response to the effects of the global cycle and the associated shifts in capital flows.[37]

THE LONG ROAD TO PRICE STABILITY

Against a backdrop of an evolving institutional and policy framework, inflation has been high and volatile during the lifespans of most of Latin America's central banks. However, there are clear differences in central bank performance for each of the three periods analyzed in this chapter, as illustrated by a snapshot of the evolution of inflation in Brazil, Chile, Colombia, and Peru during the last 100 years (Figure 2.7).

---

[37]Rey (2015) suggests that the trilemma has been replaced by a dilemma, as monetary policy remains independent only if countries directly or indirectly manage the capital account, regardless of the exchange rate regime that is in place.

Before and immediately after the creation of the central banks, inflation was low but volatile—with prices even declining significantly in several years. Monetary policy was endogenous due to the restrictions imposed by the rules of the gold standard, and thus inflation and output were determined by external shocks and the international economic cycle. The procyclical nature of the adjustment mechanism associated with the gold standard also influenced inflation and output performance.

As countries abandoned the gold standard, central banks acquired discretion to implement monetary policy. Monetary expansion accelerated mostly to finance the government, thus sowing the seeds of higher inflation. During the developmental phase, with a mandate to finance economic growth and development, central bank credit was used and abused, especially to finance government expenditure. The interventionist monetary policy took its toll on macroeconomic stability. Inflation in Latin America accelerated markedly from the 1950s onward, in particular in the Southern Cone countries (Argentina, Chile, and Uruguay) and Brazil. Eventually, a number of countries in the region entered into a spiral of monetary expansion-devaluation-monetary expansion that fueled increasing inflation until soaring prices got out of control. By the late 1980s and early 1990s inflation had reached four-digit rates in countries such as Argentina, Brazil, Nicaragua, and Peru.

With a new central bank mandate focused on a single objective, namely price stability, inflation started to decline by the mid-1990s. By 2000, annual inflation in Latin America had declined from about 500 percent in 1990 to below 10 percent.[38] But it was only in the mid-2000s that most countries in Latin America finally conquered inflation. In a region with a history of endemic inflation, this was a major achievement. Price stability was also possible because these countries simultaneously introduced, and maintained over time, sound macroeconomic policies—in particular fiscal policies—and strengthened their financial systems, and because they benefited from declining inflation globally.

After having defeated inflation and later successfully weathered the effects of the global financial crisis, central banks in Latin America may have entered into a new transition phase. They have started to move toward taking greater responsibility for securing the stability of financial systems. Central banks in Latin America may also be called upon to help stem the deceleration of economic growth or to restore its momentum.

Central banks in the region already had responsibilities in the past for helping to preserve financial stability—other than being the lender of last resort. In particular, those central banks created under the "Atlantic model" (Argentina, Brazil, Paraguay, and Uruguay), have a mandate of financial stability and thus regulate and supervise banks, and have implicit crisis management responsibilities. In general, most central banks rediscounted paper to financial institutions over the course of the 1920s to the 1990s, verifying that those institutions were on a sound

---

[38]See the IMF's *World Economic Outlook* (various issues).

financial footing. In this sense, central banks used to help keep financial stability in check and to fund financial institutions, thus minimizing the possibility of liquidity shortages. However, this practice was abandoned during the 1990s—following the latest central bank reform—to allow financial institutions to effectively play the role of financial intermediaries and central banks to focus on fighting inflation.

Today, assigning Latin American central banks financial stability responsibilities would have different implications. On the one hand, it would provide central banks with the institutional underpinnings to "lean against the wind" to moderate macroeconomic fluctuations caused by financial factors. On the other hand, central banks might be called on to develop a macroprudential policy function and thus become responsible for monitoring the buildup of systemic financial vulnerabilities and for taking decisions to prevent systemic crises—involving not only banks but also other financial intermediaries. Some Latin American countries (Chile, Mexico, and Uruguay) have already established financial stability committees, although the mandate of central banks has not been modified.[39]

The case for making central banks in Latin America responsible for economic growth and/or employment is less clear cut. In the aftermath of the recent crisis, central banks in major advanced economies have provided monetary accommodation to mitigate the recession and later to make the recovery less protracted. Central banks in Latin America had already implemented similar policies in the wake of the Great Depression, but the results became negative in the long term when their use was prolonged for normal times. Some LA5 central banks turned to this policy option during the Great Recession, but only as a last resort and in modest amounts. Operationally, should central banks in Latin America expand their monetary policy toolkit to incorporate unconventional policies as a way of boosting growth and employment?[40] In Latin America—like in other developing and emerging market economies—monetary policy is not likely to be effective in spurring growth and/or employment in the long term. Economic activity is highly dependent on external conductors in the short term, and hinges to a great extent on structural changes to feed employment and enhance productivity in the long term.

Meanwhile, some central banks in Latin America face challenges from the global economy. Specifically, it is unclear to what extent the financially integrated economies in Latin America can preserve monetary policy independence in a world of unsynchronized economic cycles. Monetary policy decisions in the region seems to be sensitive to decisions taken—and even to those only

---

[39]In all cases, the minister of finance chairs this committee, which aims at overseeing financial systems as a whole and at preventing financial crises. Jácome, Nier, and Imam (2012) describe the structure of these committees and their responsibilities.

[40]The advanced economies have already started to discuss whether to prolong accommodation and preserve unconventional instruments as part of the monetary policy toolkit, given that the Phillips curve no longer seems relevant in those economies (IMF 2013).

announced—by the U.S. Federal Reserve. These decisions and announcements can fuel capital flow reversals, and hence, exchange rate depreciations and inflation, thus generating pressure to elevate interest rates independently of domestic considerations. growing stream of literature, including Chapters 4 and 5 in this book, empirically analyzes the effect of monetary policy actions in advanced economies on central bank decisions in emerging markets.[41] Furthermore, in those countries in the region for which China is the main trading partner (Argentina, Brazil, Colombia, and Peru, among others) central banks face the dilemma of whether to increase the policy rate, as such an increase exacerbates the adverse impact of China's economic deceleration on Latin American exports and thus output.

CONCLUSIONS

It took about 80 years for Latin American central banks to achieve low and stable inflation. It was a long and rocky journey during which central banks were assigned different mandates and governments influenced monetary policy for about 50 years. As a result, many countries went through long periods of high inflation. However, following the institutional reform of monetary policy in the 1990s and the subsequent introduction of a forward-looking monetary policy focused on fighting inflation as a primary policy objective, a number of central banks finally achieved price stability. Latin American central banks later contributed decisively to helping the region successfully weather the global financial crisis.

The consequences of the global financial crisis and the Great Recession may trigger a new era of central banking in Latin America, as is already happening in advanced economies. The severity of the crisis upset a number of economic verities, including the consensus that central banks should primarily focus on controlling inflation. In response, a new paradigm has emerged, one that assigns central banks an enhanced role in preserving systemic financial stability. Central banks have also been called upon to help foster economic activity through the expansion of their balance sheets. The financial reform has just started to take hold in some Latin American countries. Learning from history might be useful in providing additional perspective as to how to shape future central bank policies in this region. The challenge is to avoid a situation where a new institutional and policy framework undermines central bank autonomy and accountability and, therefore, central banks' hard-won credibility.

---

[41]See Rey (2015), Obstfeld (2015), Aizenman, Chinn, and Ito (2016), and IMF (2015).

APPENDIX 2.1. MAIN RESPONSIBILITIES AND GOVERNANCE OF CENTRAL BANKS IN LATIN AMERICA WHEN THEY WERE FOUNDED

Country	Main Responsibilities	Composition of Board	Ownership
Argentina (1935)	- Issue the domestic currency. - Regulate the amount of money and credit in line with the needs of the economy. - Accumulate sufficient international reserves to moderate the adverse effects of exports and foreign investments and preserve the value of the currency. - Preserve appropriate conditions of liquidity and credit and apply the legislation to the banking system. - Act as fiscal agent and advisor to the government for the management of debt.	President and Vice President appointed by the President of the Republic and confirmed by the Senate; one member appointed by the executive branch; one by the Banco Nación; one by the provincial banks; three by the private banks; two by the foreign banks; and four representing the business associations.	Government and the banking system.
Chile (1925)	- Issue the national currency. - Conduct rediscount and discount operations with banks and the general public. - Provide financial assistance to the public sector on a limited basis. - Work as a fiscal agent. - Receive deposits from banks, the public sector, and the general public. - Provide clearing for payments. - Define the rediscount rate.	The President of the Republic appointed three board members; the banks appointed three; the business associations, two; the general public shareholders, one; and labor organizations, one.	Government, the banking system, and the general public.
Colombia (1922)	- Issue the national currency. - Conduct rediscount and discount operations with banks and the general public. - Provide financial assistance to the public sector on a limited basis. - Work as a fiscal agent. - Receive deposits from banks, the public sector, and the general public. - Provide clearing for payments. - Define the rediscount rate.	The President of the Republic appointed three board members; the domestic and international banks appointed four and two members, respectively; and the general public had one representative.	Government, the banking system, and the general public.
Ecuador (1927)	- Issue the national currency. - Act as lender of last resort to the banking system. - Conduct rediscount and discount operations with banks and the general public. - Provide financial assistance to the public sector on a limited basis. - Work as a fiscal agent. - Receive deposits from banks, the public sector, and the general public. - Define the rediscount rate. - Provide clearing for payments.	The President of the Republic appointed two members, commercial banks two members, business associations three members, and labor organizations one member.	The private banks, the general public, and the government (without voting rights).

(continued)

(continued)

Country	Main Responsibilities	Composition of Board	Ownership
El Salvador (1934)	- Issue the domestic currency. - Control the volume of credit and the money supply. - Preserve the external value of the currency. - Act as a fiscal agent and receive deposits from the government.	Five members designated by the central bank's shareholders.	Commercial banks and the Coffee Producers Association.
Mexico (1925)	- Issue currency. - Regulate the circulation of money, the exchange rate, and the interest rate. - Rediscount operations to banks. - Provide support to the government for Treasury operations. - Perform similar operations as the banking system.	The President of the Republic appointed five members and the shareholders appointed another four members.	Government and the general public.
Peru (1922)	- Monopoly of currency issue. - Receive deposits from banks, the public sector, and the general public. - Discount and rediscount commercial paper, treasury bonds, and other financial instruments. - Define discount rates. - Provide clearing for payments. - Provide financing to the government on a limited basis.	The President of the Republic appointed three members, the local banks four members, and the foreign banks three members.	National and international banks.

Sources: Argentina: Law 12.155 (1935); Chile: Law 486 (1925); Colombia: Sanchez, Fernández, and Armenta (2005) and Bank of the Republic website; Ecuador: Organic Law of the Central Bank of Ecuador (1927); El Salvador: Central Reserve Bank of El Salvador website; Mexico: Law that created the Bank of Mexico (1925); Peru: Law 4500 (1922).

APPENDIX 2.2. MAIN RESPONSIBILITIES AND GOVERNANCE OF CENTRAL BANKS IN LATIN AMERICA DURING THE DEVELOPMENTAL PHASE

Country	Main Objectives/Responsibilities	Composition of Board	Ownership
Argentina (1949)	Responsibilities: - Handle international reserves and execute capital controls to smooth out the impact from changes in trade and capital transactions on the currency and economic activity. - Regulate the amount of money and credit in order to secure conditions to preserve a high level of employment and the purchasing power of the currency. - Monitor liquidity and the appropriate flow of credit and implement the Banking Law. - Preserve and regulate developments in the securities market and act as fiscal agent for internal and external debt transactions.	The Minister and Vice Minister of Finance are President and Vice President of the Board; the presidents of the four following banks: Nación Argentina, Crédito Industrial Argentino, Hipotecario Nacional, and Caja Nacional de Ahorro Postal; five members appointed by the President of the Republic and who represent the agriculture, livestock, industrial, and trade sectors, as well as workers.	Government.
Chile (1953)	Objective: Orderly and continuous development of the national economy, implement monetary and credit policies to avoid inflationary and deflationary trends, and facilitate the best use of the country's productive resources.	The President of the Republic appointed three board members; banks appointed three; business associations, two; general public shareholders, one; and labor organizations, one.	Government, the banking system, and the general public.
Colombia (1951 for the objective and 1963 for the Monetary Board)	Objective: Conduct monetary, credit, and exchange rate policies with the aim of fostering the appropriate conditions for an orderly development of the Colombian economy. Responsibilities: - Issue the national currency. - Conduct rediscount and discount operations with banks and the general public. - Provide financial assistance to the public sector on a limited basis. - Work as a fiscal agent. - Receive deposits from banks, the public sector, and the general public. - Provide clearing for payments. - Define the rediscount rate.	Monetary Board comprised of the Minister of Finance; Minister of Economy; Minister of Agriculture; Head of the Planning Office; and the General Manager of the Bank of the Republic.	The banking system and the general public.

(continued)

(continued)

Country	Main Objectives/Responsibilities	Composition of Board	Ownership
Ecuador (1948)	Responsibilities: - Adapt the money supply and the flow of credit to the needs of the country. - Prevent and moderate inflationary and deflationary trends. - Promote the effective functioning of the banking system and the appropriate distribution of credit. - Coordinate with economic and fiscal activities that may affect credit and money markets. - Preserve the external value of the currency and its convertibility. - Preserve the competitiveness of the national production in international markets. -Prevent or moderate the adverse effects on the money supply and inflation from cyclical disequilibrium of the balance of payments.	Monetary Board comprised of one member appointed by Congress; the Minister of Finance; a representative of the National Economic Council; a representative of the Institute of Social Security; one member each appointed by commercial banks from the Coastal and from Andean regions; one member each appointed by business associations from the Coastal and Andean region; and one member appointed by the other members of the Monetary Board.	Government and the private banks.
Guatemala (1945)	Objective: Promote and maintain monetary, exchange rate, and credit conditions most favorable to the orderly development of the economy. Responsibilities: - Adapt the means of payment and credit policy to the needs of the country and the development of productive activities, preventing inflationary and deflationary trends. - Promote liquidity and solvency of the banking system and distribute credit according to the economic needs of the country. - Coordinate between monetary and fiscal policies as well as with other economic and financial policies. - Preserve the external value of the currency and its convertibility. - Administer international reserves. - Safeguard the international competitiveness of the domestic production.	Monetary Board comprised of the President and Vice President appointed by the President of the Republic; Ministers of Finance, Economy, and Agriculture; one representative from San Carlos University; one from the private banks; one from state-owned banks; and one from business associations (agriculture, industry, and trade).	Government.

(continued)

(continued)

Country	Main Objectives/Responsibilities	Composition of Board	Ownership
Mexico (1941 and reforms)	Objective: Issue currency and preserve credit and foreign exchange conditions that favor the stability of the purchasing power of money, financial system development, and sound economic growth. Responsibilities: - Regulate currency issue and circulation, as well as credit and the exchange rate. - Lender of last resort and operate the payments system. - Financial agent of the government for domestic and external credit operations, and provide treasury services to the government. - Advise the government on economic and financial issues. - Represent the country at the IMF and other multilateral institutions related to central banks in line with national objectives and planning, under the guidelines for monetary and credit policies defined by the Secretary of Treasury.	Governing Board comprised of 11 members: the Secretary and Under Secretary of the Treasury; the Secretary of the Budget; the Secretary of Trade and Industry; the Director General of the Bank of Mexico; the presidents of the Banking and Insurance Commission and of the Securities Commission; the president of the Banking Association; and three external members appointed by the executive branch.	Government.
Peru (1962)	Objective: Preserve monetary stability, credit, and exchange rate conditions conducive to orderly development of the economy, with the support of adequate fiscal and economic policies. Functions: - Currency issue and monetary regulation. - Regulate banks' credit. - Administer the country's international reserves.	The President of the Republic appointed three members and the other six members representing development banks, regional commercial banks, commercial banks established in Lima, the agriculture sector, the industrial sector, and trade associations.	Government.

Sources: Argentina: Law 25.120 (1949); Chile: Law 11151 (1953); Colombia: Decree 756 DE (1951), Law 21 (1963), and Decree 2206 DE (1963); Ecuador: Law of the Monetary Regime (1948); Guatemala: Law 215 (1945); Mexico: Organic Law of the Bank of Mexico (1985); Peru: Organic Law 13958 (1962).

APPENDIX 2.3. POLICY OBJECTIVES AND GOVERNANCE OF CENTRAL BANKS IN LATIN AMERICA DURING THE GOLDEN AGE

Country	Objectives	Composition of Board	Term in Office
Chile (1989)	Stability of the currency and functioning of domestic and external payments.	Five directors appointed by the executive and confirmed by the Senate for staggered terms.	Term for central bank president is five years, and for the other directors it is 10 years.
Colombia (1992)	Preserve price stability.	Minister of Finance (Chair), General Manager of central bank (appointed by the board), and five directors appointed for staggered terms by the executive branch.	The six directors, including the general manager of the central bank, serve for four years with a renewable term.
Costa Rica (1995)	Maintain the domestic and external stability of the currency.	President of the central bank and five members, appointed by the executive, plus the Minister of Finance. Five members appointed for staggered terms and confirmed by Congress.	President of the central bank has a four-year term, like the President of the Republic. The other five members' terms are 90 months.
Honduras (1996)	Maintain internal and external value of domestic currency and favor normal functioning of the payment system.	Executive appoints five directors. Minister of Finance is part of the board without decision power.	Four years simultaneously with government period.
Mexico (1993)	Ensure the stability of the currency's purchasing power; the central bank should also promote the sound development of the financial system and the functioning of the payments system.	Five members appointed by the President of the Republic with the approval of the Senate.	Governor's term is six years and for other members it is eight years, with staggered appointments.
Peru (1993)	Preserve monetary stability.	Executive nominates four directors, including the central bank president. Congress ratifies this decision and appoints three additional directors.	The same as the President of the Republic.
Uruguay (1995)	Ensure currency stability, functioning of domestic and external payments, and adequate levels of international reserves, and promote and maintain soundness, solvency, and operations of the financial system.	The executive, with the approval of the Senate, appoints the president, vice president, and a director of the central bank.	Appointed for the term of office of the President of the Republic.
Venezuela (1992)	Create and maintain monetary, credit, and exchange rate conditions favorable to monetary stability, economic equilibrium, and orderly economic development.	Executive nominates the central bank president (confirmed by Senate) and six directors, including a member from the executive (not the Minister of Finance).	The president is appointed for five years and the directors for six years staggered, except for the executive member.

Sources: Chile: Law 18840; Colombia: Law 31/1992; Costa Rica: Law 7558; Honduras: Decree 228-96; Mexico: Law of the Bank of Mexico (1993); Peru: Law 26123; Uruguay: Law 16.696; Venezuela B.R.: Law 31.

REFERENCES

Aizenman, J., M. D. Chinn, and H. Ito. 2016. "Monetary Policy Spillovers and the Trilemma in the New Normal: Periphery Country Sensitivity to Core Country Conditions." *Journal of International Money and Finance* 68: 298–330.

Barro, R., and D. Gordon. 1983. "A Positive Theory of Monetary Policy in a Natural Rate Model." *Journal of Political Economy* 91(4): 589–610.

Braun-Llona, J., M. Braun-Llona, I. Briones, J. Diaz, R. Luders, and G. Wagner. 2000. *Economía Chilena 1810–1995: Estadísticas Históricas*. Santiago: Pontificia Universidad Católica de Chile.

Bruno, M., G. Di Tella, R. Dornbusch, and S. Fischer. 1988. *Inflation Stabilization: The Experience of Israel, Argentina, Brazil, Bolivia, and Mexico*. Cambridge, Massachusetts: MIT Press.

Bruno, M., S. Fischer, E. Helpman, and N. Liviatan. 1991. *Lessons of Economic Stabilization and Its Aftermath*. Cambridge, Massachusetts: MIT Press.

Canales-Kriljenko, J., L. I. Jácome, A. Alichi, and I. de Oliveira Lima. 2010. "Weathering the Global Storm: The Benefits of Monetary Policy Reform in the LA5 Countries." IMF Working Paper 10/292, International Monetary Fund, Washington, DC.

Carbo, L. A. 1978. *Historia Monetaria y Cambiaria del Ecuador*. Quito: Banco Central del Ecuador.

Carrasco, C. 2009. *Banco Central de Chile 1925–1964: Una Historia Institucional*. Santiago: Banco Central de Chile.

Carstens, A., and L. I. Jácome. 2005. "Latin American Central Bank Reform: Progress and Challenges." IMF Working Paper 05/114, International Monetary Fund, Washington, DC.

Corbo, V. 1985. "Reforms and Macroeconomic Adjustment in Chile during 1974–1984." *World Development* 13(8): 893–916.

———, and L. Hernández. 2005. "Ochenta Años de Historia del Banco Central de Chile." Working Paper 345, Central Bank of Chile, Santiago.

Cukierman A., S. Webb, and B. Neyapti. 1992. "Measuring the Independence of Central Banks and Its Effect on Policy Outcomes." *World Bank Economic Review* 6 (September): 352–98.

Díaz, J., R. Lüders, and G. Wagner. 2010. "La República en Cifras." EH Clio Lab-Iniciativa Científica Milenio, Pontificia Universidad Católica de Chile, Santiago.

Dincer, N., and B. Eichengreen. 2014. "Central Bank Transparency and Independence: Updates and New Measures." *International Journal of Central Banking* (March): 189–253.

Dornbusch, R., and S. Edwards. 1990. "Macroeconomic Populism." *Journal of Development Economics* 32(2): 247–77.

Fernandez, R. 1985. "The Expectations Management Approach to Stabilization in Argentina during 1976–1982." *World Development* 13(8): 871–92.

Fleming, M. 1962. "Domestic Financial Policies under Fixed and Floating Exchange Rates." *IMF Staff Papers* 9: 369–79.

Frenkel, J., and H. Johnson. 1976. *The Monetary Approach to the Balance of Payments*. London: Allen & Unwin.

Grupo de Estudios de Crecimiento Económico. 2001. *El Crecimiento Económico Colombiano del Siglo XX*. Bogotá: Banco de la República.

Haddad, C. 1978. "Crescimento do Producto Real Brasileiro–1900/1947." *Revista Braileira de Economia* 29(1): 3–26.

International Monetary Fund (IMF). 2013. "The Dog That Didn't Bark: Has Inflation Been Muzzled or Was It Just Sleeping?" In *World Economic Outlook*. Washington, DC, April.

———. 2015. "To Hike or Not to Hike: Is That an Option for Latin America? Assessing Monetary Policy Autonomy." In *Regional Economic Outlook: Western Hemisphere*. Washington, DC, October.

Jácome, L. I. 2008. "Central Bank Involvement in Banking Crises in Latin America." IMF Working Paper 08/135, International Monetary Fund, Washington, DC.

———. 2015. "Central Banking in Latin America: From the Gold Standard to the Golden Years." IMF Working Paper 15/60, International Monetary Fund, Washington, DC.

———, E. W. Nier, and P. Imam. 2012. "Building Blocks for Effective Macroprudential Policies in Latin America." IMF Working Paper 12/183, International Monetary Fund, Washington, DC.

———, T. Saadi-Sedik, and S. Townsend. 2012. "Can Emerging Market Central Banks Bail Out Banks? A Cautionary Tale from Latin America." *Emerging Markets Review* 13: 424–48.

Jácome, L. I., and F. Vázquez. 2008. "Any Link between Legal Central Bank Independence and Inflation? Evidence from Latin America and the Caribbean." *European Journal of Political Economy* 24 (December): 788–801.

Kydland, F., and E. Prescott. 1977. "Rules Rather than Discretion." *Journal of Political Economy* 85(3): 473–92.

Laurens, B., M. Arnone, and J.-F. Segalotto. 2009. *Central Bank Independence, Accountability, and Transparency—A Global Perspective.* London: Palgrave Macmillan for the International Monetary Fund.

Lora, E. 2001. "Structural Reforms in Latin America: What Has Been Reformed and How to Measure It." IDB Publication 39858, Inter-American Development Bank, Washington, DC.

Mundell, R. 1963. "Capital Mobility and Stabilization Policy under Fixed and Flexible Exchange Rates." *Canadian Journal of Economic and Political Science* 29(4): 475–85.

Obstfeld, M. 2015. "Trilemmas and Tradeoffs: Living with Financial Globalization." In *Global Liquidity, Spillovers to Emerging Markets and Policy Responses*, edited by C. Raddatz, D. Saravia, and J. Ventura. Santiago: Central Bank of Chile.

Polak, J. 1957. "Monetary Analysis of Income Formation and Payments Problems." *IMF Staff Papers* 6 (November).

Rey, H. 2015. "Dilemma Not Trilemma: The Global Financial Cycle and Monetary Policy Independence." NBER Working Paper 21162, National Bureau of Economic Research, Cambridge, Massachusetts.

Rogoff, K. 1985. "The Optimal Degree of Commitment to an Intermediate Monetary Target." *Quarterly Journal of Economics* 100: 1169–89.

Sánchez, F., A. Fernández, and A. Armenta. 2005. "Historia Monetaria de Colombia en el Siglo XX: Grandes Tendencias y Episodios Relevantes." Documento CEDE 2005-30 (May), Universidad de los Andes, Bogotá, Colombia.

Suzigan, W., and A. Villela. 2001. *Política de Governo e Crescimento da Economia Brasileira 1889–1945.* Brasilia: Instituto de Pesquisa Econômica Aplicada.

CHAPTER 3

Central Banking in Latin America: The Way Forward

Yan Carrière-Swallow, Luis Jácome, Nicolás Magud, and Alejandro Werner, International Monetary Fund

The 2008 global financial crisis and its aftermath have ushered in a new era of central banking worldwide. Major changes are taking place in advanced economies. Many have introduced legal reforms that assign a more active role to central banks in preserving financial stability. These institutions have also adopted extraordinary unconventional monetary policies initially aimed at avoiding the collapse of their financial systems and later at supporting economic recovery.[1] Meanwhile, crucial new challenges have arisen for central banking in emerging market economies, and some still have to deal with more traditional problems. For Latin America's central banks, these challenges can be grouped into three categories.

First, the traditional challenge of delivering price stability still confronts a small group of economies in the region where inflation remains stubbornly high and volatile. While fiscal policy is the root cause of high inflation in many cases, strengthening central bank independence is an important aspect of disinflationary strategies.

Second, in those countries with established and credible inflation-targeting frameworks, central challenges relate to policymaking under heightened uncertainty. Specifically, implementation of the appropriate monetary policy stance is made more complex in a period of unusually high uncertainty about the level and growth of potential output, the natural interest rate, and the equilibrium real exchange rate. It will also be important to strengthen communication to better anchor inflation expectations and improve monetary policy transmission. Some countries need to clarify the role of the exchange rate and foreign exchange intervention, as well as the appropriate level of international reserves.

Finally, important challenges stem from the influence of global factors and the lessons learned from the recent financial crisis. Increasingly powerful external financial cycles have proved that they can influence and even overpower monetary

---

[1]Joyce and others (2012) offer a clear and comprehensive summary of these extraordinary measures, while Borio and Zabai (2016) and IMF (2013a) discuss their effectiveness.

policymaking at home, as well as destabilize domestic financial systems. In this context, many Latin American central banks are revisiting the role that they should play in preserving financial stability and the ways in which monetary and macroprudential policies can be coordinated.

The next section of this chapter revisits the progress made in the conduct of monetary policy in Latin America over previous decades and highlights some reversals of past progress that warrant further reforms. The following section discusses refinements that could be made to improve inflation-targeting regimes in the region. The chapter then revisits the role of the exchange rate in monetary policymaking in the region, and suggests areas where improved communication could clarify the central bank's reaction function. The chapter then turns to discussing the implications of assigning central banks the task of ensuring financial stability, before putting forth some final conclusions.

DEFEATING INFLATION: ACHIEVEMENTS AND REVERSALS

Since the 1990s, monetary policy in Latin America has achieved a remarkable transformation in terms of achieving price stability. A wave of legal reforms in the region in the first half of the decade—in some cases enshrined in national constitutions—granted independence to central banks. At their core, the changes aimed to restrict central bank financing of public sector deficits that was at the root of high inflation throughout Latin America. These reforms took place alongside determined efforts to rein in public sector deficits. At the same time, countries gradually liberalized external current and capital accounts, strengthened financial systems, and allowed price discovery in key economic sectors. Because of these reforms, high inflation has been consigned to history for most countries in the region.

Initially, central bankers were not interested in independence as a means of implementing monetary policy to stabilize the domestic business cycle under flexible exchange rates. Rather, a number of them continued to target the exchange rate as the main operational instrument of monetary policy in order to bring down high inflation or further consolidate gains in terms of already-low inflation. Only later did countries gradually and more formally adopt exchange rate flexibility and inflation targeting. After both of these processes were implemented, price stability was restored in most economies, and monetary policy eventually assumed its important countercyclical role.

Central Bank Reform

New central banking legislation in Latin America was based on four main pillars: (1) definition of a clear and narrow mandate; (2) formulation of central bank policies independent of the executive branch; (3) autonomy of monetary policy implementation; and (4) accountability of central banks. These pillars also figured prominently in the legislation that established new central banks in the transition economies of Eastern Europe during the same period. While these pillars have figured in the reforms implemented in many countries, the details of their application have varied.

In Latin America, Chile was a pioneer in changing its constitution and central bank legislation in 1989. Other countries soon followed suit. El Salvador approved new central bank legislation in 1991; Argentina, Colombia, Ecuador, Nicaragua, and Venezuela in 1992; Mexico and Peru in 1993; Bolivia, Costa Rica, Paraguay, and Uruguay in 1995; Honduras in 1996; and the Dominican Republic and Guatemala in 2002. As an exception, Brazil has not amended its central bank law since its creation in 1964, while other countries (Argentina, Bolivia, Ecuador, and Venezuela) have backtracked by passing legal changes that undermined previous central bank independence.[2]

Price stability became the single or primary objective assigned to most central banks (Table 3.1). Rather than directly promoting economic development, central banks were required by legislatures to focus on fighting inflation as a way of indirectly fostering economic growth and thus improving social welfare.[3] This narrow mandate was elevated to the constitutional level in a number of countries, including Chile, Colombia, Mexico, and Peru. Assigning a clear mandate also facilitated the task of holding central banks accountable.

In some countries (Chile, Honduras, and Nicaragua), securing the operation of the payments system was combined with a price stability mandate, whereas in others (Argentina, Brazil, Paraguay, and Uruguay) the central bank was also empowered to regulate and supervise banks. Thus, *financial stability* was an additional objective in these countries, as well as in others such as Costa Rica and Mexico. Since Brazil did not reform its central bank law, the use of monetary policy to promote economic development is not legally restricted, whereas in Argentina this objective was reintroduced to the central bank charter in 2012. In Venezuela, the central bank has been required since 2001 to coordinate monetary policy with the government in order to "achieve the highest objectives of the State and the Nation."

To achieve its price stability mandate, the new legislation also instituted *central bank autonomy* to formulate monetary policy. The rationale was to insulate monetary policy decisions made by an independent board from the short-term influences of the political cycle, which could give rise to an inflationary bias.[4]

---

[2]Recently, the Brazilian government announced its intention to submit a bill to Congress granting operational independence to its central bank.

[3]Before the reform of the central bank legislation, a monetary policy mandate to promote economic growth or economic development was a common pattern in Latin America (see Chapter 2).

[4]See the early contributions of Barro and Gordon (1983) and Rogoff (1985). Separating central bank decision making from the government required appointing board members in a two-step process in which they are nominated by the executive branch and confirmed by the legislature (Carstens and Jácome 2005). Furthermore, in most cases, board members were appointed for a longer period than the presidential term and/or overlapping with that term. Brazil is a prominent exception to this practice, as central bank board members are appointed without specifying their tenure, whereas in Peru the appointment of board members coincides with the presidential term.

TABLE 3.1

Key Features of Central Bank Legislation in Latin America, 2016						
	Primary Mandate		Political Independence	Credit to the Government		Accountability
	Price stability	Economic development	Years of tenure of board members	Banned or restricted	Weak limitations	Formal report to Congress
Argentina	✓	✓	6		✓	✓
Bolivia	✓		6/5		✓	
Brazil		✓	Open	✓		✓
Chile	✓		5/10	✓		✓
Colombia	✓		4	✓		✓
Costa Rica	✓		4/8.5	✓		
Dominican Republic	✓			✓		
Guatemala	✓	✓	4	✓		✓
Honduras	✓		4	✓		
Mexico	✓		6/8	✓		✓
Nicaragua	✓		4	✓		
Paraguay	✓		5	✓		✓
Peru	✓		5	✓		✓
Uruguay	✓		5	✓		
Venezuela	✓	✓	7		✓	

Source: Countries' central bank legislation.
Note: When they differ, the tenure is listed for presidents and for regular board members.

Furthermore, the new legislation excluded members of the government from the board of the central bank (except in a few countries like Colombia and Guatemala).[5] In several countries, a cornerstone of this political autonomy is that board members can only be removed for violations that are strictly codified in the legislation through judicial or legislative review. In addition, in most cases, central banks were empowered to autonomously formulate exchange rate policy.

With a history of high and persistent inflation, some countries in Latin America assigned central banks independence not only to select their instruments, but also *to specify their goals*. The latter implies that central banks unilaterally set their inflation target, a feature that is uncommon among advanced economies. In turn, assigning operational or instrument independence to central banks enables them to control all policy instruments required to fight inflation without government interference. Furthermore, financing the government deficit—the historical source of inflation in the region—was strictly restricted and even banned at a constitutional level in Chile, Colombia, Ecuador, Guatemala, Mexico, and Peru, among other countries.

The fourth pillar of the reform was *central bank accountability*. This typically requires that central banks submit a report to the executive and legislative branches and, in general, publicly disclose the decisions and actions taken in pursuing their policy objectives. In some countries, the central bank governor is also

---

[5] In Chile, the Minister of Finance is allowed to attend meetings of the central bank's board, but does not have voting powers.

TABLE 3.2

Central Bank Independence in Latin America Before and After the Legal Reform, Selected Countries

Country	Reform Year	Pre-reform	Post-reform	Country	Reform Year	Pre-reform	Post-reform
Argentina*	1992	0.31	0.83	Honduras	1996	0.39	0.68
Bolivia*	1995	0.33	0.83	Mexico	1993	0.39	0.81
Chile	1989	0.26	0.85	Nicaragua	1992	0.41	0.73
Colombia	1992	0.29	0.83	Paraguay	1995	0.37	0.70
Costa Rica	1995	0.51	0.74	Peru	1993	0.50	0.84
Dominican Republic	2002	0.44	0.77	Uruguay†	1995	0.44	0.70
Guatemala	2002	0.57	0.73	Venezuela*	1992	0.40	0.69

Sources: Central bank legislation; and Jácome and Vázquez (2008).
Note: The index of central bank independence is based on the legal provisions of central bank laws and related legislation. The overall value of the index fluctuates on a continuous scale from zero to one, with higher values indicating stronger legal central bank independence. Countries where subsequent legislation has reverted these reforms to some extent are marked with an asterisk, while countries that have furthered the independence of their central banks through subsequent reforms are marked with a dagger.

required to appear before Congress to report on the conduct of monetary policy and explain the central bank's performance in achieving its policy objectives.

Measuring Central Bank Independence

Legal independence of central banks increased significantly in most countries as a result of their institutional reforms. Measured by a well-known index, independence of many central banks in the region more than doubled following the reform (Table 3.2).[6] Improvements were achieved on all fronts, but in particular with respect to the definition of the central banks' mandate, limitations to grant credit to the government, and the introduction of central bank accountability. Among emerging markets, the most independent central banks in Latin America now rank highly when compared with peers in other regions (Canales and others 2010).

Greater central bank independence, in turn, is associated with lower inflation, as documented by Jácome and Vázquez (2008),[7] who found a (statistically significant) positive correlation between structural reforms and legal central bank independence. This suggests that changes to central bank legislation coincided with the broader agenda of structural reforms implemented in Latin America.[8]

---

[6]See Cukierman, Webb, and Neyapti (1992). The modified version of the index used here incorporates a broader view of political independence that includes all members of the central bank board and not only the governor, central banks' financial independence (whether central banks have capital at all times), and their accountability and transparency.

[7]The analysis uses panel regressions for the period 1985–2002 and controls for international inflation, banking crises, and exchange rate regimes.

[8]Evidence of a causal relationship between (legal) central bank independence and inflation was not established in the study. Such causality was only found for the tests based on the turnover rate of central bank governors as a measure of de facto central bank independence.

A New Policy Framework

Central bank independence was not viewed as a precondition for adopting an inflation-targeting framework, but rather as necessary for reducing inflation and durably achieving price stability. In fact, during the early phases of their autonomy a number of central banks in the region targeted the exchange rate using a crawling peg or crawling band to reduce inflation. It was the advent of currency crises in some countries (like Brazil, Colombia, and Mexico), and the impact of intellectual developments in monetary policy and central banking on others (Chile), that made floating the most prevalent exchange rate regime in the region by the early 2000s and opened the door for the implementation of fully fledged inflation-targeting regimes (Figure 3.1).

With the turn of the century, a rising number of countries in the region introduced greater exchange rate flexibility. By 2015, 10 of the 18 countries in the region had adopted a flexible regime, up from 6 in 1990, while 5 countries still kept a soft peg and 3 countries used the U.S. dollar as legal tender (Figure 3.2). Exchange rate flexibility in Latin America initially was met with significant skepticism, however, as countries repeatedly intervened in the foreign exchange market to restrict that flexibility and to build up international reserves.[9] But as hedging markets developed and nominal uncertainty declined, the costs of exchange rate volatility declined and the variability of Latin America's exchange rates converged to that of advanced small and open economies (Figure 3.3).

Strengthening international reserves was a more consistent and common trend, as countries aimed to create a buffer against recurrent real and financial shocks. Remarkable examples are Bolivia and Peru, where international reserves—measured by gross reserves minus gold—increased to more than 30 percent of GDP by 2015 from less than 5 percent in 1990. By 2015, Brazil and Mexico had also boosted international reserves to 20 and 15 percent of GDP, respectively. In most countries, reserve accumulation benefited from the favorable external conditions associated with the supercycle in global commodity prices.

As exchange rates became more flexible, inflation targeting also became more prevalent in the region. With a clear mandate on price stability and after having already reduced inflation—often via exchange rate targeting—an increasing number of central banks adopted inflation targeting to preserve price stability gains. In most cases, the adoption of inflation targeting followed a gradual path in which the main elements of transparency and accountability were introduced in piecemeal fashion. Brazil, however, followed a "cold turkey" approach in the midst of its currency crisis in early 1999. Chile and Colombia also introduced inflation targeting that year, whereas Mexico and Peru did so in 2001 and 2002, respectively.[10]

---

[9]Calvo and Reinhart (2002) called this phenomenon "fear of floating" and questioned the countries' commitment to floating the exchange rate.

[10]For a detailed description of each of the country cases, see Schmidt-Hebbel and Werner (2002) for Brazil, Chile, and Mexico; Gómez, Uribe, and Vargas (2002) for Colombia; and Armas and Grippa (2005) for Peru. Costa Rica, the Dominican Republic, Guatemala, and Paraguay adopted inflation targeting later.

Figure 3.1. Inflation, Central Bank Independence, Exchange Rate Regimes, and Inflation Targeting in Selected Latin American Countries
(Percent)

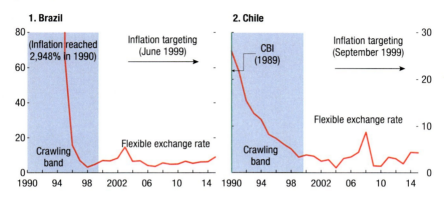

Sources: Central bank websites; IMF, *Annual Report on Exchange Arrangements and Exchange Restrictions*; and IMF, *International Financial Statistics*.
Note: The shaded area covers the years that countries targeted the exchange rate to defeat inflation. Brazil did not approve legislation to grant independence to the central bank. CBI = central bank independence.

Inflation targeting provided an anchor for inflationary expectations while allowing for enhanced monetary policy flexibility. To monitor policy success, the LA5 countries (Brazil, Chile, Colombia, Mexico, and Peru) chose a point target with a certain tolerance band for inflation (Table 3.3), using the consumer price index as the measure of price stability.

Central banks also enhanced communication and transparency to strengthen the effectiveness of monetary policy. Policy rates are decided during pre-announced monetary policy meetings, mostly held on a monthly basis (Table 3.3). All LA5 central banks issue a communique announcing the policy decision and, except for Peru, later issue minutes of the policy meetings. Information about how votes

Figure 3.2. Exchange Rate Regimes in Latin America

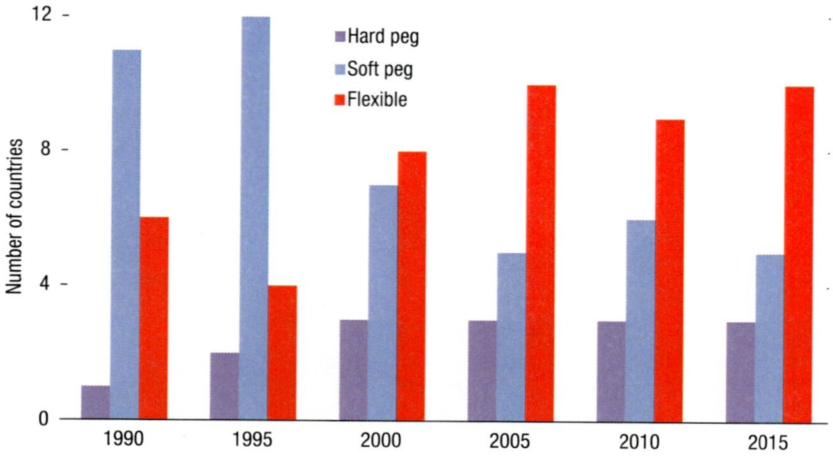

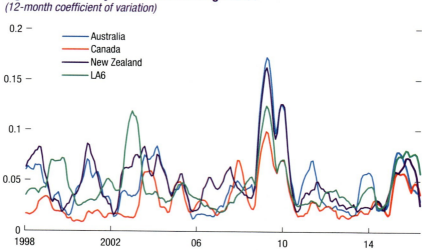

Sources: Central bank websites; IMF, *Annual Report on Exchange Arrangements and Exchange Restrictions*.

Figure 3.3. Volatility of Nominal Exchange Rates
(12-month coefficient of variation)

Sources: IMF, Information Notice System database; and IMF staff calculations.
Note: LA6 represents the simple average of Brazil, Chile, Colombia, Mexico, Peru, and Uruguay.

TABLE 3.3

Inflation Targets, Decision Making, Communication, and Transparency						
	Inflation Target	Frequency of Policy Meetings	Issue Press Release	Issue Minutes	Publication of Votes	Inflation Report
Brazil	4.5% (+/−2)	Eight times a year	Yes	Yes	Balance of votes	Four times a year
Chile	3% (+/−1)	Monthly	Yes	Yes	Balance of votes	Four times a year
Colombia	3% (+/−1)	Monthly	Yes	Yes	Whether majority or consensus	Four times a year
Mexico	3% (+/−1)	11 times a year	Yes	Yes	No	Four times a year
Peru	2% (+/−1)	Monthly	Yes	No	No	Four times a year

Sources: Central bank websites; and Hammond 2009.

were cast is provided in Brazil and Chile. In addition, all central banks issue a quarterly inflation report explaining the rationale of the monetary policy stance in the context of the broad internal and external macroeconomic environment and stressing the upside and downside risks for the inflation forecast.

Central banks in Latin America also revamped their operational frameworks. When they introduced their inflation targets, Brazil, Chile, and Colombia all established a short-term interest rate as their operational target. The Bank of Mexico adopted a policy rate as its operational target only in January 2008, after having followed some steps to replace its previous quantity-based operational target (a borrowed reserves target, the so-called *corto*) (Carstens and Werner, 1999). In Peru, where the financial system is highly dollarized, the central bank moved to a policy rate as an operational target in late 2003, after going through a gradual transition away from the use of monetary aggregates. Peru also used reserve requirements as a capital flow management measure and to discourage financial dollarization. The LA5 central banks all chose a target for a market-based overnight interest rate as their policy rate.[11]

Achieving Low and Stable Inflation, and Some Reversals

The institutional and policy reform of central banks paid off, as inflation plunged across the region by the mid-1990s. After decades of very high inflation, most Latin American countries brought inflation down to single digits and eventually achieved low and stable inflation during the mid-2000s (Figure 3.4, panels 1 and 2). This outcome allowed a number of central banks—particularly those that had adopted inflation targeting as their monetary policy regime at the

---

[11]Central banks also set up standing facilities offered for liquidity provision and for liquidity absorption, thus creating an interest rate corridor around the policy rate to help keep market interest rates close to the target.

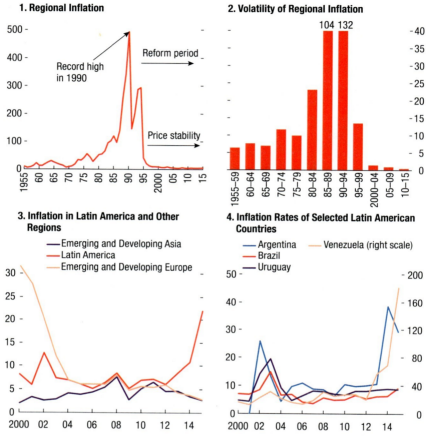

Figure 3.4. Inflation in Latin America
(Percent)

Sources: IMF, *International Financial Statistics;* and IMF, *World Economic Outlook.*
Note: Data refer to period average consumer price inflating. Starting in 2007, inflation for Argentina corresponds to IMF staff estimates.

beginning of the century—to build credibility by keeping inflation within their target band most of the time.

Yet, average inflation in Latin America remains above that in other regions with similar levels of development (Figure 3.4, panel 3), largely due to the recent acceleration of prices in a small number of countries. In particular, inflation has surged to triple digits in Venezuela, while in Argentina it is estimated to have averaged more than 30 percent since 2014. As of mid-2016, these two countries hold the dubious distinction of having the highest rates of inflation in the world. These developments reflect a significant deterioration in public finances and fiscal dominance, as governments pressure central banks to finance fiscal deficits. In turn, inflation in Brazil and Uruguay has recently hovered around 10 percent (Figure 3.4, panel 4). There are many causes behind this outcome that apply to one or both countries, including institutional weaknesses in central banks, lax fiscal policies that place downward pressure on the exchange rate and upward pressure on inflation expectations, and wage indexation.

Against this backdrop, Latin American central banks face important challenges ahead. In high-inflation economies, central bank independence must be consolidated while governments strengthen their fiscal frameworks, thus laying the basis for achieving price stability. And despite having successfully stabilized inflation in their economies, Latin America's inflation targeters confront important challenges of their own, which we turn to in the following sections.

MAKING INFLATION TARGETING MORE EFFECTIVE

Assessing the right stance for monetary policy has become an even harder task for central banks in the region in the face of a very uncertain international environment that has coincided with significant changes on the domestic front. Unusually accommodative global financial conditions, falling commodity prices, and a lower neutral rate of interest in advanced economies are key external sources of uncertainty. Meanwhile, on the domestic front, the level and growth rate of potential output are being reassessed. These external and domestic sources of uncertainty complicate determining the appropriate monetary policy stance, as policymakers try to determine the new equilibrium levels of the real exchange rate, the neutral interest rate, and the level of slack in the economy. Amidst these challenging developments, the inflationary impact of a large and persistent exchange rate depreciation has prompted a difficult discussion regarding the appropriate monetary policy response from Latin America's central banks, and how these decisions should be communicated.

Improving Assessments of Economic Slack and the Policy Stance

Clearly communicating the central bank's estimate of the output gap has been shown to improve the effectiveness of inflation-targeting regimes. It provides market participants with information on the assumptions underlying monetary policy, thus allowing them to better anticipate the future path of policy decisions. But before the output gap can be clearly communicated, central banks around the world—including in advanced economies—face an operational challenge: the output gap must first be reliably estimated. Since an economy's potential output is unobservable, assessing it is inevitably subject to uncertainty and relies on judgment. At the core of the exercise is being able to determine whether the shocks hitting the economy and driving inflation are transitory or permanent.

As Orphanides and van Norden (2002) document for the United States, and Grigoli and others (2015) extend for a large sample of countries using the IMF's

World Economic Outlook vintages, real-time estimates of the output gap tend to suffer substantial revisions. With the benefit of hindsight, there seems to be a bias toward overestimating economic slack in real time, with initial diagnoses of slack often revised to overheating in subsequent years. Estimation errors stem from two main factors. First, initial data releases for economic output tend to be substantially revised in subsequent periods. Second, it is difficult to distinguish transitory from permanent shocks, which introduces errors in assessments of potential output. Surprisingly, revisions to output gap estimates happen long after the initial data release.[12]

Across countries, output gap revisions are significantly smaller among advanced economies than emerging market economies and are smaller among inflation-targeting countries. Even among the established inflation-targeting economies of Latin America, the size of historical revisions to output gap estimates suggest that it has been extremely difficult to assess excess capacity in real time with any degree of precision. Given these large revisions, policy interest rate decisions often deviate substantially from those that might have been chosen with the benefit of hindsight.

Over time, the difficulties associated with measuring the output gap, and the size of possible policy missteps that can result, are heightened in periods when potential output—usually a slow-moving variable—is itself subject to substantial revisions. As Figure 3.5 shows, the end of the commodity price supercycle has led to very large downward revisions to the outlook for medium-term growth in Latin America and the Caribbean. In this context, recent assessments of economic slack have been subject to considerable uncertainty.

A recent literature has argued that variables with a longer cycle, such as world commodity prices or global financial variables, can lead output to deviate from its sustainable potential for prolonged periods without necessarily generating inflationary pressures, further complicating estimates of the output gap.[13] Promisingly, Borio, Disyatat, and Juselius (2013) and Borio and others (2016) show that adjusting for the financial cycle generates real-time estimates of the output gap that are less prone to subsequent revisions. Alberola and others (2016) estimate that the recent supercycle in global commodity prices caused real-time estimates of the output gap in Latin America to be excessively procyclical, leading monetary policy to follow suit in some cases. But while adjusting output gap estimates for these lower-frequency factors may be conceptually appealing under certain conditions, it is unclear how such decisions should be communicated within a coherent monetary policy framework. In particular, doing so may require lengthening the horizon at which monetary policy is

---

[12]During the first year, the median revision reaches 0.9 percentage points, and even after two years additional revisions are almost 0.5 percentage points. This bias is larger during recessionary periods.

[13]For instance, Rabanal and Raheri Sanjani (2015) illustrate how the presence of financial frictions amplifies measures of the output gap in the European context.

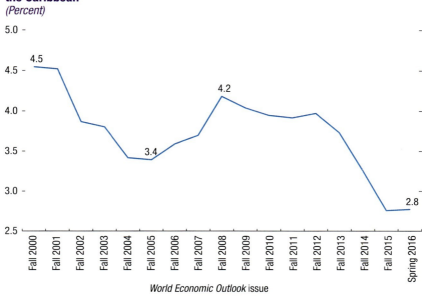

Figure 3.5. Forecasts of Medium-Term Growth in Latin America and the Caribbean
(Percent)

Source: IMF, *World Economic Outlook* (various issues).

expected to return inflation to its target, further testing the limits of central bank credibility.

Of course, the challenge intrinsic in making policy decisions based on imperfect real-time data and estimates does not mean that central banks should abandon the use of the output gap. Rather, they should strive to improve measurement of the output gap and, above all, supplement their information with more detailed studies and indicators, especially of the country's labor market and capacity utilization. While estimation of economic slack based on each of these indicators is subject to similar limitations as estimation of the output gap, the use of a wider information set may help in making a more accurate real-time assessment. Central banks must focus on improving their reading of tightness in product and factor markets. This could be achieved through better understanding of labor markets and capacity utilization, with less of a focus on univariate estimates of the output gap.

A related issue is the assessment of the monetary policy stance. Since 2013, central banks in Latin America have kept policy rates on hold or implemented relatively modest hikes in response to prolonged inflationary pressures largely attributable to exchange rate depreciations. The stated intention of this policy has been to maintain accommodative monetary policy conditions in order to support weak aggregate demand amid rapidly slowing growth rates. But how accommodative have policy rates been? The answer depends crucially on the level of the neutral rate of interest.

Highly accommodative global financial conditions since the 2009 crisis and the trends that have contributed to the global savings glut are estimated to have systematically and substantially lowered the neutral real interest rate in Latin America (Magud and Tsounta 2012). But in standard models, the neutral rate of interest is expected to be an increasing function of the growth rate of potential output and the international neutral rate. As such, rapidly slowing potential growth rates largely related to the end of the commodities boom and a declining neutral rate in advanced economies may be further reducing neutral interest rates throughout Latin America.[14] If this is the case, a seemingly accommodative policy of steady policy rates may in fact correspond to a gradually tightening monetary stance.

Strengthening Nominal Anchors

Along with the reduction of inflation and its volatility since the adoption of inflation-targeting regimes in the region, market expectations about future inflation have come to reflect an increased credibility of central banks' commitment to their targets. This hard-earned asset is thought to be a crucial determinant of monetary transmission and efficiency.[15] But the task of anchoring expectations is not complete, and ensuring that inflation expectations converge with the central bank's inflation target remains a challenge in some countries.

At least two aspects of inflation forecasts are thought to provide relevant information about the credibility of the central bank's nominal anchor. First, to what extent do forecasts of inflation tend to *agree with the central bank's target?* Figure 3.6 displays the deviations of inflation expectations from central bank targets since January 2006 in selected economies, at short- and medium-term horizons. Panel 1 is based on expectations at a short-term horizon of 12 months. Strong central bank credibility does not necessarily imply that short-term forecasts remain equal to announced targets, since they capture the inflationary effects of transitory shocks. But where expectations are well-anchored, short-term inflation expectations are expected to fluctuate more or less symmetrically around the inflation target, as they do in Australia and Chile. In turn, panel 2 shows deviations of inflation forecasts at a medium-term horizon of two years, which are expected to fluctuate far less on account of transitory shocks. A problem may arise when deviations of expectations persist in one direction, since this suggests a bias in the perceptions of the central bank's commitment to the inflation target.

---

[14] Magud and Sosa (2015) show that potential output in emerging market economies has been affected by decelerating commodity terms of trade and slow investment growth, which in turn reduce the growth rate of the capital stock. Moreover, Adler and Magud (2015) document that Latin American commodity exporters saved little of the large and unprecedented windfall income accrued during the recent boom, lowering their prospects for medium-term growth.

[15] See Woodford (2003) for a comprehensive discussion. Citing experience from Chile, Céspedes and Soto (2007) describe how gains in credibility associated with the transition to inflation targeting increased the efficiency of the central bank's monetary policy, in part by allowing decisions to become more forward-looking.

Figure 3.6. Deviations of Short-Term Inflation Expectations from Central Bank Targets
(Percent)

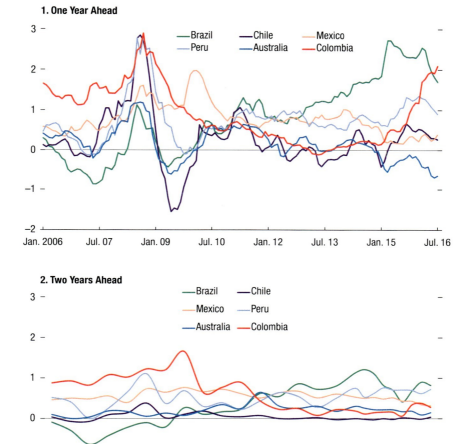

Source: Authors' calculations based on data from Consensus Economics and national central banks.
Note: One-year-ahead forecasts are monthly and are computed as the linear combination of current- and following-year fixed-event forecasts. Two-year-ahead forecasts are quarterly and correspond to expected annual inflation during the calendar year two years hence.

In some cases, inflation expectations have spent prolonged periods well above the midpoint of the central bank's target. In Brazil, inflation expectations have exceeded the central bank's target for the past six years, reaching deviations of up to 250 basis points at a one-year horizon during 2015. In Peru, inflation expectations have also been above the target since early 2010 and seem to have settled around 75 basis points above the midpoint of the range. In Mexico, market participants have not expected inflation to reach the central bank's target in a two-year horizon since early 2006. Even amid strong deflationary pressures from low global oil prices since early 2015, inflation expectations still have not reached the midpoint of the central bank's target. Achieving greater convergence between inflation expectations and the central bank's target can be facilitated—at least in part—by improving the central bank's communication of monetary policy and clarifying the primacy of the price stability objective.

Another relevant aspect of inflation expectations is the degree to which market participants agree with each other about the future path of inflation. In this respect, progress has been more even in Latin America. A growing literature has documented that disagreement about inflation is correlated with the level and volatility of inflation (Mankiw, Reis, and Wolfers 2003). But as Dovern, Fritsch, and Slacalek (2012) argue, even for a given level and variability of inflation, disagreement among forecasters contains additional information about the degree to which a credible monetary policy has anchored expectations about nominal variables, and they document how disagreement has been greater where central banks face constraints to their independence.[16] Among developing economies, Capistrán and Ramos-Francia (2010) find that the adoption of inflation-targeting regimes reduces forecast disagreement, reflecting better-anchored inflation expectations. This work suggests that disagreement among forecasts of inflation captures the degree to which the central bank's reaction function is well understood.

Figure 3.7 shows the evolution of normalized disagreement among professional forecasters of inflation over the next 12 months, using monthly surveys compiled by Consensus Economics. Since the early 2000s, the degree to which private agents agree on the future evolution of inflation is in line with advanced economies such as Australia and Canada, which represents an important achievement. That is to say, even in those countries where forecasters do not anticipate that future inflation will coincide with the central bank's announced target, they do seem to agree among themselves about what future inflation will be. Carrière-Swallow and Gruss will return to the concept of forecast disagreement in Chapter 4, where they estimate that it has been a key determinant of a central bank's ability to implement an autonomous monetary policy, and of the degree of exchange rate pass-through to inflation.

---

[16]These results are estimated for G7 economies. See Brito, Carrière-Swallow, and Gruss (forthcoming) for an exploration of forecast disagreement in a large set of countries, and relationships between this metric and alternative indicators of monetary performance.

Figure 3.7. Disagreement among Forecasters of Inflation at a 12-Month Horizon

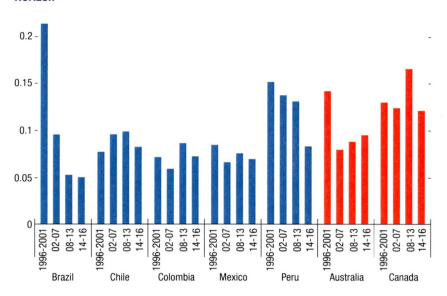

Source: Authors' calculations based on data from Consensus Economics.
Note: Bars correspond to average normalized disagreement within each period, equal to the ratio of the standard deviation across forecasts to the mean inflation forecast.

REVISITING THE ROLE OF THE EXCHANGE RATE

When characterizing the policy frameworks of Latin American inflation targeters, care should be taken to incorporate the specific features that distinguish these emerging small and open economies from their advanced economy counterparts, such as less-developed and shallower financial markets, higher intrinsic volatility, and weaker institutions. As a result, policymakers in Latin American inflation targeters have displayed considerable flexibility in the face of these challenging situations. As Céspedes, Chang, and Velasco (2014) document, recent monetary policy decisions taken by the region's central banks have gone considerably beyond standard interest rate movements, involving a good dose of currency intervention, capital account measures, and the use of unconventional policies. These measures have been deployed to deal with booms—during which capital inflows lead to currency appreciation and generate fears of financial vulnerability—and also during times of crisis, when the interest rate instrument has been deemed insufficient to support domestic demand and meet inflation objectives.[17]

---

[17]See also Calani, Cowan, and Garcia-Silva (2011) for an account of unconventional policy measures deployed by Latin American central banks following the global financial crisis, and De Gregorio (2014) for a comprehensive account of economic policymaking in the region before, during, and after the crisis.

During the prolonged period of high commodity prices and strong capital inflows that followed the global financial crisis, many Latin American countries deployed a plethora of tools to mitigate the impact of global push factors on their capital accounts and exchange rates. More recently, the past few years have seen a sudden correction of global commodity prices and the start of the uncertain process of normalization in global financial conditions, which have been important determinants of the deterioration in Latin America's medium-term outlook discussed above (Figure 3.5). These developments have revived the traditional challenge of setting appropriate interest rate policy in the midst of large exchange rate movements.

Monetary Policy Following Large External Shocks

For Latin America's inflation targeters, recent shifts in global commodity prices and financial conditions have triggered substantial exchange rate depreciations. This change in relative prices helps the economy adjust to a less favorable external environment and helps avoid the accumulation of imbalances that could otherwise lead to balance of payment crises. By allowing a flexible exchange rate to play a critical role as a shock absorber, monetary policy can remain oriented toward the objectives of stabilizing domestic demand.[18] But these developments pose a test for the inflation-targeting regimes, since they have led to a prolonged increase in inflation—though more modest in size than during past episodes of large depreciations—despite weak domestic demand.

A depreciation of the exchange rate places upward pressure on inflation by raising the price of tradable goods and inputs in domestic currency. However, in the absence of widespread indexation practices, this adjustment of relative prices is expected to generate only a one-off increase in the price level. Monetary policy should overlook the short-term effects on inflation and clearly explain the shock's transitory nature. Policy decisions should be accompanied by a forward-looking communication strategy that emphasizes the need to set monetary policy according to underlying demand pressures—which are a better predictor of future inflation—rather than realized inflation.

Consistent with these arguments, the region's inflation targeters initially met recent depreciations by keeping monetary policy accommodative to support weak domestic demand. However, two characteristics of the exchange rate adjustments have created tension for monetary policy. First, recent depreciations against the U.S. dollar have been large. Panel 1 of Figure 3.8 plots 18-month episodes of depreciation against the U.S. dollar over a fan-chart constructed using the historical trajectories of this variable since 1995. For oil producers Brazil, Colombia, and Mexico, the current episode corresponds to a start date of June 2014, coinciding with the steep fall in global prices. For metals producers Chile and Peru,

---

[18]Recently, Rey (2015) has questioned the extent to which a flexible exchange rate allows central banks to implement an autonomous monetary policy in the face of global financial shocks. See Chapter 4 for a discussion of these issues as they apply to Latin America.

the terms-of-trade shock hit earlier, such that the window of interest begins in March 2013. In all cases, with the exception of Peru, the recent exchange rate depreciation is among the largest since the shift to more flexible exchange rate regimes.

Second, recent depreciations have been prolonged, likely reflecting a sequence of shocks in the same direction. In comparison, the response of Latin American exchange rates following the bankruptcy of Lehman Brothers—which triggered the global financial crisis in September 2008—was equally sharp on impact but much more short-lived. In Brazil, Chile, Colombia, and Peru, large initial depreciations had completely reverted to their preshock levels within one year. This is in stark contrast to the current episodes, in which currencies continuously lost value against the dollar for a period of over two years.

The size and duration of the recent depreciations have pushed inflation above central bank target ranges for a sustained period. This has left central bankers with the task of justifying how a particular constellation of shocks led them to miss their inflation objectives repeatedly. Policymakers have faced a tension between either (1) keeping policy supportive of weak domestic demand and admitting that inflation may remain above target for some time, thus exposing themselves to allegations that they lack commitment to their price stability mandate; or (2) implementing procyclical monetary tightening to offset the inflationary pressures from the currency, thus worsening economic slack.

A credible monetary policy that keeps inflation expectations well anchored at the relevant policy horizon is crucial to the successful implementation of the first strategy. This has been more challenging to accomplish in countries where the policy horizon is shorter, since one-off inflationary shocks move expectations at short horizons. Going forward, central banks may need to be more flexible regarding the horizon to which they commit to return inflation to target when confronted with a multiplicity of shocks that move inflation in the same direction, thus preserving their credibility. A useful example is the Bank of England, which commits to returning inflation to its target "within a reasonable time period without creating undue instability in the economy."[19] The Monetary Policy Committee normally interprets this horizon as two to three years, allowing it to tolerate relatively lengthy deviations from the target in the face of particular circumstances. Between 2008 and 2011, this flexibility allowed the Monetary Policy Committee to communicate the need for aggressive expansionary policy in spite of a prolonged period of above-target inflation, basing its argument on the transitory nature of price shocks facing the economy, the underlying degree of economic slack, and the fact that longer-term market expectations remained anchored.

While inflation has been running above inflation targets for the past few years in several Latin American countries, two mitigating factors have helped to keep the size of these deviations small and inflation expectations well anchored in most

---

[19]See "Monetary Policy Framework," available at bankofengland.co.uk/monetarypolicy.

Figure 3.8. Recent Exchange Rate Depreciations in Historical Context
(Index, episode start date = 100; increase corresponds to appreciation)

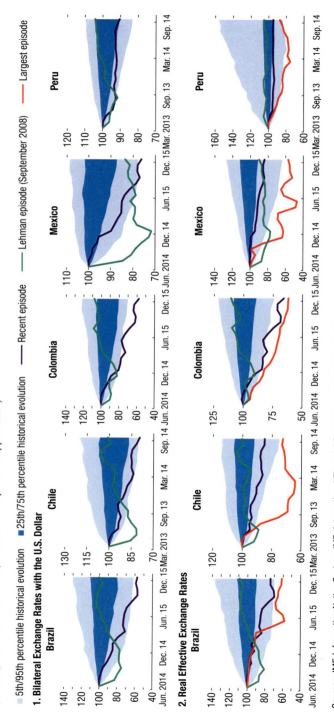

Sources: IMF, Information Notice System; IMF, *International Financial Statistics*; and IMF staff calculations.
Note: Confidence bands report the empirical distribution of changes in the exchange rate, based on all 18-month trajectories for the given country since January 1995 (nominal exchange rate) and January 1980 (real effective exchange rate). Largest episode corresponds to the largest year-on-year real effective exchange rate depreciation since January 1980, with start date varying by country: March 1998 (Brazil), March 1982 (Chile), March 1985 (Colombia), October 1981 (Mexico), and September 1984 (Peru).

cases. Indeed, when compared to episodes of large currency depreciations in previous decades, the current increases in inflation have been smaller in magnitude.

The first mitigating factor is that the sensitivity of domestic prices to the exchange rate has fallen throughout Latin America over the past few decades. As documented in Chapter 4, exchange rate pass-through coefficients are estimated to have declined substantially, and particularly among the region's inflation targeters. Exchange rate pass-through partly reflects an economy's openness: the larger the share of imports in the domestic consumption basket, the greater the impact of a given depreciation on consumer prices. On this score, the gradual opening of Latin American economies over the past few decades would be thought to increase the sensitivity of inflation to the exchange rate. Crucially, however, the degree of pass-through also appears to be endogenous to the monetary policy framework and its credibility. Where inflation expectations are well anchored, such that private agents agree on the future evolution of inflation, exchange rate pass-through has been lower. In contrast, where expectations start becoming unanchored, exchange rate pass-through can rise.

As we have argued, Latin America's inflation targeters have made considerable progress in anchoring inflation expectations. These gains have coincided with substantial reductions in exchange rate pass-through, which in Chile, Colombia, Mexico, and Peru has fallen to levels that are in line with advanced economies. But in many countries in the region that continue to struggle with delivering price stability, pass-through estimates are much higher than can be explained by their openness to imports. In these cases, there is scope for reducing pass-through by lowering inflation and better anchoring private agents' expectations through clear communication of a monetary policy that is committed to delivering price stability.

A second mitigating factor has come from the fact that the region's trade partners have also seen large depreciations of their exchange rates, in the context of a strong U.S. dollar. Bilateral depreciations are relevant for a number of aspects of monetary policymaking, including the formation of *expectations about future inflation* and the health of balance sheets. However, multilateral exchange rates are important drivers of *actual inflation*. Panel 2 of Figure 3.8 plots the evolution of real effective exchange rates over the same period, and compares it to the distribution of their historical trajectories since 1980. The global strength of the dollar has meant that multilateral exchange rates in Latin America have weakened somewhat less than the bilateral rates against the dollar, which has limited external adjustment in some cases. But in Brazil and Colombia, recent movements remain large with respect to each country's historical experience.

While these mitigating factors have limited pressure on inflation in the region, they both underscore the risks associated with the formation of inflation expectations. Central banks must be extremely attentive to the evolution of inflation expectations, since exchange rate pass-through can rise when these become unanchored. Meanwhile, the technical difference between multilateral and bilateral exchange rates is not widely understood by the general public. As a result, the large magnitude of the depreciation against the dollar can generate excessive concerns about rising inflation, inflation expectations, and, potentially, financial stability risks. If the short-term inflationary effects are large and persistent enough, or experience with historical depreciations against the dollar continue to shape inflation expectations, a forward-looking communication policy may need to be supported by interest rate actions. Indeed, concerns that inflation expectations may become unanchored have motivated recent policy rate increases in Colombia and Mexico.

Foreign Exchange Intervention and International Reserves

Why Do Countries Intervene in Foreign Exchange Markets?

Foreign exchange intervention is typically aimed at achieving either one, two, or all of the following: (1) price stability; (2) financial stability; and (3) buffer building. To achieve these objectives, monetary authorities deem foreign exchange intervention to be more effective and/or complementary to the interest rate instrument in certain circumstances. Containing excessive depreciation of the exchange rate makes it easier to achieve the price stability objective by avoiding inflationary pressures from pass-through, thus preserving the credibility of the central bank. Limiting excessive exchange rate volatility contributes to preserving financial stability by mitigating risks from currency mismatches, in turn supporting economic growth by avoiding the financial market disruptions and elevated uncertainty associated with episodes of financial instability. Finally, accumulating international reserves helps to build stronger buffers to respond to external shocks and to reduce the possibility of multiple equilibria driven by foreign currency liquidity shortages.

From a theoretical perspective, the literature has suggested the following four channels through which foreign exchange intervention may affect the exchange rate:

- *Signaling.* Central banks may want to signal their future monetary policy intentions by conveying information to the market. Specifically, banks may want to signal the exchange rate that would be consistent with the future monetary policy stance (Mussa 1981).
- *Portfolio balance channel.* To the extent that domestic assets are not perfect substitutes for foreign assets, domestic assets carry a risk premium. Thus, a central bank that intervenes by selling domestic assets to buy foreign assets (i.e., a sterilized intervention) would increase the (domestic assets) risk premium given higher relative stock of such assets (and vice versa when buying domestic assets to appreciate the currency). Portfolio arbitrage implies that domestic assets will be worth less, depreciating the domestic currency (Kouri 1976).
- *Market microstructure.* The microstructure-exchange rate literature has documented the positive relationship between market volume trading and exchange rate volatility (Frankel and Froot 1990). News, external shocks, and liquidity problems usually result in a larger volume of trading, increas-

ing exchange rate volatility. This could dislocate financial markets and asset allocation and pricing. Moreover, Aghion and others (2009) show that higher exchange rate volatility reduces growth by lowering total factor productivity growth. The transmission channel is as follows: higher exchange rate volatility increases uncertainty, thus reducing investment (given nonfinancial firms' credit constraints).

- *Precautionary saving channel.* The Asian financial crises in the 1990s and the effects of the global financial crisis pushed central banks to build up international reserves in order to have larger buffers against external shocks.[20]

Focusing on the region, inflation-targeting central banks in Latin America use foreign exchange intervention to react to large movements in exchange rates and excessive exchange rate volatility. The intervention is subordinated to the traditional interest rate policy, aimed at achieving the inflation target through an aggregate demand channel while also affecting inflation expectations.

Intervening to limit excessive exchange rate volatility or excessive depreciations can support the main role of the central bank—inflation targeting—if the mechanism used to form those expectations puts greater emphasis on these movements than what is warranted by the underlying structural price formation process. Also, when intervention is associated with the financial stability objective, central banks can intervene to mitigate exchange rate volatility (as has been done, for example, by Colombia, Mexico, and Peru) to address currency mismatches in assets and liabilities, as well as liquidity problems. For its part, Chile added a liquidity facility in 2009 to smooth the effects of the global financial crisis. It is worth mentioning that, although financial stability is not the aim of many central banks in the region, a lack of it could deanchor inflation expectations.

An additional motive for foreign exchange intervention is building buffers via the accumulation of international reserves. Countries usually prefer to have stronger buffers against unexpected shocks, following the precautionary motive channel mentioned above. For small and open economies, higher international reserves serve that purpose—despite the fact that pure floating exchange rate regimes would not theoretically require a high level of reserves. In fact, during the period from 2010 to 2015, LA5 central banks accumulated a substantial amount of international reserves, including up to about 7 percentage points of GDP in the case of Brazil (Figure 3.9). In some cases, there were explicit objectives, as in the case in 2011 of Chile, which aimed at pairing its level of reserves to GDP with countries of similar development and policy frameworks. However, the accumulation of international reserves should be sterilized to avoid higher inflation that can potentially deanchor inflation expectations.

Looking into recent evidence of the objectives of foreign exchange intervention, Adler and Tovar (2014) survey intervention motives in 15 economies in Latin America between 2004 and 2010. They document that reducing excess

---

[20]See Heller (1966) and Frenkel and Jovanovic (1981) for early models; see Jeanne and Rancière (2011) and Bianchi, Hatchondo, and Martinez (2013) for more recent contributions.

Figure 3.9. Change in Gross International Reserves, 2010–15
(Percentage points of GDP)

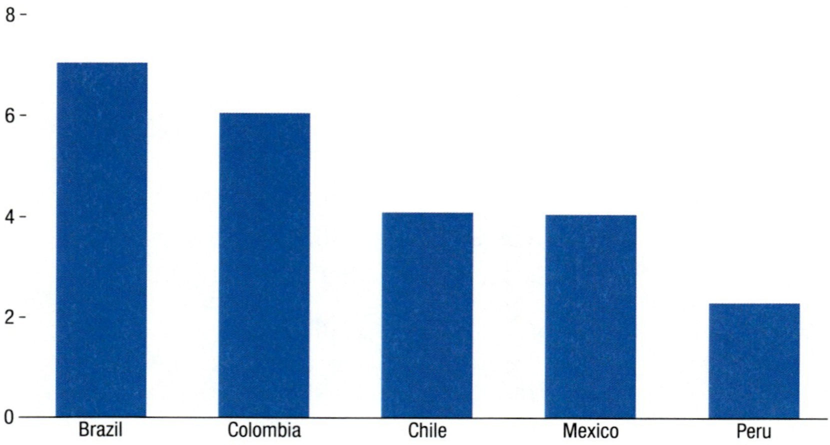

Sources: IMF, World Economic Outlook database (July 2016); and IMF staff calculations.

volatility is typically the main stated motive for foreign exchange interventions, while the most frequently argued reasons for intervening are building reserves for self-insurance purposes and containing exchange rate volatility.

How Do Central Banks Intervene?

To look into how foreign exchange intervention is actually implemented, we need to focus on several aspects. The first is the foreign exchange intervention framework, as some countries operate under a rules-based framework, while others operate based on discretionary decisions—with potential pros and cons. In turn, countries can change over time in terms of whether they use rules or discretion. Another aspect is the actual instrument. Some countries intervene in the spot market; others do so using swaps in futures markets. We discuss below how the choice of instrument is mostly dictated by the objective. The frequency of interventions, in turn, is affected by the choice of framework in most cases. Finally, we focus here on sterilized foreign exchange intervention. We look into each of these issues below, examining when different instruments would better serve the objectives of the central bank.

It is worth highlighting that for Latin America, foreign exchange intervention has been mostly concentrated in achieving the objectives of financial stability and prevention (i.e., building buffers). The objective of price stability has been the focus only in episodes of large exchange rate depreciations—even in countries with low pass-through of exchange rates to domestic prices, given the sheer size of the fall in the exchange rate.

In terms of the foreign exchange intervention framework, some Latin American countries follow a rules-based approach. Those rules can specify the size of the intervention and its modality, as well as contingent triggers. For example, Colombia and Mexico used rules that conditioned the intervention on a sufficiently large daily change in the exchange rate, but these were discontinued in May and February 2016, respectively. For a short period, Brazil also employed a rules-based foreign exchange intervention policy. Following the so-called "taper tantrum," Brazil's central bank started a program of pre-announced interventions in August 2013 involving daily auctions of foreign exchange swaps and repos equivalent to US$3 billion per week. While the initial program was set to expire at the end of 2013, it was extended repeatedly—though with lower auction volumes—before ending in March 2015. At its peak, the foreign exchange outstanding balance was about US$110 billion.

Other countries in the region prefer discretionary foreign exchange intervention, including Brazil (with the exception of the program described above) and Peru, but also, more recently, Colombia and Mexico (see panels 1 and 2 of Table 3.4).[21] Under discretion, while market participants usually realize that the central bank is buying/selling dollars, they may only learn the actual size of that involvement after it has taken place.

There are pros and cons to the different approaches. Announcing the intervention should be preferable at least from a signaling perspective—an issue that is especially relevant for inflation-targeting central banks. Greater transparency helps alleviate fears that interventions will send mixed signals about the commitment to inflation targeting. To put Latin America in perspective, the Reserve Bank of New Zealand employs a transparent rule to determine when to intervene, which is conditional on not affecting monetary policy objectives. Foreign exchange intervention is only triggered if its preconditions are met, and is aimed at limiting excessive exchange rate volatility as well as overly appreciated or depreciated levels of the exchange rate with respect to its fundamentals.[22]

Panel 1 of Table 3.4 also summarizes the foreign exchange intervention instruments that have been used in Latin America. Chile, Colombia, and Mexico

---

[21]In Peru, for example, the central bank has a policy of moderating excessive exchange rate volatility to limit the negative effects of large exchange rate fluctuations. In general, the central bank intervenes in three ways: (1) spot intervention, by directly buying or selling dollars in the market; (2) certificates of deposits (CDs), indexed to the exchange rate, that are denominated in domestic currency but adjusted for foreign currency price movements (aimed at providing the market with a hedging asset); and (3) currency swaps, which are nondeliverable forwards settled in local currency. Foreign exchange swaps are settled in local currency, and any adjustment related to exchange rate movements (gains and losses from valuation) goes to an account called "Article 89."

[22]For details, see the *RBNZ Bulletin*, No. 68, Issue 1 (January 2005). For foreign exchange intervention to be triggered "…[the] Bank will need to be satisfied that all of the following criteria are met: (i) the exchange rate must be exceptionally high or low; (ii) the exchange rate must be unjustified by economic fundamentals; (iii) intervention must be consistent with the PTA (inflation target); and (iv) conditions in markets must be opportune and allow intervention a reasonable chance of success." These conditions are defined precisely in the same volume to guide policymakers' decisions.

TABLE 3.4

Foreign Exchange Intervention Frameworks and Main Instruments and Gross Sales and Purchases

Country	1. Intervention Frameworks			
	Rules vs. Discretion		Spot vs. Swaps	
	Rules	Discretion	Spot	Swap
Brazil	✓	✓	✓	✓
Chile		✓	✓	
Colombia	✓	✓	✓	
Mexico	✓	✓	✓	
Peru		✓	✓	✓

	2. Gross Sales and Purchases (Billions of U.S. dollars)											
	Gross Foreign Exchange Sales						Gross Foreign Exchange Purchases					
	2010	2011	2012	2013	2014	2015	2010	2011	2012	2013	2014	2015
Brazil	0	6.7	26.2	130.4	153.3	122.6	42.0	66.4	30.4	5.5	16.8	8.3
Chile	0	0	0	0	0	0	0	12.0	0	0	0	0
Colombia	0	0	0	0	0	0	3.1	3.7	4.8	6.8	4.1	0
Mexico	0	0	0.7	0	0.2	24.5	20.6	23.2	16.9	17.3	14.3	2.8
Peru	0.04	10.3	2.9	10.5	16.9	22.2	9.2	10.3	13.0	6.3	6.3	8.7

Sources: National authorities.
Note: Gross sales and purchases include spot transactions and swap contracts.

intervene mostly through the spot exchange rate, especially owing to their financial stability objectives. Brazil and Peru intervene using both types of instruments. In the case of Brazil, as mentioned above, swaps are especially used owing to the signaling objective. For Peru, currency mismatches are particularly relevant for financial stability.

While spot interventions can help meet foreign exchange liquidity shortages, swap interventions are mainly useful to alleviate foreign exchange hedging demand. When a bank or firm has foreign exchange liabilities coming due, it needs actual spot dollars to pay those liabilities. In the presence of an economy-wide shortage of foreign exchange liquidity, intervention through swaps would be less effective than spot interventions. However, if the increase in the demand for foreign exchange is driven by hedging concerns (e.g., as foreign exchange risk is reassessed), then intervention through swaps could meet that need. That said, if forward and spot markets are not segmented, the choice of instrument for intervention might not be as important. Swaps, which are usually settled in domestic currency, are especially useful to mitigate changes in international reserves resulting from foreign exchange intervention. Whether swaps settled in domestic currency precommit the stock of reserves remains the subject of debate, since they do not do so in an accounting sense, but may do so from an economic point of view or from the perspective of market participants.

The frequency of the intervention depends on two factors. On the one hand, it depends on whether interventions hinge on rules or discretion. If intervention is rules-based, only market outcomes would trigger the intervention, affecting its frequency, which can be at least partially assessed. Discretion-based interventions would tend to amplify instability, as the probability of intervention given the observed market developments is more difficult to estimate. As such, discretionary intervention is likely to exacerbate instability. On the other hand, the core fundamentals and credibility of the authorities could either increase or reduce how often foreign exchange intervention is used. In either case, an increase in transparency and better communication would tend to mitigate both factors, therefore reducing the likelihood of the central bank actually intervening in the foreign exchange market.

The case for using sterilized foreign exchange sales is usually stronger when the exchange rate clearly overshoots its equilibrium level, currency mismatches are large, and reserves are adequate. Overshooting may be a symptom of distress in foreign exchange markets, in which case the potential benefits from intervention may be large. Also, all else being equal, foreign exchange intervention against overshooting reduces its expected cost, because the monetary authority profits if the intervention succeeds.

Sterilized foreign exchange sales are costlier when the exchange rate adjusts gradually to a more depreciated equilibrium, without overshooting. Using foreign exchange intervention to smooth that adjustment can generate large expected losses for the central bank and delay fundamentally warranted adjustment. Thus, it should be considered mainly in the face of financial stability risks (such as in the presence of currency mismatches in balance sheets) and disorderly market conditions. An important consideration when deciding whether and how much to intervene is the adequacy of international reserves. If reserves are barely or less than adequate, foreign exchange intervention can be counterproductive, since further reserve losses would increase vulnerability.

What Have Been the Effects of Intervention?

The evidence on the effectiveness of foreign exchange intervention in reducing volatility is mixed, as is the case for its impact on the level of the exchange rate. One reason for limited effectiveness may be that the details of these policy decisions are not being clearly explained to markets. For instance, what is understood by volatility is rarely defined in policy announcements. Likewise, not a single country that implemented foreign exchange intervention surveyed by Adler and Tovar (2014) mentioned the level of the exchange rate as an objective of its policy. A lack of communication and transparency—key ingredients of strong inflation-targeting regimes—may be limiting the effectiveness of foreign exchange interventions.[23]

The early empirical work on foreign exchange intervention focused on advanced economies, mostly consisting of portfolio balance models to identify changes in exchange rate levels. The studies found little evidence of the effectiveness of foreign exchange intervention.[24] This is not surprising given the limits of

---

[23]Recently, Adler, Lama, and Medina (2016) have studied optimal foreign exchange interventions.

[24]See Sarno and Taylor (2001) for a survey, or Fatum and Hutchison (2005), on sterilized intervention in Japan that systemically affects the exchange rate only in the short term.

portfolio effects, since the size of the interventions was very small with respect to the depth of the bond markets in these economies.[25]

In contrast, the recent empirical literature on emerging markets has found some supportive evidence.[26] For instance, Adler and Tovar (2014) and Adler, Lama, and Medina (2016) examine cross-country evidence and find that sterilized intervention indeed had a meaningful economic impact, reducing the pace of appreciation when the intervention responded to capital inflows. Similar results are obtained by Daude, Levy-Yeyati, and Nagendgast (2014). Barroso (2014) and Chamon, Candido de Souza, and Garcia (2015) report that foreign exchange intervention had limited appreciation pressures in Brazil, with varying degrees of economic impact. These studies assess exchange rate levels, implicitly or explicitly testing for the portfolio balance approach. Fratzscher and others (2015) find that foreign exchange intervention works very well in terms of smoothing the path of exchange rates, and in stabilizing the exchange rate in countries with narrow band regimes.

IMF (2015) shows that foreign exchange intervention reduced volatility in Brazil during the 2013 "taper tantrum" event. Barroso (2014) also examines the exchange rate volatility issue, testing the effectiveness of foreign exchange intervention in achieving the financial stability objective. Likewise, Tashu (2014) finds that foreign exchange intervention was effective in reducing exchange rate volatility in Peru, while Domac and Mendoza (2004), Chamon (2015), and IMF (2015) find similar evidence in Mexico. Although there are fewer cases—and thus studies—covering foreign exchange intervention in Chile, Claro and Soto (2013) study the effectiveness of reserve purchases in 2008 and 2011. They find that, though successful, these foreign exchange interventions were not cost-free.

However, Disyatat and Galati (2005) find that in the Czech Republic intervention had a weakly statistically significant impact on the spot rate and the risk reversal, but that this impact was small. They also find that intervention had an influence on short-term exchange rate volatility, and that Czech authorities appeared to intervene mainly in response to an acceleration of the speed of appreciation of the koruna.

In terms of instrument assessment, recent work by Nedeljkovic and Saborowski (forthcoming) compares the relative effectiveness of spot and nondeliverable futures in Brazil. They find both instruments to be effective in affecting the level and volatility of the exchange rate, with a significant link between both instruments. They also document that Brazil's central bank tends to rely more on spot foreign exchange intervention to contain capital flows pressures, while using futures to affect the trend of the exchange rate.

---

[25] To put matters in perspective, the total amount of interventions in the Plaza Agreement was about US$18 billion, which, even corrected for inflation, is smaller than the amount of foreign exchange intervention in the LA5 in recent years.

[26] See Menkhoff (2013) for a recent survey. See Appendix 3.1 for a list of papers and estimates.

Challenges for Foreign Exchange Interventions: Transparency Is Key

Going forward, what are the main challenges for enhancing inflation-targeting regimes in Latin America in relation to foreign exchange intervention? Given the apparent conflict between the use of standard interest rate policy and foreign exchange intervention, there is ample room for improving this aspect of monetary policy.

In part, the efficacy of inflation targeting strongly relies on the credibility that transparency and clear communication provide to coordinate and anchor inflation expectations. Transparency and proper communication enable economic agents to infer with minimal error the central bank's interest rate reaction function. In this sense, coordination is achieved, anchoring inflation expectations. But this clarity is lacking with regard to foreign exchange intervention, including in those central banks operating under rules-based foreign exchange intervention. Clearer objectives (be they exchange rate levels, financial stability, or reserve accumulation) and operational frameworks (using rules or discretion) will be necessary to make the foreign exchange intervention process easier to unveil for the market. Eventually, the signaling objective should gain relevance on the back of central bank credibility. This is particularly relevant because in some cases foreign exchange intervention policies could actually amplify financial instability instead of mitigating it.

Once policies become more transparent, private sector actors will be better equipped to understand the foreign exchange intervention policy reaction function of the central bank. A better communicated, transparent, and thus more credible foreign exchange intervention policy could reduce the need to actually intervene, as market participants would anticipate the central bank's action in response to movements in the exchange rate. Market microstructure effects on exchange rates would be mitigated. In turn, this would strengthen the effectiveness of inflation targeting.

CENTRAL BANKS AND SYSTEMIC FINANCIAL STABILITY

In line with a global trend, central banks in Latin America are rethinking their role in preserving financial stability. The depth and costs of the financial crisis have led to a global consensus about the need to develop a macro dimension for financial regulation—or macroprudential regulation—with a view toward preserving financial stability and avoiding another systemic crisis. This new approach to financial regulation has two elements: one that stresses the importance of looking at the financial system as a whole and not as the sum of individual institutions; and another that expands the perimeter of regulation to include the entire financial industry and not only banks. The consensus also suggests that central banks should play a central role in the formulation of macroprudential policy. In response, most advanced countries are already implementing macroprudential policies, while emerging markets are gradually moving in the same direction.²⁷ Yet, while macroprudential policy brings undeniable benefits, it can potentially induce costs if it is not appropriately designed. The challenge for central banks in Latin America is thus to design an effective macroprudential policy function that minimizes costs while avoiding undermining the independence of central banks in the conduct of monetary policy.

Macroprudential Policy in Latin America: The State of Play

Latin America has been prone to large and recurrent banking crises like no other region worldwide. From 1970 to 2012, as many as 28 systemic banking crises occurred in the region and no large country remained immune. Compared to other regions, Latin America ranks third in terms of total number of crises, but first on a crises-per-country basis (Figure 3.10). Moreover, in some countries, banking crises occurred more than once in the same period, with Argentina leading this group with four episodes (1981, 1989, 1995, and 2002), and many countries suffering banking crises twice. In 14 of these episodes, a currency crisis took place simultaneously, and in nine of them sovereign debt crises occurred as well.²⁸

Yet, Latin America weathered the adverse impact of the global financial crisis relatively well. For the first time in decades, disorderly conditions were largely averted despite the impact of a large external financial shock. The financial systems in the commodity-exporting countries also did well in resisting the impact of the strong external shock induced by the terms-of-trade deterioration associated with the end of the commodities' supercycle, and the large capital outflows that followed the possible normalization of monetary policy in the United States. These two shocks generated large currency depreciations, but financial systems have largely remained on solid ground.

This outcome should not lead to complacency, however, as no country is immune to financial crises. The global financial crisis has shown that vulnerabilities can develop with systemic connections and can move between different activities of the financial industry (banks, insurance companies, securities markets).

Latin America has taken a cautious approach with respect to macroprudential policy. The countries have made progress, although at a slower pace than the advanced economies. Chile, Mexico, and Uruguay have formally established financial stability committees, which differ in some ways across countries (Box 3.1). Brazil has also created a similar arrangement within the central bank as well as other committees with a view toward coordinating information with

---

²⁷The United Kingdom and the United States, as well as the European Union and several of its member countries, approved legal reforms to their financial stability framework to lay the groundwork for macroprudential policies. A number of emerging markets—including Malaysia, Thailand, and Turkey—did as well.

²⁸See Laeven and Valencia (2013) for a database of systemic banking crises.

Figure 3.10. Systemic Banking Crises in Latin America and Other Regions, 1970–2012

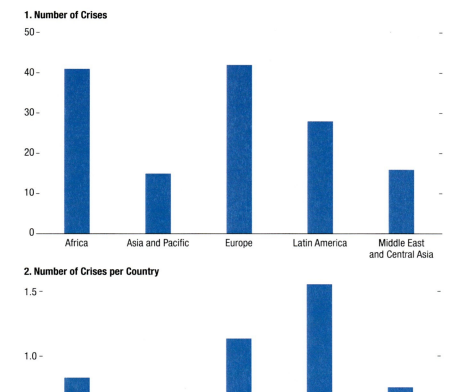

Source: Laeven and Valencia (2013) database of banking crises.

> **Box 3.1. Financial Stability Committees in Chile, Mexico, and Uruguay**
>
> There is increasing interest in Latin America in how to design an effective macroprudential policy framework. Since the global financial crisis, some decisions have already been taken in that direction. Chile, Mexico, and Uruguay have made progress toward improving financial stability frameworks, laying the groundwork for the implementation of macroprudential policies. Chile created the Financial Stability Council in 2011, Mexico the Financial System Stability Council in 2010, and Uruguay the Financial Stability Committee in 2011. These new institutional arrangements have a number of common features:
>
> - They all have a mandate to prevent the buildup of systemic risks and, if necessary, recommend implementation of macroprudential policies to the relevant agencies. They do not have decision-making powers and are not held accountable—although in Mexico the council is required to prepare and publish a report assessing financial stability and the measures taken toward this end. The three institutional arrangements are vested with powers to obtain information from all financial industries and their participating institutions and to play a coordinating role to secure the consistency of financial stability efforts.
> - The financial stability committees in Mexico and Uruguay have explicit powers to manage financial crises. In Chile, the crisis management powers reside with the individual institutions, and the council operates as a coordination mechanism. Crisis management was explicitly stated as a key consideration for establishing the council. In all three countries the committee is presided over by the Minister of Finance and the other members are the heads of the financial supervisory agencies and the central bank (except in Chile, where the governor is invited to participate but is not formally a member of the council). Thus, to a great extent, the councils mirror the structure of the Financial Stability Oversight Council in the United States. Mexico's council is comprised of another eight members, including the heads of the National Commission of Banks and Securities, National Commission of Insurance, National Commission for Savings for Retirement, Executive Secretary of the Institute of Bank Savings Protection, Undersecretary of Finance, and Governor of the Bank of Mexico and two Deputy Governors. Uruguay's committee is comprised of the Governor of the Central Bank of Uruguay, Superintendent of Financial Services, and President of the Corporation for the Protection of Bank Savings. Chile's council is comprised of the heads of the Superintendence of Securities and Insurance, Superintendence of Banks and Financial Institutions, and Superintendence of Pensions. The Governor of the Central Bank of Chile is not formally a member of the council because this was seen to conflict with the independence and mandate of the central bank, as sanctioned in the constitution.
>
> Some of the committees have additional specific responsibilities, such as recommending criteria for the determination of the budget of the supervisory agencies in Chile, and coordinating with other international institutions on issues of financial stability in Uruguay. The three committees are required to meet regularly: at least every month in Chile, at least quarterly in Mexico, and at least once a year in Uruguay.

other regulatory agencies in the financial industry.[29] In the first three cases, the institutional arrangement for macroprudential policy mirrors the type of structure of the U.S. Financial Stability Oversight Council, although in Chile, the

---

[29]See Jácome, Nier, and Imam (2012) for an explanation of the Brazilian institutional arrangement.

central bank is not a formal member of the Financial Stability Committee, but rather participates only as an invited member.

The toolkit for macroprudential policy is comprised primarily of the same regulatory instruments that existed before the global financial crisis. Dynamic provisioning had already been in place in Bolivia, Colombia, Peru, and Uruguay, and a larger number of countries used other instruments such as limits on net open positions and interbank exposures, although in general with a microprudential approach. The most active country in the implementation of macroprudential instruments is Brazil, where changes in loan-to-value ratios and risk-weight factors, and sometimes both, have also been used to cope with financial vulnerabilities (Afanasieff and others 2015). Interestingly, imposing extraordinary capital requirements on systemic financial institutions is not common in Latin America, despite the fact that in most countries the two largest banks have a market share that together exceeds 40 percent.

The Challenge of Establishing an Effective and Balanced Macroprudential Policy Function

While Latin American countries have in general made important strides over the last 15 years to increase the soundness of their financial systems and their resilience to real and financial shocks, additional efforts may be needed to cope with systemic vulnerabilities. Because of the large toll inflicted by banking crises in the 1980s and 1990s, most countries enacted new legislation to upgrade prudential supervision and regulations. Capital requirements are higher than Basel standards, and large liquidity buffers are in place. Regulatory agencies have moved from supervision based on compliance checking toward implementation of risk-oriented procedures. Countries have also modernized legislation to cope with bank failures and strengthened financial safety nets. Yet, Latin American countries still need to establish an effective macroprudential policy to monitor and tackle systemic vulnerabilities in a timely fashion and in terms of structural dimensions. The global financial crisis has shown that the sources and level of systemic risk are likely to evolve over time, while the distribution of risks can shift quickly given the static nature of traditional prudential regulations. In addition, regulations must factor in that financial sector risks interact strongly with macroeconomic developments.

Progress is needed on the design of a macroprudential policy function in Latin America within the existing institutional environment—the Atlantic and Pacific models—and taking key aspects of these structures as given.[30] In the Atlantic model (Argentina, Brazil, Paraguay, and Uruguay), the central bank is responsible for both monetary policy and prudential regulation and supervision. In the Pacific model (Chile, Colombia, Mexico, and Peru, among others), these two responsibilities are carried out by the central bank and by a separate agency.[31]

---

[30]These institutional arrangements have historical roots (see Chapter 2) and are enshrined in law—in some countries in the constitution.

[31]These two institutional models are discussed in Jácome, Nier, and Imam (2012).

Depending on what model countries use, they present different starting points for establishing an effective macroprudential policy function. As for other areas of the financial industry that are relevant for macroprudential policy, the institutional structures vary across countries.[32]

The key issue for the countries under the Atlantic model is to clarify the legal mandate and to establish clear accountability. Countries should make a distinction between the objectives of macroprudential policy (financial stability) and monetary policy (price stability). This distinction is relevant for assigning the corresponding powers to take macroprudential policy decisions. Countries should also further coordination efforts to address systemic risks with other supervisory agencies. Holding policymakers accountable for the policy decisions they have taken is a difficult endeavor in itself. This is because accountability needs to be based on a clear and measurable objective against which the policy actions can be gauged. However, financial stability is inherently difficult to measure. What is more easily measured is instability—exactly what macroprudential authorities would hope to avoid—at which point the exercise of accountability is reduced to assigning blame rather than preventing negative outcomes in advance.

In countries where the starting point is the Pacific model, there are additional challenges to strengthening macroprudential policies. This is because the relevant information, expertise, and regulatory powers are distributed across the central bank and the banking authority—as well as across other regulatory agencies, like in the Atlantic model—making the success of macroprudential policy harder to achieve because it depends on cooperation across several agencies (Nier and others 2011). The response in some countries has been to enact a financial stability committee. However, these committees lack macroprudential policy effectiveness, so while they may recommend the adoption of macroprudential measures, their recommendations are not legally binding. Presumably, legislators tried to preserve the independence of the central bank and financial regulatory agencies by avoiding interference from the executive power—financial stability committees are chaired by the Minister of Finance—but at the cost of making accountability ineffective, since no agency is ultimately responsible for macroprudential policy. An alternative to strengthen the effectiveness of these committees is to vest them with "comply or explain" powers associated with the existing recommending provisions.

Regardless of which institutional arrangement model the Latin American countries employ, strengthening or establishing a macroprudential framework should be guided by the following criteria: (1) achieving effective identification, analysis, and monitoring of systemic risk; (2) ensuring timely and effective use of

---

[32]In Argentina and Brazil, insurance companies and securities markets are regulated by dedicated agencies, and in Chile by a single regulator. In Colombia, they are regulated by the banking supervision authority, and in Mexico banks and securities are regulated jointly. In Peru, banks and insurance companies are regulated together, while in Uruguay, banks, insurance companies, and securities markets are all regulated by the central bank.

macroprudential policy tools by creating appropriate mandates and assuring strong powers and accountability; and (3) ensuring effective coordination in risk assessments and mitigation so as to reduce gaps and overlaps, while preserving the autonomy of separate policy functions.[33] This said, the institutional setup supporting macroprudential policy should not undermine the hard-won independence of central banks and their credibility. Since preserving financial stability inevitably involves government involvement—given that financial crises are paid for with taxpayers' money—it is important to keep monetary policy decisions insulated from government interference. One alternative is to maintain distinct decision-making bodies with clear and separate objectives, and different primary instruments (interest rates for monetary policy and macroprudential tools for financial stability). Enhancing communication to explain the central bank's role in executing these responsibilities is also essential.

Countries in Latin America must also define how they can better coordinate macroprudential policies with other economic policies, especially monetary and microprudential policies (IMF 2013b). It is widely accepted that monetary and macroprudential policies feature strong complementarities and interactions. However, there is no standard recipe to ensure effective coordination. Thus, it is essential to understand the interactions between these policies, their potential conflicts and synergies, and how best to deploy them to achieve the goals of price stability (associated with monetary policy) and financial stability (associated with macroprudential policy). As a principle of coordination the two policies should be used to complement each other—primarily assigning the use of interest rates to affect aggregate demand and achieve the objective of price stability, and using macroprudential instruments primarily to achieve the objective of financial stability. Macroprudential and microprudential regulation are even more closely interrelated. As in their relation with monetary policy, in principle macroprudential and microprudential policies have different objectives (stability of the financial system as a whole and protection of depositors, respectively) and, although they have complementary features, the two objectives can be mutually conflicting at certain times. For example, a country might need to introduce a macroprudential measure, such as the release of special provisions in banks to maintain credit flows in the downswing of the business cycle. In contrast, the microprudential authority may recommend a more conservative policy and believe macroprudential regulation could endanger the security of deposits or the solvency of institutions. The challenge is to design an institutional framework that can effectively coordinate the two policies, keeping in mind that their mutual boundary is unclear, as the two types of regulation use similar instruments.

---

[33]See a discussion of these principles in Nier and others (2011).

CONCLUSIONS

Latin America's independent central banks have made substantial progress in delivering an environment of price stability that supports sustainable economic growth. This chapter has reviewed the underpinnings of these achievements and discussed remaining challenges facing central banking in the region.

For those countries where inflation remains high and volatile, achieving durable price stability will require not only addressing fiscal imbalances but also strengthening the independence of central banks. In countries where inflation-targeting regimes are well established, remaining challenges involve assessing economic slack and the policy stance, further anchoring inflation expectations, communicating monetary policy in a context of long-lived transitory shocks, and clarifying the role of the exchange rate in the monetary policy framework. Finally, the role of macroprudential policy in preserving financial stability must be coordinated with existing objectives, and care must be taken to preserve the independence of central banks and the primacy of the price stability objective.

APPENDIX 3.1. EMPIRICAL EVIDENCE ON FOREIGN EXCHANGE INTERVENTIONS

Study	Impact
Cross-Country	
Adler and Tovar (2014)	0.1 percent of GDP foreign exchange intervention slows the pace of domestic currency appreciation by 0.3 percent.
Adler, Blanchard, and Carvalho (2015)	0.25 percent of GDP foreign exchange intervention reduces appreciation on impact by 1.5 percent.
Adler, Lisack, and Mano (2015)	1 percent of GDP foreign exchange intervention depreciates the nominal and real exchange rates by between 1.7 and 2.0 percent, and between 1.4 and 1.7 percent, respectively.
Daude, Levy-Yeyati, and Nagengast (2014)	1 percent increase in foreign exchange intervention weakens the domestic currency by 0.18 percent.
Brazil	
Barroso (2014)	US$1 billion buying intervention = >0.45–1.18 percent depreciation. US$1 billion selling intervention = >0.46–0.66 percent appreciation. Average: 0.5 percent change in domestic currency valuation.
Chamon, Candido de Sousa, and Garcia (2015)	Appreciation in excess of 10 percent following the 2013 Swap Program Announcement.
Mexico	
Domac and Mendoza (2004)	Foreign exchange sale of US$100 million strengthens the peso by 0.08 percent.
Chamon (2015)	Appreciation of about 2½ percent following 2015 foreign exchange intervention announcements.
Peru	
Tashu (2014)	Foreign exchange sales effective in reducing volatility and depreciation. Foreign exchange purchases not effective.
Turkey	
Domac and Mendoza (2004)	Foreign exchange sale of US$100 million strengthens the lira by 0.2 percent.

REFERENCES

Adler, G., O. Blanchard, and I. de Carvalho Filho. 2015. "Can Foreign Exchange Intervention Stem Exchange Rate Pressures from Global Capital Flow Shocks?" NBER Working Paper 21427, National Bureau of Economic Research, Cambridge, Massachusetts.

Adler, G., R. Lama, and J. P. Medina. 2016. "Foreign Exchange Intervention Under Policy Uncertainty." IMF Working Paper 16/67, International Monetary Fund, Washington, DC.

Adler, G., N. Lisack, and R. Mano. 2015. "Unveiling the Effects of Foreign Exchange Intervention: A Panel Approach." IMF Working Paper 15/130, International Monetary Fund, Washington, DC.

Adler, G., and N. Magud. 2015. "Four Decades of Terms-of-Trade Booms: A Metric of Income Windfall." *Journal of International Money and Finance* 55: 162–92.

Adler, G., and C. E. Tovar. 2014. "Foreign Exchange Interventions and their Impact on Exchange Rate Levels." *Monetaria* II(1): 1–48.

Afanasieff, T., R. L. P. Coelho, E. C. de Castro, J. Gregrio, and F. L. C. A. Carvalho. 2015. "Implementing Loan-to-Value Ratios: The Case of Auto Loans in Brazil (2010-11)." Working Paper 380, Central Bank of Brazil, Brasilia.

Aghion, P., P. Bacchetta, R. Rancière, and K. Rogoff. 2009. "Exchange Rate Volatility and Productivity Growth: The Role of Financial Development." *Journal of Monetary Economics* 56: 494–513.

Alberola, E., R. Gondo, M. Lombardi, and D. Urbina. 2016. "Output Gaps and Policy Stabilization in Latin America: The Effect of Commodity and Capital Flow Cycles." BIS Working Paper 568, Bank for International Settlements, Basel.

Armas, A., and F. Grippa. 2005. "Targeting Inflation in a Dollarized Economy." IDB Working Paper 538, Inter-American Development Bank, Washington, DC.

Barro, R. J., and D. B. Gordon. 1983. "Rules, Discretion and Reputation in a Model of Monetary Policy." *Journal of Monetary Economics* 12(1): 101–21.

Barroso, J. B. 2014. "Realized Volatility as an Instrument to Official Intervention." Working Paper 363, Central Bank of Brazil, Brasilia.

Bianchi, J., J. C. Hatchondo, and L. Martinez. 2013. "International Reserves and Rollover Risk." NBER Working Paper 18628, National Bureau of Economic Research, Cambridge, Massachusetts.

Borio, C., P. Disyatat, M. Drehmann, and M. Juselius. 2016. "Monetary Policy, the Financial Cycle, and Ultra-Low Interest Rates." BIS Working Paper 569, Bank for International Settlements, Basel.

Borio, C., P. Disyatat, and M. Juselius. 2013. "Rethinking Potential Output: Embedding Information About the Financial Cycle." BIS Working Paper 404, Bank for International Settlements, Basel.

Borio, C., and A. Zabai. 2016. "Unconventional Monetary Policies: A Re-appraisal." BIS Working Paper 570, Bank for International Settlements, Basel.

Brito, S., Y. Carrière-Swallow, and B. Gruss. Forthcoming. "Disagreement about Inflation and Monetary Policy Performance." IMF Working Paper, International Monetary Fund, Washington, DC.

Calani, M., K. Cowan, and P. Garcia-Silva. 2011. "Inflation Targeting in Financially Stable Economies: Has It Been Flexible Enough?" In *Monetary Policy under Financial Turbulence*, edited by L. F. Céspedes, R. Chang, and D. Saravia. Santiago: Central Bank of Chile.

Calvo, G. and C. Reinhart. 2002. "Fear of Floating." *Quarterly Journal of Economics* 67(2): 379–408.

Canales-Kriljenko, J., L. I. Jácome, A. Alichi, and I. de Oliveira Lima. 2010. "Weathering the Global Storm: The Benefits of Monetary Policy Reform in the LA5 Countries." IMF Working Paper 10/292, International Monetary Fund, Washington, DC.

Capistrán, C., and M. Ramos-Francia. 2010. "Does Inflation Targeting Affect the Dispersion of Inflation Expectations?" *Journal of Money, Credit and Banking* 42(1): 113–34.

Carstens, A., and L. I. Jácome. 2005. "Latin American Central Bank Reform: Progress and Challenges." IMF Working Paper 05/114, International Monetary Fund, Washington, DC.

Carstens, A., and A. Werner. 1999. "Mexico's Monetary Policy Framework under a Floating Exchange Rate Regime." Documento de Investigación 9905, Banco de México, Mexico City.

Céspedes, L. F., R. Chang, and A. Velasco. 2014. "Is Inflation Targeting Still on Target? The Recent Experience of Latin America." *International Finance* 17(2): 185–207.

Céspedes, L. F., and C. Soto. 2007. "Credibility and Inflation Targeting in Chile." In *Monetary Policy under Inflation Targeting*, edited by F. Mishkin and K. Schmidt-Hebbel. Santiago: Central Bank of Chile.

Chamon, M. 2015. "The Effects of FX Intervention in Mexico." IMF Country Report 15/314 (November), International Monetary Fund, Washington, DC.

———, L. Candido de Souza, and M. Garcia, 2015. "FX Interventions in Brazil: A Synthetic Control Approach." Textos para discussão 630, PUC Department of Economics, Rio de Janeiro.

Claro, S., and C. Soto. 2013. "Exchange Rate Policy and Exchange Rate Interventions: The Chilean Experience," *BIS Papers* 73: 81-94.

Cukierman A., S. Webb, and B. Neyapti. 1992. "Measuring the Independence of Central Banks and Its Effect on Policy Outcomes." *World Bank Economic Review* 6 (September): 352–98.

Daude, C., E. Levy-Yeyati, and A. Nagendgast. 2014. "On the Effectiveness of Exchange Rate Interventions in Emerging Markets." Working Paper 324, Organization for Economic Cooperation and Development, Paris.

De Gregorio, J. 2014. *How Latin America Weathered the Global Financial Crisis*. Washington, DC: Peterson Institute for International Economics.

Disyatat, P., and G. Galati. 2005. "The Effectiveness of Foreign Exchange Intervention in Emerging Market Economies: Evidence from the Czech Koruna." BIS Working Paper 172, Bank for International Settlements, Basel.

Domac, I., and A. Mendoza. 2004. "Is There Room for Foreign Exchange Interventions under an Inflation Targeting Framework? Evidence from Mexico and Turkey." Policy Research Working Paper 3288, World Bank, Washington, DC.

Dovern, J., U. Fritsche, and J. Slacalek. 2012. "Disagreement Among Forecasters in G7 Countries." *Review of Economics and Statistics* 94(4): 1081–96.

Fatum, R., and M. Hutchison. 2005. "Foreign Exchange Intervention and Monetary Policy in Japan, 2003-04." *International Economics and Economic Policy* 2(2–3): 241–60.

Frankel, J., and K. A. Froot. 1990. "Exchange Rate Forecasting Techniques, Survey Data, and Implications for the Foreign Exchange Market." NBER Working Paper 3470, National Bureau of Economic Research, Cambridge, Massachusetts.

Fratzscher, M., O. Gloede, L. Mekhoff, L. Sarno, and T. Stohr. 2015. "When Is Foreign Exchange Intervention Effective? Evidence from 33 Countries." Discussion Paper 1518, German Institute for Economic Research, Berlin.

Frenkel, J., and B. Jovanovic. 1981. "Optimal International Reserves: A Stochastic Framework." *Economic Journal* 91: 507–14.

Gómez, J., J. D. Uribe, and H. Vargas. 2002. "The Implementation of Inflation Targeting in Colombia." Paper presented at the conference "Inflation Targeting, Macroeconomic Modeling and Forecasting," Banco de la República and Bank of England, Bogotá, January.

Grigoli, F., A. Herman, A. Swiston, and G. Di Bella. 2015. "Output Gap Uncertainty and Real-Time Monetary Policy." IMF Working Paper 15/14, International Monetary Fund, Washington, DC.

Hammond, G. 2009. "State of the Art of Inflation Targeting." Handbook No. 29, Centre for Central Banking Studies, Bank of England, London.

Heller, R. H. 1966. "Optimal International Reserves." *Economic Journal* 76: 296–311.

International Monetary Fund (IMF). 2013a. "Unconventional Monetary Policies—Recent Experience and Prospects." IMF Policy Paper, International Monetary Fund, Washington, DC.

———. 2013b. "Key Aspects of Macroprudential Policy." IMF Policy Paper (June), International Monetary Fund, Washington, DC.

———. 2015. "Selected Issues Papers for the 2015 Article IV Consultation with Brazil." IMF Country Report 15/122, International Monetary Fund, Washington, DC.

Jácome, L. I., E. W. Nier, and P. Imam. 2012. "Building Blocks for Effective Macroprudential Policies in Latin America." IMF Working Paper 12/183, International Monetary Fund, Washington, DC.

Jácome, L. I., and F. Vázquez. 2008. "Any Link Between Legal Central Bank Independence and Inflation? Evidence from Latin America and the Caribbean." *European Journal of Political Economy* 24: 788–801.

Jeanne, O., and R. Rancière. 2011. "The Optimal Level of International Reserves for Emerging Market Countries: A New Formula and Some Applications." *Economic Journal* 121(555): 905–30.

Joyce, M., D. Miles, A. Scott, and D. Vayamos. 2012. "Quantitative Easing and Unconventional Monetary Policy—an Introduction." *Economic Journal* 122: 1–88.

Kouri, P. 1976. "The Exchange Rate and the Balance of Payments in the Short Run and in the Long Run: A Monetary Approach." *Scandinavian Journal of Economics* 78: 280–308.

Laeven, L., and F. Valencia. 2013. "Systemic Banking Crises Database." *IMF Economic Review* 61(2): 225–70.

Magud, N., and S. Sosa. 2015. "Investment in Emerging Markets: We Are Not in Kansas Anymore, Or Are We?" IMF Working Paper 15/77, International Monetary Fund, Washington, DC.

Magud, N., and E. Tsounta. 2012. "To Cut or Not to Cut? That Is the (Central Bank's) Question: In Search of the Neutral Interest Rate in Latin America." IMF Working Paper 12/243, International Monetary Fund, Washington, DC.

Mankiw, N. G., R. Reis, and J. Wolfers. 2003. "Disagreement about Inflation Expectations." In *NBER Macroeconomics Annual*, Vol. 18, edited by M. Gertler and K. Rogoff. Cambridge, Massachusetts: MIT Press.

Menkhoff, L. 2013. "Foreign Exchange Intervention in Emerging Markets: A Survey of Empirical Studies." *World Economy* 36: 1187–208.

Mussa, M. 1981. "The Role of Official Intervention." Group of Thirty Occasional Paper, New York.

Nedeljkovic, M., and C. Saborowski. Forthcoming. "The Relative Effectiveness of Spot and Derivatives Based Intervention: The Case of Brazil." IMF Working Paper, International Monetary Fund, Washington, DC.

Nier, E. W., J. Osinski, L. I. Jácome, and P. Madrid. 2011. "Institutional Models for Macroprudential Policy." IMF Staff Discussion Note 11/180, International Monetary Fund, Washington, DC.

Orphanides, A., and S. van Norden. 2002. "The Unreliability of Output-Gap Estimates in Real Time." *Review of Economics and Statistics* 84(4): 569–83.

Rabanal, P., and M. Raheri Sanjani. 2015. "Financial Factors: Implications for Output Gaps." IMF Working Paper 15/153, International Monetary Fund, Washington, DC.

Rey, H. 2015. "Dilemma Not Trilemma: The Global Financial Cycle and Monetary Policy Independence." NBER Working Paper 21162, National Bureau of Economic Research, Cambridge, Massachusetts.

Rogoff, K. 1985. "The Optimal Degree of Commitment to an Intermediate Target." *Quarterly Journal of Economics* 100(4): 1169–89.

Sarno, L., and M. P. Taylor. 2001. "Official Intervention in the Foreign Exchange Market: Is It Effective, and, If So, How Does It Work?" *Journal of Economic Literature* 39(3): 839–68.

Schmidt-Hebbel, K., and A. Werner. 2002. "Inflation Targeting in Brazil, Chile, and Mexico: Performance, Credibility, and the Exchange Rate." Working Paper 171, Central Bank of Chile, Santiago.

Tashu, M. 2014. "Motives and Effectiveness of Forex Interventions: Evidence from Peru." IMF Working Paper 14/217, International Monetary Fund, Washington, DC.

Woodford, M. 2003. *Interest and Prices: Foundations of a Theory of Monetary Policy*. Princeton, New Jersey: Princeton University Press.

PART II

Monetary Independence in an Integrated World

CHAPTER 4

Implications of Global Financial Integration for Monetary Policy in Latin America

YAN CARRIÈRE-SWALLOW AND BERTRAND GRUSS, INTERNATIONAL MONETARY FUND

Financial asset markets around the world have grown increasingly interconnected, and many economies in Latin America have been no exception. This chapter assesses two aspects of monetary policy in the region for which financial integration is expected to have important implications: monetary autonomy from global financial conditions, and exchange rate pass-through. It also explores how improving the credibility of policy frameworks and establishing a strong nominal anchor has helped the region to deal with the trade-offs along these two aspects that financial integration has likely accentuated.

The first aspect that we will consider is the degree to which monetary policy in Latin America has been constrained by monetary policy decisions taken abroad. In discussions surrounding the normalization of U.S. monetary policy after the global financial crisis, a range of observers have questioned whether Latin American central banks would be able to maintain an accommodative stance—and thus allow the exchange rate to adjust in response to a larger interest rate differential—or if they would see the need to follow U.S. monetary policy despite weak domestic demand.

The second aspect is a reexamination of the relationship between exchange rate movements and inflation in the region. In a context of increased financial integration and volatile exchange rates, the ability of central banks to deliver stable inflation depends crucially on a limited degree of exchange rate pass-through. Indeed, a concern during the adoption of inflation-targeting regimes was precisely that exchange rate pass-through had historically been high in the region.

As monetary policies in many advanced economies have resorted to unconventional measures since the global financial crisis, and emerging market exchange rates have undergone large fluctuations in response to a series of global shocks, these topics have attracted a good deal of attention in the recent literature and policy debate.

FINANCIAL INTEGRATION AND ITS IMPLICATIONS FOR MONETARY POLICY

Latin American economies have gradually removed restrictions on the movement of international capital over the past four decades. Panel 1 of Figure 4.1 shows how de jure measures of capital account policies have evolved in selected Latin American countries since 1970—the index ranges from zero to one, where a larger number represents greater openness. While restrictions have gradually become less pervasive over this period, a particularly marked movement toward greater openness has taken place since the early 1990s.

In a region long characterized by low savings rates, opening the capital account offered the promise of allowing more plentiful foreign savings to finance productive investment, thus spurring development. As foreign financial intermediaries entered domestic markets, increased competition would improve efficiency among local incumbents. And finally, the ability of governments and firms to borrow abroad would allow them to smooth the impact of idiosyncratic shocks.

The removal of restrictions on the movement of international capital has indeed been accompanied by a gradual increase in capital flows to and from the region. Panel 2 of Figure 4.1 reports a de facto measure of financial integration, which corresponds to the sum of external assets and external liabilities over gross domestic product, based on data compiled by Lane and Milesi-Ferretti (2007).

Increased financial integration with global markets was also expected to carry certain well-recognized costs. In terms of risks, integrated economies face increased exposure to shocks from abroad such as sudden capital reversals, which can impose large costs and even trigger financial crises in extreme cases (see a discussion in Obstfeld 1998).

The move to greater openness had important implications for monetary policymaking. As international arbitrage of domestic assets became ever more prevalent under more interconnected financial markets, policymakers were confronted with a choice under the open-economy trilemma: either control the exchange rate but give up monetary policy, or maintain the autonomy to set policy interest rates in line with domestic objectives for inflation and activity while letting the exchange rate fluctuate.

During the financial liberalization agendas implemented in parts of Latin America during the 1970s, authorities had opted to keep exchange rates fixed. The transition to greater openness during the 1990s was characterized by a more eclectic and gradual approach that, in most cases, involved an increasing degree of exchange rate flexibility. This was in part due to memories of the accumulation of external imbalances that culminated in the debt crisis of the early 1980s. But it also responded to recognition of the importance of retaining monetary policy autonomy in the face of large external shocks, especially as countercyclical fiscal policy had often proved difficult to implement.

Panel 1 of Figure 4.2 shows that the number of countries with pegged exchange rates had declined by the 1990s. In some cases, the exchange rate arrangement evolved into a managed float or soft peg, rather than a fully flexible

Figure 4.1. Measures of Financial Integration in Latin America since 1970

1. De Jure (Chinn and Ito 2008)

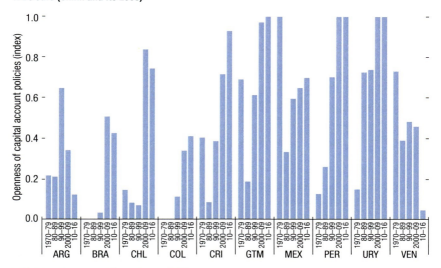

2. De Facto (Lane and Milesi-Ferretti 2007)

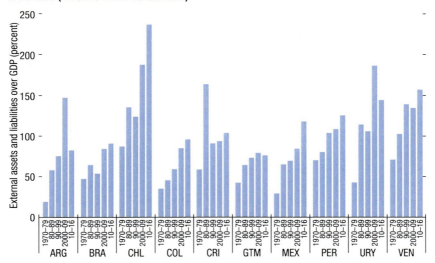

Sources: Chinn and Ito (2008); Lane and Milesi-Ferretti (2007); and authors' calculations.
Note: The Chinn and Ito (2006, 2008) index is based on information regarding restrictions in the International Monetary Fund's *Annual Report on Exchange Arrangements and Exchange Restrictions*. It is normalized between zero and one, and a higher value indicates more openness to cross-border capital transactions.

exchange rate, and the number of pegs in Latin America has actually increased somewhat recently—including due to the adoption of the U.S. dollar as legal tender in some countries. But the de facto degree of exchange rate flexibility in the region generally increased over the past few decades, as shown in panel 2 of Figure 4.2—where a lower reading of the exchange rate stability index denotes more flexibility.

While there has been no recipe, gradual transitions toward greater financial openness have allowed regulation and supervision regimes to mature and local financial markets to deepen alongside the increasing participation of nonresidents. In many cases, countries have opted to maintain some degree of discretion in the use of capital flow measures—a strategy that the International Monetary Fund has come to broadly endorse in light of international experience (IMF 2012).

In many countries, there has been an effort to extend the availability and use of financial instruments to hedge the currency mismatches that can make corporate and bank balance sheets vulnerable in a context of greater exchange rate volatility. As policy frameworks have allowed greater exchange rate flexibility, this generates an endogenous incentive for private actors to pay the price of insuring against exchange rate risk. In turn, this has reduced pressure on independent central banks to intervene in foreign exchange markets.

Regulatory and prudential reforms also helped address financial vulnerabilities in a context of more volatile currencies. One clear example is the de-dollarization agenda implemented in several Latin American countries. The set of policies included the introduction of prudential measures to create incentives to internalize the risks of dollarization.[1] These measures included active management of reserve requirement differentials and setting higher provision requirements for foreign currency loans and tighter limits on the banks' net open position. An explicit strategy for the development of a capital market in local currency through the issuance of long-term public bonds in domestic currency also played a key role, as it facilitated bank funding and pricing of long-term loans in domestic currency. In a context of macroeconomic stability—with a notable reduction of inflation levels—and sustained exchange rate appreciation, financial dollarization ratios in Bolivia, Paraguay, Peru, and Uruguay decreased by almost 30 percentage points on average (García-Escribano and Sosa 2011). Despite this progress, however, dollarization levels are still relatively high in some countries.

In order to successfully transition to a new monetary regime geared toward domestic price stability under flexible exchange rates, establishing a strong nominal anchor was critical. Many countries in the region adopted inflation targeting in the late 1990s and early 2000s as a means of establishing such an anchor in the form of a simple, easily communicated policy framework. However, adopting a formal target for inflation with some degree of legislative oversight meant that

---

[1] See Armas, Ize, and Levy (2006) for a discussion of policies to deal with financial dollarization, and Chapter 9 for an in-depth discussion of the Peruvian case.

Figure 4.2. Transitioning toward More Exchange Rate Flexibility

1. Exchange Rate Regime Classification (Klein and Shambaugh 2008)

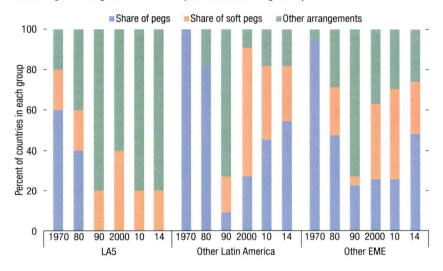

2. Exchange Rate Stability Index (Aizenman, Chinn, and Ito 2008)

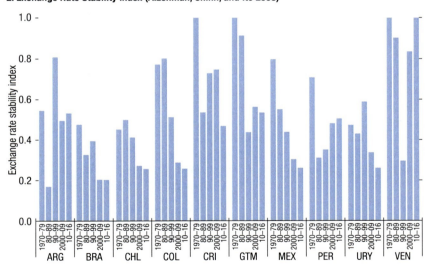

Sources: Aizenman, Chinn, and Ito (2008); Klein and Shambaugh (2008); and authors' calculations.
Note: The Klein and Shambaugh (2008) classification of pegs and soft pegs closely follows the method employed by Obstfeld and Rogoff (1995). The Aizenman, Chinn, and Ito (2008) index is based on the annual standard deviation of each country's monthly exchange rate with respect to its base country, and has been normalized to take values between zero and one. A larger value denotes less exchange rate flexibility. EME = emerging market economies. LA5 = Brazil, Chile, Colombia, Mexico, and Peru.

scrutiny would befall the central bank in the event that the target went unmet. In a region where currency adjustments had been historically associated with periods of hyperinflation, containing high exchange rate pass-through presented a challenge for meeting inflation objectives.

How have these countries fared in their pursuit of a domestic nominal anchor? As we have shown, the change toward openness was followed by larger capital flows and higher exchange rate volatility. Panel 1 of Figure 4.3 shows the evolution of inflation in selected Latin American countries since 1990, where bars correspond to average inflation in 1990–95, 1996–2001, 2002–07, 2008–13, and 2014–16. In those countries that have adopted an inflation target, average inflation has decreased markedly. But the figure also makes clear that in other countries, reducing inflation to levels consistently below 10 percent—a threshold that some empirical work has identified as imposing high costs from misallocation in terms of output and employment (Reis 2013)—remains a challenge.

Since price instability is the ultimate source of welfare costs that central banks seek to reduce, the variability of inflation matters alongside the average rate of inflation. Panel 2 of Figure 4.3 shows the standard deviation of inflation during the same time periods. Importantly, the reduction of the level of inflation has also been accompanied by a marked decrease in the volatility of inflation. Finally, as was noted in Chapter 3, these achievements have been accompanied by an increased anchoring of inflation expectations, with average forecasts falling in line with targets, and the degree of disagreement among forecasters being strongly reduced. That is to say, private agents increasingly tend to agree on the future trajectory of prices, and their projections broadly coincide with central banks' stated objectives.

Whether this improved monetary performance can be attributed to the adoption of inflation targeting is open to debate, as international evidence on the impact of implementing such a monetary framework is somewhat mixed.[2] We now turn to the analysis of two aspects of monetary policymaking in Latin America that can shed light on the link between their evolving policy frameworks and observed monetary performance.

The first aspect is related to the ability of central banks to tailor monetary policy to domestic objectives in a context of greater financial integration. The impossible trinity or policy trilemma in open economies (Mundell 1963; Obstfeld and Taylor 1998) states that if the monetary authority of a financially open economy fixes the exchange rate, they will be unable to tailor monetary policy according to domestic objectives such as ensuring output and price

---

[2] For instance, Gonçalves and Salles (2008) find that developing countries that adopted inflation targeting benefited from a larger fall in inflation and inflation volatility than those that did not. However, Brito and Bystedt (2010) find that this reduction in inflation came at the cost of lower average output growth. So while it may be true that inflation targeting allowed central banks to fight inflation more aggressively, it may not have reduced the costs associated with disinflation in terms of economic activity. See Céspedes, Chang, and Velasco (2014) for a review of the recent experience with inflation targeting in a subset of Latin American countries.

Figure 4.3. Reduction in the Level and Volatility of Inflation since 1990

1. Inflation
(Period average, percent)

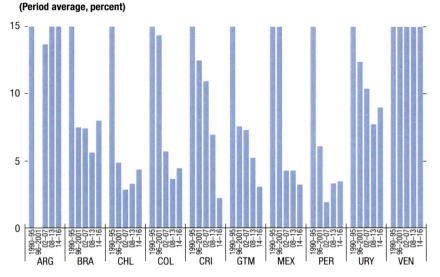

2. Inflation volatility
(Period standard deviation, percentage points)

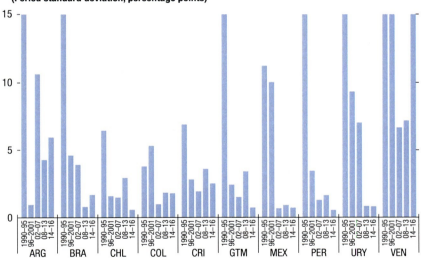

Source: IMF, Information Notice System.
Note: For clarity, values in panel 1 and 2 have been capped at 15. Argentina's CPI data after December 2006 correspond to private analysts' estimates.

stability. The corollary is that autonomous monetary policy is possible as long as the exchange rate is allowed to float. However, many studies have found that the pass-through of international to domestic interest rates remains significant even for countries with flexible exchange rates (see, for instance, Edwards 2015). Some have even questioned the validity of the trilemma based on the large co-movement of interest rates and other asset prices across integrated economies (Rey 2015). Have Latin American central banks been able to pursue autonomous monetary policy after opening up their capital accounts?

The second aspect is related to the ability to deliver price stability in a context of greater exchange rate variability. Even if the central bank retains autonomy to set policy interest rates in line with domestic objectives, higher exchange rate variability may result in excessive inflation volatility if the consumer prices are highly sensitive to the exchange rate. Under such a scenario, it may not be possible to effectively offset such price variability with monetary policy given its lengthy transmission mechanism, resulting in difficulties to anchor inflation expectations. The extent of exchange rate pass-through had indeed been historically large in the region, so a natural question is how it was possible to deliver low and stable inflation with more exchange rate volatility. Have the monetary reforms been accompanied by a reduction in pass-through rates in the region?

SPILLOVERS AND MONETARY POLICY AUTONOMY IN LATIN AMERICA

Since the early 2000s, there has been substantial co-movement of interest rates across a large sample of advanced and emerging market economies.[3] We analyze this aspect of the global financial cycle by estimating a global factor of short- and long-term interest rates, real output growth, and Consumer Price Index (CPI) inflation, which corresponds to the principal component of the time series of each variable across a panel of 60 countries.[4]

Short-term interest rates exhibit a positive correlation with the global component in most countries. Within Latin America, the largest degree of co-movement with the global component is observed among those economies that have become the most integrated with global financial markets (Brazil, Chile, Colombia, Mexico, and Peru, denoted LA5). In these countries, the average correlation of short-term interest rates with the global factor has been slightly above 0.7, which is comparable to that of financially integrated economies in Asia. The degree of co-movement with global short-term rates is smaller for other Latin American countries, such as Costa Rica, Honduras, and Paraguay. The patterns are similar in the case of long-term interest rates.

---

[3] The analysis in this section was originally reported in IMF (2015).

[4] This principal component corresponds to the linear combination of the underlying series that best summarizes the total variance in the data.

Figure 4.4. Rolling Correlation across Selected Latin American Economies and the Global Common Factor

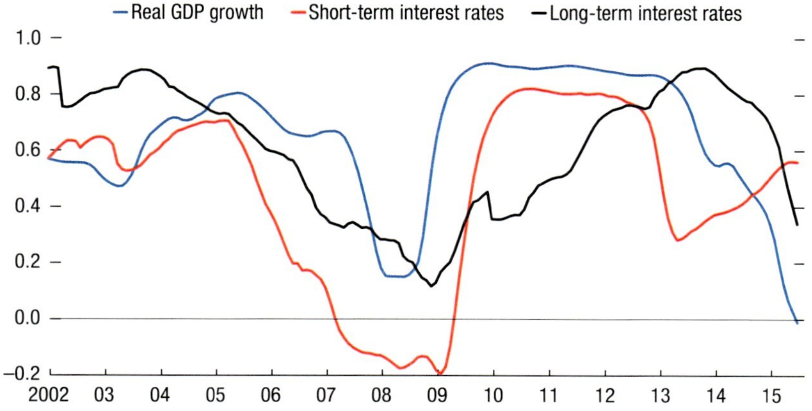

[Chart showing Real GDP growth, Short-term interest rates, and Long-term interest rates from 2002 to 2015, y-axis ranging from -0.2 to 1.0]

Source: Authors' calculations.
Note: Average correlation across selected macroeconomic variables in Brazil, Chile, Colombia, Mexico, and Peru (LA5) against the global component for the corresponding variable; four-year moving average.

But does a high correlation of global and domestic interest rates indicate that open economies with flexible exchange rates lack the autonomy to set an independent monetary policy? As we will argue, not necessarily.

As shown in Figure 4.4, the degree of co-movement of interest rates with respect to the corresponding global factor varies over time, and fluctuations tend to mimic the variations in synchronization of business cycles across countries. For instance, the degree of synchronicity of short-term interest rates in the LA5 economies with the global factor reached particularly high levels following the common shock from the global financial crisis and has since moderated somewhat as real cycles have diverged during the postcrisis period. This observation highlights the importance of accounting carefully for the co-movement in business cycles if we want to infer the extent of monetary policy autonomy from estimates of interest rate interdependence—an exercise to which we turn later in this section.

We first use a set of country-specific vector autoregressions (VARs) and monthly data since the early 2000s to quantify the linkages between interest rates in the United States and those in a sample of 43 advanced and emerging market economies.[5] All models include changes in short- or long-term interest rates as domestic variables—depending on the question—and changes in the U.S. federal funds rate or in the 10-year Treasury bond yields as external or exogenous

---

[5]The quantitative exercises in this chapter are focused on the effects of changes in U.S. interest rates, as these are a key driver of global financial conditions (see, for instance, Rey, 2015).

variables.[6] Following the results in Chen, Mancini-Griffoli, and Sahay (2014), we also include the Chicago Board Options Exchange Volatility Index (VIX) as an external variable to account for changes in global risk sentiment.

We start by exploring the reaction of domestic short-term rates to changes in the U.S. federal funds rate.[7] Short-term rates react quite differently across our sample of countries in response to a movement in the federal funds rate (circles in panel 1 of Figure 4.4).[8] The average response to a 100-basis-point hike in the federal funds rate for a broad sample of emerging markets outside Latin America is less than 10 basis points, while the average response for advanced economies is about 30 basis points. Within Latin America, the response of Mexican and Peruvian short-term rates to the same shock is as high as 95 basis points and 80 basis points, respectively. Short-term rates in Argentina, Bolivia, Chile, Costa Rica, and Uruguay react only by 20 to 40 basis points. In Colombia, in turn, their response is close to zero, and it is negative—though not statistically significant—in the case of Brazil.

There is nothing necessarily surprising or inherently undesirable about domestic financial conditions being synchronized with those of international financial markets. For instance, countries with strong trade and financial linkages with the United States—such as Canada and Mexico—will tend to have an economic cycle that is highly synchronized with the U.S. cycle. In such cases, changes in domestic financial conditions may be broadly aligned with U.S. financial conditions, without compromising price and output stabilization objectives.

The situation would be different, however, if domestic financial conditions are driven by foreign conditions that are out of sync with the domestic business cycle. In this case, monetary policy may deviate from the inward-looking policy objectives of local central banks, with consequent costs in terms of output and price stability.

To narrow our analysis to spillovers from U.S. interest rates that would signal constrained monetary autonomy, we follow the two-stage procedure presented in Caceres, Carrière-Swallow, and Gruss (2016), which partials out the systematic policy response to changes in domestic macroeconomic conditions.[9] The intuition behind the procedure is as follows. We first impose the null hypothesis that domestic monetary policy is inward-looking, focusing exclusively on stabilizing domestic output and prices. But at times, monetary policy decisions will have deviated from what the central bank's policy rule would predict on the basis of

---

[6]All model specifications share the assumption that domestic variables do not affect global variables, as is thought to be the case for Latin America's small and open economies.

[7]We use interest rates on short-term government bonds (with a maturity of about three months). Even if this is not the monetary policy instrument, the short-term market interest rate should be closely linked to changes in the monetary policy stance.

[8]Throughout the chapter we focus on the estimated cumulative impulse response functions after 12 months to allow transmission to be fully realized.

[9]The justification for the use of this procedure over other empirical methods for assessing monetary autonomy is described in detail in Caceres, Carrière-Swallow, and Gruss (2016).

local developments alone. We then estimate whether these deviations can be accounted for by movements in U.S. monetary policy. If so, we conclude that monetary autonomy is constrained to some degree.

More specifically, in the first stage we estimate a Taylor-type rule for the dynamic relationship between domestic interest rates and 12-month-ahead forecasts of inflation and output growth, as reported by Consensus Economics. These market forecasts are meant to capture changes in the economic outlook due to both idiosyncratic and global factors.

Ideally we would employ the central banks' internal forecasts used to inform the policy decision, but these are publicly available for only a small number of countries. Using market forecasts instead is subject to two potential limitations. First, there is a timing problem because they are not collected on the day of monetary policy decisions, such that information sets will differ from those available to policymakers. This could potentially bias the assessment of monetary autonomy.[10] As a robustness check, we verify that using alternative forecast vintages does not significantly alter the results. The second concern is that market forecasts may incorporate expected policy responses. If the central bank is fully credible, the argument goes, market forecasts might not react to a shock that affects domestic conditions, as agents anticipate that the central bank will do whatever is necessary to neutralize its effects. However, it is generally believed that monetary policy affects economic outcomes with a significant delay, such that movements in 12-month-ahead market forecasts should be highly correlated with movements in the central bank's internal forecasts.

The residuals or unexplained components from the first-stage estimations can be interpreted as deviations from the historical policy reaction function that characterizes the central bank's efforts to stabilize the domestic cycle. Of course, these unexplained interest rate movements likely reflect other central bank objectives beyond preserving price stability, including financial stability concerns related to exchange rate fluctuations, and could well be welfare-enhancing.[11] Nonetheless, they entail changes in domestic monetary conditions beyond what can be attributed to the central bank's usual response to inflation and output developments.

In the second stage, we seek to quantify to what extent these unexplained interest rate movements can be attributed to changes in U.S. interest rates. To do so, we estimate a second set of country-specific VAR models including the residuals from the first-stage estimation, the federal funds rate, and the VIX. As before,

---

[10]To ensure that forecasts are predetermined with respect to policy decisions, we use lagged market forecasts, even though this may come at the cost of reducing their information content further.

[11]Consider the case of a central bank that decides to increase interest rates in the face of a shock that would otherwise lead to exchange rate depreciation. Our procedure identifies the part of the rate increase that can be explained by its concern for the second-round effects on inflation, as captured by its historical behavior. The remainder is considered unexplained, even though it could correspond to an explicit intent to contain vulnerabilities from balance sheet mismatches in order to preserve financial stability.

the coefficient matrices are restricted to ensure that global variables are not affected by domestic variables. We expect the impulse response of the Taylor-rule residuals to shocks from the federal funds rate to be nonzero where monetary autonomy is constrained, so we denote these responses *autonomy-impairing spillovers*.

The autonomy-impairing spillovers from U.S. to domestic short-term interest rates (depicted with bars in panel 1 of Figure 4.5) are generally smaller than the overall responses reported earlier (20 basis points lower on average). This suggests that an important portion of the co-movement in interest rates is simply a reflection of synchronized business cycles, and thus cannot be taken to mean that the central bank lacks monetary autonomy.

However, the estimated autonomy-impairing spillovers are statistically significant in 8 of the 46 advanced and emerging market economies in the sample: Canada, Hong Kong Special Administrative Region, Israel, Mexico, Peru, Saudi Arabia, Singapore, and Taiwan Province of China.[12] The average spillover among these economies is quite large—about 40 basis points—but there is substantial heterogeneity across countries. Interestingly, these economies include some with fully flexible exchange rates and well-established central bank credibility, such as Canada and Israel.

In Latin America, spillovers associated with limited autonomy are significant and large in the cases of Mexico and Peru—about 70 basis points and 50 basis points, respectively—but smaller and not statistically significant in the other countries. This is likely related to the tight financial linkages with the United States in the former and the high degree of dollarization in the latter. In a context in which the U.S. and Latin American business cycles are out of sync, our results would suggest that a co-movement with U.S. rates would be more likely in Mexico and Peru than elsewhere.

In sum, we find that a large portion of the response of short-term interest rates to movements in U.S. rates can be attributed to the synchronicity of business cycles across countries. However, we also find that movements in U.S. rates generate significant spillovers to domestic short-term rates in several countries—including a few in Latin America—above and beyond what can be explained by standard business-cycle co-movement. Overall, there seems to be an important amount of heterogeneity in terms of the ability to set short-term rates according to domestic objectives, which motivates an analysis of the determinants of monetary autonomy in the next section.

Many important economic decisions taken by firms, households and financial institutions depend on longer-term interest rates. Moreover, the U.S. Federal Reserve has conducted monetary policy by influencing the longer end of the yield curve through quantitative easing and forward guidance since the policy rate hit the zero lower bound during the global financial crisis. So before turning to the

---

[12]It should be noted that these estimates reflect historical average effects, and thus cannot fully capture improvements in policy frameworks that have been implemented since 2000.

Figure 4.5. Spillovers to Short- and Long-Term Interest Rates

1. From the Federal Funds Rate to Domestic Short-Term Interest Rates

2. From 10-Year U.S. Treasury Bond Yields to Domestic Long-Term Interest Rates

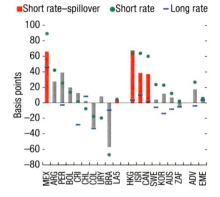
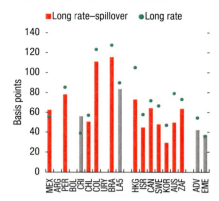

Source: Authors' calculations.
Note: Responses in basis points following a 100 basis point increase in the corresponding U.S. rate. ADV = advanced economies; EME = emerging market economies; LA5 = Brazil, Chile, Colombia, Mexico, and Peru.

determinants of monetary autonomy, we explore the response of domestic interest rates at the longer-end of the yield curve to changes in U.S. interest rates. To this end, we estimate country-specific VAR models that include the long-term interest rate as the domestic variable of interest, and U.S. interest rates (the federal funds rate or the 10-year U.S. Treasury bond yields, depending on the question) and the VIX as external variables.

We find that changes in the federal funds rate do not have an important impact on domestic long-term interest rates elsewhere (dashes in panel 1 of Figure 4.5). A notable exception in Latin America is Mexico, where long-term rates are estimated to rise by about 40 basis points following a 100 basis point hike in the U.S. policy rate.

However, movements in 10-year U.S. bond yields typically have a greater impact on corresponding domestic rates, and the responses are more similar across countries (dots in panel 2 of Figure 4.5). After a 100 basis point increase in U.S. bond yields, long-term rates in emerging market and advanced economies increase by an average of 35 and 55 basis points, respectively. The average response of long-term rates in the LA5 economies is even larger, at about 90 basis points. Brazil stands out with a response of about 130 basis points, followed by Colombia at 120 basis points. The response in the other LA5 countries lies between 55 and 75 basis points.

For completeness, we also report estimates of spillovers to long-term rates obtained by implementing the two-stage procedure described above—shown with bars in panel 2 of Figure 4.5—but find that they are essentially the same as the overall response from simple VAR models. An interpretation of this result is that the short-term domestic macroeconomic outlook has little bearing on long-term sovereign interest rates, which are in turn heavily impacted by movements in corresponding U.S. rates.

In an additional exercise (not reported here due to space considerations), we reestimate the country-specific VAR models including long-term interest rates in the domestic block, but substituting the U.S. bond yields in the external block with its decomposition into the expected path of short-term interest rates and the term premium. We find that the term premium is a much more important driver of Latin American long-term rates than the expected path for short-term rates, suggesting that conventional U.S. Federal Reserve policy has not been a major driver of international long-term rates. While this might suggest a secondary role for U.S. monetary policy in driving the global financial cycle in this asset class, it should be noted that unconventional monetary policy measures adopted since the global financial crisis appear to have influenced the term premium by reducing uncertainty surrounding the future rate path.

Determinants of Monetary Autonomy

In the previous section we reported that the response of domestic short-term rates to changes in the U.S. federal funds rate varies significantly across countries even after controlling for domestic economic conditions, suggesting that monetary autonomy is limited in some cases but not in others. What explains this heterogeneity in monetary policy autonomy? According to the trilemma theory, the main determinants of autonomy are the degree of exchange rate flexibility and capital account openness. More recently, Rey (2015) has argued that autonomy can only be achieved by restricting the capital account, challenging the dimensions of the trilemma's central trade-off. Our results seem to lay somewhere in between. Some countries with flexible exchange rates are constrained by significant spillovers from global financial conditions. Meanwhile, many other countries in Latin America do seem to enjoy full autonomy to set monetary policy according to domestic objectives, regardless of the global financial cycle. We should note that this does not imply that these countries are isolated from financial conditions abroad, since these likely have important impacts on their domestic macroeconomic variables. Rather, these global developments do not cause domestic financial conditions to deviate from the objectives of stabilizing output and inflation and are thus indistinguishable from a fully inward-looking monetary policy.

The large variability in estimates of spillovers associated with limited autonomy across countries suggests that there may also be other factors affecting the trade-offs underlying monetary autonomy. This section reports the results from a panel VAR estimation approach that exploits the differences in spillovers across countries and explores how these are affected by policy frameworks and other characteristics. Following the setup used in Towbin and Weber (2013), an interacted-panel VAR (IPVAR) model is used to exploit heterogeneity in fundamentals across countries and also over time. The model includes the same variables that are in the country-specific

VAR models—that is, the first-stage Taylor-rule residuals, the U.S. federal funds rate, and the VIX—but estimates the dynamic relationships in a panel setting.

A regular panel VAR would force the coefficient matrices to be the same for all countries. In the IPVAR model, instead, the model coefficients are functions of country-specific fundamentals that can, in addition, vary over time. Once the model is estimated, we can then obtain different impulse response functions that are conditional on particular values of each country-specific fundamental.

We start by verifying the basic predictions of the trilemma by conditioning the impulse-response functions on the exchange rate regime. Panel 1 of Figure 4.6 compares the estimated autonomy-impairing spillovers under alternative exchange rate regimes (as defined in Reinhart and Rogoff, 2004, and Ilzetzki, Reinhart, and Rogoff, 2009), conditional on an open capital account. We find that maintaining a fully flexible exchange rate regime sharply reduces the degree of spillovers to domestic short-term rates. For a country with high financial openness, the spillover effect declines from about 40 basis points under a fixed exchange rate to about 14 basis points under a floating exchange rate and to only four basis points under a fully flexible regime—and the response under a fully flexible exchange rate regime is actually indistinguishable from zero at a 10 percent confidence level.[13]

Other results (not reported here due to space considerations) also confirm that constraining capital mobility reduces the extent of autonomy-impairing spillovers: when we condition on a floating exchange rate and the degree of capital account openness is set to match the value of the index corresponding to the first decile in our sample, the spillover drops from 14 basis points to practically zero.

Finally, we explore whether the strength of policy frameworks affects the extent of autonomy-impairing spillovers. To this end, we extend the model to include a third fundamental and construct a country-specific index for the degree of anchoring of inflation expectations and monetary policy credibility.[14] Panel 2 of Figure 4.6 shows that, for a given policy choice along the capital account openness and exchange rate flexibility dimensions, a smaller degree of disagreement among professional forecasters of inflation reduces the extent of spillovers that are associated with limited monetary autonomy. The spillover response drops by about 10 basis points when the index of policy credibility moves from a value corresponding to the third decile of its distribution to its maximum level in our sample. We interpret a smaller degree of forecast disagreement as suggesting that inflation expectations are better anchored, probably as a result of more predictable and credible monetary policy.

---

[13]This finding is in line with the panel analysis of Obstfeld (2015) for a similar broad sample of countries, and with the narrative approach in Claro and Opazo (2014) and De Gregorio (2014) for the case of Chile.

[14]The degree of anchoring of inflation expectations is constructed as the inverse of a four-year moving average of the standard deviation of inflation forecasts reported by Consensus Economics at a 12-month fixed horizon. This metric is thought to provide a proxy for monetary policy credibility, since the more predictable a central bank's reaction function is, the less likely are forecasters to disagree about the future path of inflation. Disagreement has also been found to be closely related to de jure measures of central bank independence (Dovern, Fritsche, and Slacalek 2012).

Figure 4.6. Determinants of Monetary Autonomy

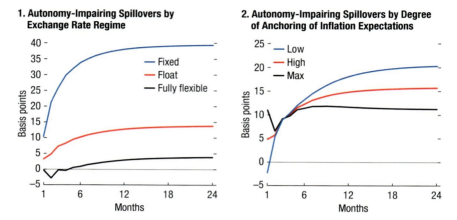

Sources: Authors' calculations.
Note: The impulse responses are estimated with an interacted-panel vector autoregression. The exchange rate regime classification used for the conditional impulse responses in panel 1 follows Ilzetzki, Reinhart, and Rogoff (2009). The impulse responses reported in panel 2 are conditional on different values of an index capturing the degree of anchoring of inflation expectations that is inversely related to the disagreement among Consensus Economics inflation forecasts. "Low" (High) corresponds to the third (seventh) decile of the distribution of this index in the sample, while "Max" corresponds to its maximum value.

This result is important for understanding the benefits of inflation targeting. While alternative policy frameworks could be implemented under a policy of flexible exchange rates, the benefits in terms of monetary autonomy are greatest when the framework delivers better-anchored inflation expectations. By helping to align private agents' expectations about the future path of inflation, inflation-targeting regimes may have helped to deliver greater monetary autonomy from global financial conditions.

So, have Latin American countries been able to implement autonomous monetary policy despite greater financial integration? Edwards (2015) suggests that policy autonomy in the region has been quite limited recently, with monetary policy in the region's inflation-targeting countries following the Federal Reserve to a considerable extent. Our results are more mixed: while Mexico and Peru do exhibit spillovers from U.S. monetary policy, Brazil, Colombia, and Chile do not. They also suggest that anchoring inflation expectations in a context of more flexible exchange rates has helped to increase the extent of monetary autonomy in the region.

EXCHANGE RATE PASS-THROUGH

A key question for Latin America at the time of transitioning to more flexible exchange rate regimes was the implications it would carry in terms of inflation volatility.[15] The sensitivity of domestic prices to changes in the exchange rate had historically been high—indeed, pegging the currency to the U.S. dollar had been extensively used in the region to stabilize prices after periods of high inflation. Delivering price stability under flexible exchange rates in a context of high exchange rate pass-through to consumer prices would naturally pose an important challenge to the region's incipient inflation-targeting regimes.

As we have shown, the region's inflation-targeting regimes have generally been able to deliver lower and more stable inflation. This took place in spite of these regimes being characterized—by design—by increased volatility of the exchange rate (Figure 4.2). This is an indication that more stable inflation does not seem to be due to a more stable external environment over this period.

We begin by exploring whether the rate of exchange rate pass-through has changed over time in Latin America. Our empirical estimation of exchange rate pass-through to consumer prices is based on a standard specification (Campa and Goldberg 2005; and Gopinath 2015). The cumulative response is estimated for each country using Jordà's (2005) local projection method (LPM):

$$p_{i,t+h-1} - p_{i,t-1} = \alpha^h + \sum_{j=0}^{6} \beta_j^h \Delta NEER_{i,t-j} + \sum_{j=1}^{6} \rho_j^h \Delta p_{i,t-j} + \gamma_j^h \Delta X_{i,t} + \varepsilon_{i,t}^h,$$

where $p_{i,t}$ denotes the natural logarithm of the domestic price level in country i at period t; $NEER$ is the natural logarithm of the import-weighted nominal effective exchange rate;[16] Δ is a first difference operator; h denotes the horizon of the cumulative response; and $\varepsilon_{i,t}$ is a random disturbance. The vector X includes a set of control variables (and their lags) that may affect both the exchange rate and inflation, to reduce concerns about omitted variable bias: international oil and food prices in U.S. dollars; the cost of production in countries from which country i imports (proxied by the import-weighted producer price index of trading partners, as in Gopinath 2015);[17] and local demand conditions (proxied by the Hodrick-Prescott cyclical component of industrial production).

Figure 4.7 reports our exchange rate pass-through estimates β_0^h across regional country groupings for estimations carried out in three overlapping time periods: 1995–2007, 1999–2011, and 2003–15. Pass-through estimates have declined substantially from the first to the last estimation period, with particularly marked declines among emerging market economies. In Latin America, declines in exchange

---

[15]The analysis in this section was originally reported in IMF (2016). The transition to flexible exchange rates in the region was not always an orderly and gradual process, and in many cases came amid a traumatic event characterized by a sharp depreciation, aggravating concerns about pass-through. See Carstens and Jácome (2005) and Chapter 2 in this volume for discussions of central bank reforms in the region.

[16]Similarly to Gopinath (2015), we use a nominal effective exchange rate metric with weights given by imports rather than by total trade, and allow these weights to vary each year.

[17]World inflation or trade-weighted consumer prices are common alternatives to control for changes in exporting countries' production costs. The drawback of those alternatives is the preponderance of nontraded goods and services in consumer price indices. Trade-weighted export prices are also problematic, as they may already reflect pricing decisions by exporters.

Figure 4.7. Estimated Exchange Rate Pass-Through over Time

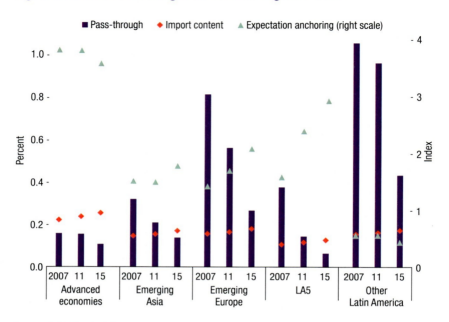

Source: Authors' calculations.
Note: Exchange rate pass-through coefficients refer to the estimated increase in the price level two years after a 1 percent increase (depreciation) of the nominal effective exchange rate. LA5 = Brazil, Chile, Colombia, Mexico, and Peru.

rate pass-through have been broad-based, but pass-through has reached particularly low levels among the region's large inflation targeters. The pass-through in those countries has become comparable to estimates among advanced economies.

What may explain the downward trend in exchange rate pass-through in emerging markets and, in particular, in Latin America? We next explore whether this phenomenon can be related to the transformation of monetary policy frameworks and its implications for the inflationary environment.

The exchange rate pass-through to consumer prices can be considered as a two-stage process. In the first stage, the prices at the border and in local currency of imported goods adjust to variations in the exchange rate. In the second stage, this gets reflected in consumer prices. The overall pass-through to consumer prices will thus depend on the sensitivity of import prices in local currency to exchange rate movements, and on the degree of import content in domestic consumption.[18] In consequence, the product of the exchange rate pass-through to

---

[18]The import content of domestic consumption includes the share of imported goods in the consumption basket, but also the share of intermediate inputs in the production of domestic goods and services that are consumed domestically.

import prices and the import content of final household consumption provides a rough benchmark for the expected *first-round* effects of currency depreciations on consumer prices.[19] As a first approximation and in line with the results in Gopinath (2015), we can assume complete pass-through to import prices, in which case the benchmark would simply correspond to the import content of consumption.[20]

But the overall pass-through to consumer prices might differ from this benchmark related to the adjustment of tradable prices if, for instance, rigidities in the labor or product markets, or poorly anchored inflation expectations, lead to *second-round* effects of currency movements. In an unstable monetary environment, in particular, the impact of currency depreciation on inflation can be amplified by changes in inflation expectations that, in turn, affect price- and wage-setting decisions, feeding back into actual inflation.

Figure 4.7 also plots the import content of domestic consumption alongside our estimates of exchange rate pass-through. A few observations are noteworthy. First, the import content has increased gradually over time in all countries, reflecting a process of increased trade integration. Second, the gap between exchange rate pass-through estimates and the import content benchmark has declined in all regions, including Latin America. Among the LA5 economies, exchange rate pass-through estimates in the most recent period are actually smaller than the import share of consumption—a feature that had previously been true only among advanced economies. We interpret this as evidence that second-round effects have become less pervasive.

The fact that second-round effects seem to have eased over time points to improvements in monetary frameworks as one of the factors behind the decline in pass-through to consumer prices. Starting by effects at the border, and given that prices are generally assumed to be sticky in the currency they are invoiced, the literature has documented how exchange rate pass-through depends on whether the price of imported goods is set in foreign or domestic currency. As such, the larger the fraction of imports that are invoiced in foreign currency, the higher the pass-through of the exchange rate to import prices in local currency. Indeed, Gopinath (2015) finds a strong correlation between the rate of pass-through to import prices and the share of foreign currency invoicing, both at short and long horizons, for a sample of 18 advanced and 6 emerging market economies.

There is scarce data on the currency of invoicing in Latin America, but what is available points to widespread usage of the U.S. dollar. For instance, Gopinath (2015) reports that the average fraction of imports invoiced in dollars over the last few years in Argentina and Brazil has been about 88 and 84 percent, respectively.

---

[19]Similarly to Burstein, Eichenbaum, and Rebelo (2005) and Gopinath (2015), we measure the total import content of households' final demand using input-output tables. See Carrière-Swallow and others (forthcoming) for more details.

[20]Carrière-Swallow and others (forthcoming) report an alternative benchmark constructed by estimating the exchange rate pass-through to import prices in local currency.

In the case of Colombia and Peru, this share is as high as 99 and 94 percent. The share in other Latin American countries is likely to also be very high, which would suggest that the pass-through to import prices is large. Indeed, Gopinath (2015) estimates nearly complete import price pass-through for Argentina, Brazil, and Mexico.

The currency of invoicing is precisely one channel through which improvements in monetary frameworks may lead to lower pass-through to import prices and, ultimately, to consumer prices. Devereux, Engel, and Storgaard (2004) argue that the currency of invoicing is an endogenous decision, with agents choosing to price their goods in the currency that most reliably holds its value. By this argument, delivering price stability would deliver an endogenous fall in the pass-through of the exchange rate to import prices.

But a change in the currency of invoicing is only one of the reasons that may explain a reduction in pass-through to consumer prices, and arguably not the most important in Latin America so far. There are other factors that are particularly relevant for the extent of second-round effects. For instance, the explicit indexation of contracts for goods and services can trigger adjustments in the price of nontradables as well. Where nominal anchors are weak and market participants doubt the central bank's commitment to price stability, indexation practices may become more widespread. More generally, a perception that an observed change in the price of tradables may actually reflect underlying inflationary pressures, rather than a transitory relative-price adjustment following an external shock, is more likely to lead price-setters to raise their prices in turn if nominal anchors are not well established.

Along these lines, Taylor (2000) argues that lower and more stable inflation is a factor behind the decline in exchange rate pass-through. In particular, he argues that an environment of lower inflation is associated with lower expected persistence of cost and price changes. Using a microeconomic model of price setting, he shows that more stable inflation leads to a reduction in the extent to which firms pass through cost increases—including those that are due to exchange rate movements—to the price of their products. A straightforward implication of this argument is that variations in pass-through should not be taken as exogenous to the inflationary environment.

One way to explore the validity of this hypothesis is to see how the extent of second-round effects is related to the inflationary environment. Figure 4.8 shows the correlation of our estimated second-round effects—that is, the difference between pass-through estimates and their benchmark—at the country level with average inflation during the estimation sample, the volatility of inflation, and the metric of the degree of inflation expectation anchoring mentioned in the previous section.

Indeed, the extent of second-round effects seems to depend on the inflationary environment. In particular, the higher and the more volatile inflation is, the larger the gap between the exchange rate pass-through and its benchmark. Also, second-round effects are larger where inflation expectations are less anchored. In a more formal analysis of these relationships, Carrière-Swallow

Figure 4.8. The Inflationary Environment and Second-Round Effects from Depreciations

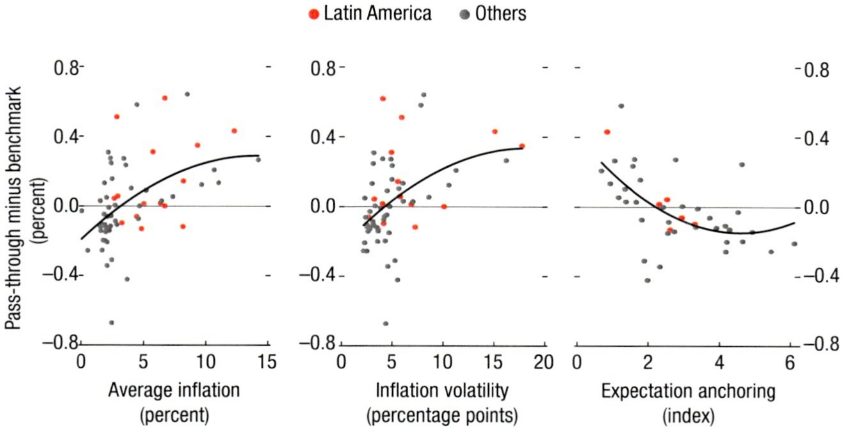

Source: Authors' calculations.
Note: The vertical axis shows the estimated second-round effects, constructed as the difference between the exchange rate pass-through estimate and the benchmark based on the import content of consumption for each individual country over 2000–15. The variables in the horizontal axis denote averages over the sample used to estimate the exchange rate pass-through.

and others (forthcoming) address possible reverse causality concerns. The results support the view that the degree of anchoring of inflation expectations is a key determinant of the extent of second-round effects from depreciations on consumer prices.

How were better-anchored inflation expectations achieved in Latin America? Many central banks have adopted an inflation-targeting regime precisely in order to anchor inflation expectations. We explore the relationship between the level of pass-through and monetary regimes by comparing the pass-through estimate for two groups of emerging market economies, with and without inflation-targeting regimes. The pass-through estimates, as well as the average degree of anchoring of expectations over each estimation sample, are reported in Figure 4.9. Inflation expectations are better anchored among countries with inflation-targeting regimes, and the extent of exchange rate pass-through is smaller in these economies. The comparison of results across samples also reveals that, as the degree of anchoring of inflation expectations improved over time, the extent of exchange rate pass-through decreased in both groups.

Of course, causal relationships cannot be inferred from these results. But the correlation of pass-through estimates with the inflation environment—and in particular the degree of anchoring of inflation expectations—and with the monetary regime suggests that credible monetary policy, supported by an institutional

Figure 4.9. Inflation Targeting, Anchored Inflation Expectations, and Exchange Rate Pass-Through

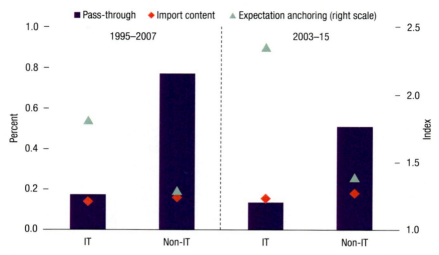

Source: Authors' calculations.
Note: Exchange rate pass-through coefficients refer to the estimated increase in the consumer price level two years after a 1 percent increase (depreciation) of the nominal effective exchange rate. Expectation anchoring is inversely related to the disagreement among Consensus Economics inflation forecasts; a higher value is associated with better-anchored inflation expectations. IT denotes countries with inflation-targeting regimes in place. The sample is restricted to 31 emerging markets.

framework that allows central banks to fulfill their mandate independently of fiscal and other considerations, effectively lowers the exchange rate pass-through to consumer prices. In doing so, it attenuates trade-offs and makes monetary policy easier to implement.

As Figure 4.10 makes clear, exchange rate pass-through continues to vary a great deal across Latin American countries. In many countries in the region, pass-through estimates remain substantially above the import-content benchmark, suggesting that second-round effects remain relevant. Some of these economies have been reluctant to let their exchange rates float for a variety of reasons, including the difficulty they might have in delivering price stability under a more volatile exchange rate. Our results suggest that the recent experience of other emerging market economies offers hope in this regard. As frameworks oriented toward price stability become well established and inflation expectations are anchored, exchange rate pass-through appears to decline substantially. In line with Taylor's (2000) argument, it seems that there may be virtuous endogeneity between the monetary policy regime and the ease with which it can reach its price stability objectives.

Figure 4.10. Exchange Rate Pass-Through Estimates in Latin America, by Country
(Percent)

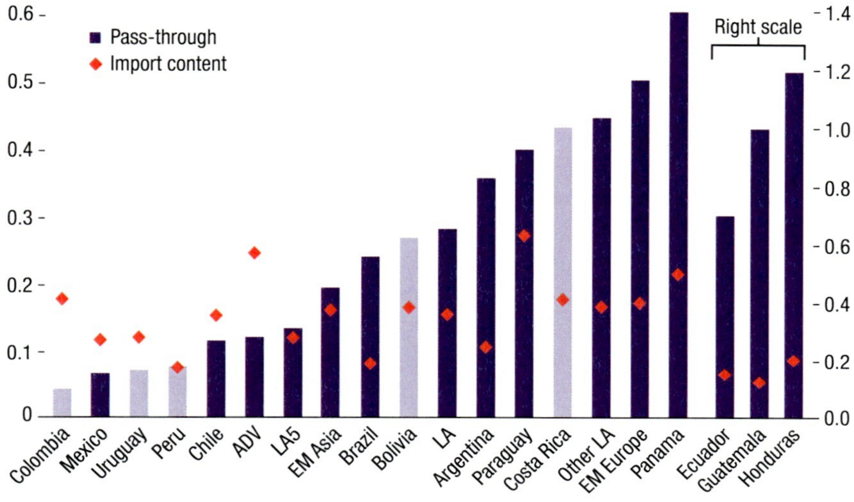

Source: Authors' calculations.
Note: Exchange rate pass-through coefficients refer to the estimated increase in the consumer price level two years after a 1 percent increase (depreciation) of the nominal effective exchange rate. Pass-through estimates for individual countries are obtained from country-specific regressions, while average regional pass-through correspond to panel model estimates. Solid bars denote statistically significant responses at the 10 percent confidence level. ADV = advanced economies; EM = emerging market economies; LA = Latin America; LA5 = Brazil, Chile, Colombia, Mexico, and Peru.

CONCLUSIONS

Over the past few decades, Latin America has embarked on a process of removing restrictions on the movement of international capital, leading to stronger integration with global financial markets. This brought important implications for monetary policymaking in the region and required an overhaul of macroeconomic frameworks. Most notably, many countries in the region moved from fixed exchange rate regimes to more flexible arrangements—a necessary condition to maintain monetary policy autonomy in a context of unrestricted capital mobility. The transition to greater financial integration and more flexible exchange rate regimes required, in turn, the establishment of a strong nominal anchor to deliver price stability. Many Latin American countries adopted inflation-targeting frameworks in the late 1990s and early 2000s as a means to establish such an anchor.

Despite claims to the contrary and widespread doubts prior to its implementation, inflation-targeting regimes with flexible exchange rates seem to have delivered the goods, in the sense that they have facilitated a reduction of inflation and inflation volatility and have been associated with increasingly well-anchored inflation expectations. Two considerations underpinned doubts about whether such a monetary framework would be able to succeed in delivering price stability in the region. First, many argued that the predictions of the classical monetary trilemma did not necessarily hold. That is, small and open economies could lack monetary autonomy even if they let their exchange rates fluctuate freely. Second, even if the central bank is able to set policy rates autonomously, monetary policy may fail to deliver price stability and anchor inflation expectations if the sensitivity of domestic prices to the exchange rate is large.

This chapter has presented evidence suggesting that the region's inflation targeters seem to have overcome these concerns through a virtuous cycle of increased credibility, lower exchange rate pass-through, and stronger autonomy. By better anchoring inflation expectations, the new frameworks facilitated a larger degree of monetary autonomy and a decline in the extent of exchange rate pass-through. This, in turn, enhanced the ability of monetary policy to reach its price stability objectives.

This study has found that the large degree of correlation of interest rates across countries does not necessarily reflect a lack of monetary autonomy, but is largely a consequence of co-movement in business cycles. After controlling for domestic economic conditions, there is much weaker evidence that interest rates in small and open economies—and in Latin America in particular—respond to global financial variables such as U.S. policy rates. But we also find evidence suggesting that certain Latin American economies do not enjoy full autonomy to set monetary conditions according to domestic price and output stability objectives, and are led to follow the financial conditions prevailing abroad.

Importantly, the analysis of cross-country heterogeneity reveals that the degree of monetary autonomy is related to the economic policy framework that is in place. Our results support the predictions of the classical trilemma: more exchange rate flexibility allows for greater monetary autonomy, even when the capital account is unrestricted. But they also emphasize the importance of predictable and credible monetary policy. A stronger nominal anchor—captured by better-anchored inflation expectations—is associated with a higher degree of monetary autonomy.

These findings do not mean that financial spillovers are irrelevant for the region—we do find, for instance, particularly large spillovers to domestic long-term interest rates from fluctuations in the U.S. term premium. But they suggest that, with careful design and implementation of their policy frameworks, central banks in Latin America can enjoy the substantial monetary autonomy they need to achieve their domestic objectives even in the face of shifting foreign financial conditions.

The ability to deliver price stability in Latin America has also been made possible by a substantial reduction in the extent of exchange rate pass-through to consumer prices. Our findings suggest that second-round effects from currency depreciations have reached unperceivable levels in many countries. This, in turn, seems to be largely due to improvements in the inflation environment and, in particular, to the anchoring of inflation expectations that resulted from monetary reforms and the implementation of inflation-targeting frameworks in the region.

REFERENCES

Aizenman, J., M. D. Chinn, and H. Ito. 2008. "Assessing the Emerging Global Financial Architecture: Measuring the Trilemma's Configurations over Time." NBER Working Paper 14533, National Bureau of Economic Research, Cambridge, Massachusetts.

Armas, A., A. Ize, and E. Levy, eds. 2006. *Financial Dollarization—The Policy Agenda*. New York: Palgrave Macmillan for the International Monetary Fund.

Brito, R. D., and B. Bystedt. 2010. "Inflation Targeting in Emerging Economies: Panel Evidence." *Journal of Development Economics* 91(2): 198–210.

Burstein, A., B. Eichenbaum, and S. Rebelo. 2005. "Large Devaluations and the Real Exchange Rate." *Journal of Political Economy* 113(4): 742–84.

Caceres, C., Y. Carrière-Swallow, and B. Gruss. 2016. "Global Financial Integration and Monetary Policy Autonomy." IMF Working Paper 16/108, International Monetary Fund, Washington, DC.

Campa, J. M., and L. S. Goldberg. 2005. "Exchange Rate Pass-Through into Import Prices." *Review of Economics and Statistics* 87(4): 679–90.

Carrière-Swallow, Y., B. Gruss, N. Magud, and F. Valencia. Forthcoming. "Exchange Rate Pass-Through: First- versus Second-Round Effects." IMF Working Paper, International Monetary Fund, Washington, DC.

Carstens, A., and L. I. Jácome. 2005. "Latin American Central Bank Reform: Progress and Challenges." IMF Working Paper 05/114, International Monetary Fund, Washington, DC.

Céspedes, L. F., R. Chang, and A. Velasco. 2014. "Is Inflation Targeting Still on Target? The Recent Experience of Latin America." *International Finance* 17(2): 185–207.

Chen, J., T. Mancini-Griffoli, and R. Sahay. 2014. "Spillovers from United States Monetary Policy on Emerging Markets: Different This Time?" IMF Working Paper 14/240, International Monetary Fund, Washington, DC.

Chinn, M. D., and H. Ito. 2006. "What Matters for Financial Development? Capital Controls, Institutions, and Interactions." *Journal of Development Economics* 81(1): 163–92.

———. 2008. "A New Measure of Financial Openness." *Journal of Comparative Policy Analysis* 10(3): 309–22.

Claro, S., and L. Opazo. 2014. "Monetary Policy Independence in Chile." BIS Working Paper 78, Bank for International Settlements, Basel.

De Gregorio, J. 2014. "Some Challenges for Financial Policies in Emerging Markets." Paper presented at the Conference on Financial Sector Development: Policies to Promote and Strengthen Local Capital Markets, October 2–3, Graduate Institute, Geneva.

Devereux, M. B., C. Engel, and P. E. Storgaard. 2004. "Endogenous Exchange Rate Pass-Through When Nominal Prices Are Set in Advance." *Journal of International Economics* 63: 263–91.

Dovern, J., U. Fritsche, and J. Slacalek. 2012. "Disagreement among Forecasters in G7 Countries." *Review of Economics and Statistics* 94(4): 1081–96.

Edwards, S. 2015. "Monetary Policy Independence under Flexible Exchange Rates: An Illusion?" *World Economy* 38: 773–87.

García-Escribano, M., and S. Sosa. 2011. "What Is Driving Financial De-dollarization in Latin America?" IMF Working Paper 11/10, International Monetary Fund, Washington, DC.

Gonçalves, C. E., and J. M. Salles. 2008. "Inflation Targeting in Emerging Economies: What Do the Data Say?" *Journal of Development Economics* 85: 312–18.

Gopinath, G. 2015. "The International Price System." NBER Working Paper 21646, National Bureau of Economic Research, Cambridge, Massachusetts.

Ilzetzki, E., C. M. Reinhart, and K. Rogoff. 2009. "Exchange Rate Arrangements Entering the 21st Century: Which Anchor Will Hold?" University of Maryland, College Park, and Harvard University, Cambridge, Massachusetts. Unpublished.

International Monetary Fund (IMF). 2012. "The Liberalization and Management of Capital Flows: An Institutional View." IMF Policy Paper, Washington, DC.

———. 2015. "To Hike or Not To Hike: Is That an Option For Latin America? Assessing Monetary Policy Autonomy." Chapter 3 in *Regional Economic Outlook: Western Hemisphere*. Washington, DC, October.

———. 2016. "Exchange Rate Pass-Through in Latin America." Chapter 4 in *Regional Economic Outlook: Western Hemisphere*. Washington, DC, April.

Jordà, Ò. 2005. "Estimation and Inference of Impulse Responses by Local Projections." *American Economic Review* 95(1): 161–82.

Klein, M. W., and J. C. Shambaugh. 2008. "The Dynamics of Exchange Rate Regimes: Fixes, Floats, and Flips." *Journal of International Economics* 75(1): 70–92.

Lane, P., and G. M. Milesi-Ferretti. 2007. "The External Wealth of Nationals Mark II: Revised and Extended Estimates of Foreign Assets and Liabilities." *Journal of International Economics* 73: 223–50.

Mundell, R. 1963. "Capital Mobility and Stabilization Policy under Fixed and Flexible Exchange Rates." *Canadian Journal of Economics and Political Science* 29(4): 475–85.

Obstfeld, M. 1998. "The Global Capital Market: Benefactor or Menace?" *Journal of Economic Perspectives* 12(4): 9–30.

———. 2015. "Trilemmas and Tradeoffs: Living with Financial Globalization." In *Global Liquidity, Spillovers to Emerging Markets and Policy Responses,* edited by C. Raddatz, D. Saravia, and J. Ventura, 13–78. Santiago: Central Bank of Chile.

———, and K. Rogoff. 1995. "The Mirage of Fixed Exchange Rates." *Journal of Economic Perspectives* 9(4): 73–96.

Obstfeld, M., and A. M. Taylor. 1998. "The Great Depression as a Watershed: International Capital Mobility over the Long Run." In *The Defining Moment: The Great Depression and the American Economy in the Twentieth Century,* edited by M. D. Bordo, C. Golden, and E. M. White. Cambridge, Massachusetts: National Bureau of Economic Research.

Reinhart, C., and K. Rogoff. 2004. "The Modern History of Exchange Rate Arrangements: A Reinterpretation." *Quarterly Journal of Economics* 119(1): 1–48.

Reis, R. 2013. "Central Bank Design." *Journal of Economic Perspectives* 27(4): 17–44.

Rey, H. 2015. "Dilemma Not Trilemma: The Global Financial Cycle and Monetary Policy Independence." NBER Working Paper 21162, National Bureau of Economic Research, Cambridge, Massachusetts.

Taylor, J. B. 2000. "Low Inflation, Pass-Through, and the Pricing Power of Firms." *European Economic Review* 44(7): 1389–408.

Towbin, P., and S. Weber. 2013. "Limits of Floating Exchange Rates: The Role of Foreign Currency Debt and Import Structure." *Journal of Development Economics* 101: 179–94.

CHAPTER 5

The Impact of the U.S. Term Premium on Emerging Markets

Alberto Naudon and Andrés Yany, Central Bank of Chile

Undoubtedly, one important and ongoing challenge for central banks in Latin America—and of small open economies in general—is how to deal with the global financial cycle. The increasing complexity and interconnectedness of financial systems have made this challenge more relevant than ever, as local financial conditions become more dependent on what happens abroad. Of course, this reality is not new, as evidenced by an extensive literature that has tried to unravel the connection between fluctuations of financial conditions in advanced economies and the economic cycle in emerging market economies. However, the aggressive monetary policy pursued by the major advanced economies to combat the negative effects of the global financial crisis and its aftermath has given new impetus to the issue. Some scholars conclude that an open capital account is simply incompatible with an independent monetary policy (Rey 2013). In this context, this chapter will focus on the two following questions:

- How relevant has the global financial cycle been for emerging market economies?
- How have central banks reacted, and what are the main issues going forward?

This chapter presents new evidence on the importance of the global financial cycle in emerging market economies and on how central banks are addressing the challenges involved. In particular, the focus is the macroeconomic and financial effects of variations of the U.S. term premium on small and open economies. The motivation for analyzing the impact of changes in the U.S. term premium, rather than on the more common topic of changes in U.S. monetary policy, is twofold. First, there is already a substantial amount of work on the impact of U.S. monetary policy on the global economy (Mackowiak 2007; Canova 2005). Second, during the last decade we have learned that the term premium is often a more important determinant of medium- and long-term interest rates, that this premium can vary substantially over time, and that it often varies for reasons unrelated to monetary policy. The "Greenspan conundrum" during the second part of the 2000s and the "taper tantrum" of 2013 are good examples of this issue.

To conduct the analysis, we study the response of financial and macro variables in nine small and open economies to a change in the U.S. term premium since 2003. The sample includes three advanced economies (Australia, Canada, and

Switzerland), and six emerging market economies, of which three are from Latin America (Chile, Colombia, and Mexico), two from Asia (Korea and Thailand), and one from Africa (South Africa).

We first decompose each country's long-term interest rate into two elements: the expected path of future short-term rates, and a term premium. Separating both elements allows us to independently study the monetary policy response and the financial channel, since the first is more related to the expected path of the short-term rate, and the latter to the behavior of the term premium. Then we study the response of several variables to a shock to the U.S. term premium.[1] We estimate a structural vector autoregression (SVAR) model with a particular identification scheme following the "agnostic" approach of Arias, Rubio-Ramirez, and Waggoner (2014), where the shock is identified imposing sign and zero restrictions directly on the impulse response functions (IRFs). This approach allows us to identify cross-country patterns and compare the differences in the impulse responses.

The analysis of the SVAR shows the large influence of global financial shocks on small open economies. In particular, our results indicate that a U.S. term premium shock has a clear pass-through to local term premiums, thus raising long-term yields. In some countries we also find inflationary effects on consumer prices through nominal depreciation of the exchange rate, and adverse effects on output. Finally, we show how central banks react to mitigate the effects of the U.S. term premium shock. We observe heterogeneity of monetary policy responses across countries, with some cutting local interest rates and others increasing them. This heterogeneity might reflect the existence of a degree of fear of floating, with some central banks worrying about potential adverse effects of local currency depreciation on inflation or financial stability.

The next section presents the theoretical framework for the computation of the term premium and reviews the evolution of long-term interest rates in the nine selected countries and its relation to the evolution of U.S. interest rates. The chapter then outlines the empirical methodology and results before presenting conclusions.

DECOMPOSITION OF YIELDS

Theoretical Framework

A central piece of our analysis is the idea that long-term interest rates can be decomposed into the two elements in the following equation:

$$R_t^n = \frac{1}{n} E_t \left\{ \sum_{s=0}^{n-1} r_{t+s} \right\} + \rho_t^n, \tag{5.1}$$

---

[1]Ceballos, Naudon, and Romero (2015) conduct a similar analysis for the case of Chile. They show that most of the fall of long-term interest rates as well as their dynamics are related to the term premia, and that the latter is driven primarily by uncertainty about nominal variables (expected inflation and the U.S. term premia).

where R_t^n is the n-period nominal interest rate, r_{t+s} is the one-period nominal interest rate, and ρ_t^n is the associated term premium.

The first element on the right-hand side of the equation is the expected future value of the short-term interest rate during the lifespan of the bond. As is common in the literature, we call this the risk-neutral rate. Since the short-term interest rate is typically used by central banks as a monetary policy instrument, we use this component as a measure of the monetary policy stance. It is important to note that, in contrast to most previous studies, we do not use the monetary policy rate, but the expected value of its future path to quantify the monetary policy. In our view, this is—at least conceptually—a better indicator of the monetary policy stance, since monetary policy is not only about setting the interest rate each month, but about guiding the market as to what the authorities will do in the future, a point that has been emphasized by the idea of forward guidance.

The second element on the right-hand side of equation (5.1) is the term premium, which captures the additional return that an investor requires to hold a long-term bond instead of rolling over a sequence of short-term bonds, since the first strategy involves interest rate risk. The term premium varies a great deal over time, and the mechanisms that determine it are not entirely clear. At times, it responds directly to changes in monetary policy. But often it moves independently, posing a challenge for monetary authorities to the extent that it causes financial conditions to deviate from the desired stance of monetary policy. A good example of this situation is the Greenspan conundrum of the mid-2000s, when a declining term premium offset a series of significant increases in the federal funds rate, leaving long-term interest rates unchanged (Bernanke 2013).

The variation of the term premium in the United States has been extensively studied (Ang and Piazzesi 2003; Wright 2011; Adrian, Crump, and Moench 2013; Joslin, Priebsch, and Singleton 2014). More recently, the large-scale asset purchase programs—or quantitative easing—pursued aggressively by the U.S. Federal Reserve have been associated with the reduction in long-term yields via a compression of the term premium. Recent estimates suggest that the first two quantitative-easing programs reduced 10-year yields by a total of about 100 basis points, attributing most of the drop in yields to a reduction in the term premium (Gagnon and others 2011).

Equation (5.1) also helps to explain how changes in the U.S. term premium can impact the long-term interest rate in other economies. First, the change in the long-term local rate depends on the reaction of monetary policy in each country. For example, if local authorities respond to an increase in the U.S. term premium by increasing their own policy rate—perhaps because they want to moderate the depreciation of their currency—then the expected path for the short-term rate will increase, and so will the long-term rate. Alternatively, term premiums in local economies could change—for instance, if the movement in the U.S. term premium generates portfolio reallocation that prompts some investors to sell domestic bonds—putting upward pressure on local long-term rates.

Figure 5.1. Ten-Year Nominal Interest Rates in the United States and Selected Countries
(Percent)

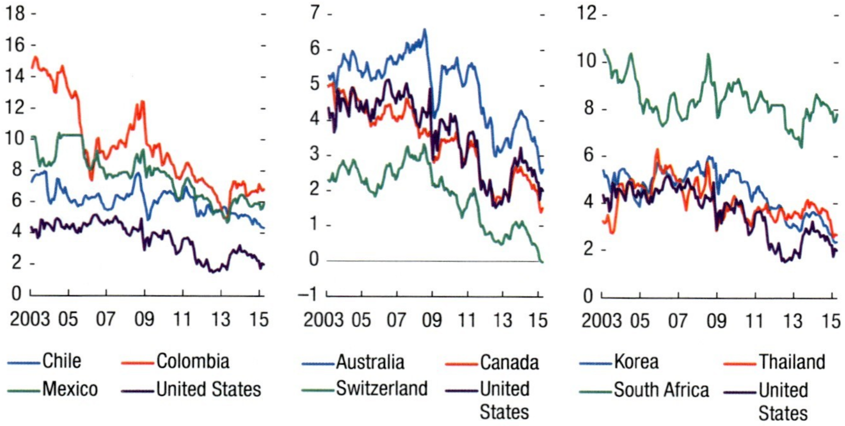

Chile — Colombia — Australia — Canada — Korea — Thailand
Mexico — United States — Switzerland — United States — South Africa — United States

Source: Bloomberg L.P.

Evolution of Yields and the Term Premium in Small Open Economies

This section reviews the evolution of long-term interest rates in the nine small open economies and their relation with movements in U.S. long-term rates. For each country, we separate the movements of long-term interest rates into those associated with term premiums and those associated with changes in the risk-neutral interest rate. We use these two elements to study the behavior of the long-term interest rates in each economy and analyze their co-movement with corresponding series in the United States.

Figure 5.1 shows the evolution of the 10-year nominal interest rates in all nine selected countries since 2003, along with the 10-year interest rate in the United States. It is clear that long-term interest rates fell in most countries after the global financial crisis, although with varying intensity. It is also clear that, in general, the declines have coincided with the evolution of the interest rate in the United States. The falls have been substantial: in most cases the rates are now about half of their 2003–05 average. In the United States, the reduction has been almost 250 basis points. In advanced open economies, the fall has been of similar magnitude. In Latin American economies, changes have been somewhat larger, particularly in Colombia, where the 10-year rate fell more than 600 basis points during this period. In Mexico the fall was also large, at 350 basis points, while in Chile it was about 250 basis points.

Figure 5.2 shows the evolution of estimated term premiums in selected economies since 2003. Beyond the well-known downward trend of the term premium in the United States, it is evident that term premiums have fallen in almost all

Figure 5.2. Term Premiums in the United States and Selected Countries
(Percent)

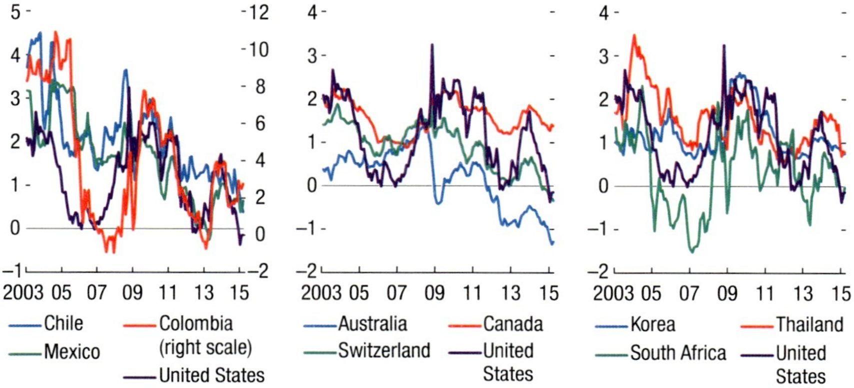

[Figure 5.2: Three panels showing term premiums over 2003–2015. Left panel: Chile, Mexico, Colombia (right scale), United States. Middle panel: Australia, Switzerland, Canada, United States. Right panel: Korea, South Africa, Thailand, United States.]

Source: Authors' calculations based on the methodology explained in the text and in Appendix 5.1.

economies considered in our analysis. In most cases, the decline of the term premiums corresponds to more than two-thirds of the fall in long-term interest rates documented in Figure 5.1.

The importance of the term premium for the evolution of long-term interest rates in each economy is more formally analyzed in Table 5.1. For each economy, the variance of the long-term interest rate is decomposed into (1) its covariance with the term premium, and (2) its covariance with the risk-neutral rate. Results of this exercise are shown in panel 1. In all cases except Switzerland, the term premium accounts for a significant share of the variance of long-term interest rates. In most cases, the portion explained by the term premium is larger than 50 percent. In the case of Latin American economies, the importance of term premiums is among the highest in our sample. The case of Chile is particularly noticeable, with the term premium explaining all the variation of the long-term interest rate, since the covariance between the risk-neutral interest rate and the long-term interest rate is slightly negative. The results are stronger still when we analyze monthly differences of long-term rates (panel 2), indicating that the variation of term premiums is important in explaining movements at higher frequency, beyond the downward trend in interest rates that has been seen in recent years.

The relationship between the interest rates in small open economies and the interest rates in the United States is analyzed in Table 5.2. Panel 1 shows the correlations between long-term interest rates in each of these economies and their U.S. counterpart, as well as the correlation between the term premiums and between risk-neutral rates. Consistent with the visual examination of Figure 5.1, the correlation between the long-term interest rates is high, at 0.75 on average. The high correlation between interest rates of advanced economies is remarkable, with a coefficient of about 0.9. In emerging market economies, the correlations are

TABLE 5.1

Variance Decomposition of Long-Term Interest Rates

	Australia	Switzerland	Canada	Chile	Colombia	Mexico	Korea	Thailand	South Africa	United States
					1. Levels					
Term premium	0.66	0.04	0.56	1.06	0.87	0.60	0.23	0.35	0.74	0.25
Risk-neutral rate	0.34	0.96	0.44	−0.06	0.13	0.40	0.77	0.65	0.26	0.75
					2. First difference					
Term premium	0.54	0.06	0.61	0.99	1.43	0.69	0.45	0.51	0.98	0.82
Risk-neutral rate	0.46	0.94	0.39	0.01	−0.43	0.31	0.55	0.49	0.02	0.18

Source: Authors' calculations.

Note: The covariance decomposition is based on the fact that for each country $VAR(R) = Cov(R, RNR) + Cov(R, TP)$, where R is the long-term interest rate, RNR is the risk-neutral rate, and TP is the term premium.

TABLE 5.2

Correlations between Local Long-Term Interest Rates, Term Premiums, and Risk-Neutral Rates with Their U.S. Counterparts

	Australia	Switzerland	Canada	Chile	Colombia	Mexico	Korea	Thailand	South Africa
1. Correlations (levels)									
10-year yield	0.89	0.94	0.91	0.62	0.70	0.82	0.83	0.67	0.49
Term premium	0.30	0.83	0.67	0.64	0.55	0.34	0.55	0.47	0.64
Risk-neutral rate	0.34	0.81	0.82	0.14	0.43	0.56	0.64	0.62	0.69
2. Share of covariance (levels)									
Term premium	0.38	0.30	0.34	0.74	0.56	0.32	0.41	−0.18	1.10
Risk-neutral rate	0.62	0.70	0.66	0.26	0.44	0.68	0.59	1.18	−0.10
3. Correlations (first difference)									
10-year yield	0.52	0.59	0.50	0.21	0.10	0.31	0.31	0.27	0.32
Term premium	0.31	0.42	0.63	0.20	0.13	0.26	0.02	0.22	0.28
Risk-neutral rate	0.22	0.41	0.49	0.06	0.13	0.11	0.17	0.26	0.10
4. Share of covariance (first difference)									
Term-premium	0.72	0.76	0.79	0.69	2.02	0.79	0.58	0.56	0.92
Risk-neutral rate	0.28	0.24	0.21	0.31	−1.02	0.21	0.42	0.44	0.08

Source: Authors' calculations.

Note: Covariance decomposition is based on the fact that $Cov(R, RUS) = Cov(R, RNRUS) + Cov(R, TPUS)$, where R is the long-term interest rate, RNR is the risk-neutral rate, and TP is the term premium.

somewhat lower, but still show levels that denote a high degree of co-movement. Among the economies of Latin America, Mexico shows the highest correlation, followed by Colombia and Chile. These rankings could be associated with the relative importance of foreign participants in each of these markets.

When we focus on cross-country correlations for each component of long-term interest rates, the results are somewhat mixed. In general, the correlations between the local components and their U.S. counterparts remain high for both the term premiums and the risk-neutral rates. Indeed, for both variables the coefficients are greater than 0.5 in most cases. Panel 2 in Table 5.2 shows the contributions of the U.S term premium and the risk-neutral rate to the co-movement between the local and the U.S. long-term interest rates. In general, the covariance between the local interest rate and the U.S. term premium accounts for more than a third of the covariance. In the Latin American countries, the share tends to be higher. Panels 3 and 4 repeat the exercise for monthly differences, and the results remain essentially unchanged.

The evidence presented above shows that long-term interest rates have fallen since the crisis, and that this decline is related to prospects of more dovish monetary policy and a reduction of term premiums. Additionally, a significant degree of correlation is observed between the evolution of long-term rates in the analyzed economies and what has happened in the United States. This correlation is due both to co-movement of monetary policies and the co-movement of term premiums.[2]

---

[2] Of course we are not the first to report the important correlation between rates in emerging market economies and the United States. See Turner (2014) and Miyajima, Mohanty, and Chan (2012).

In the Latin American economies, these patterns tend to be even more significant, as most of the movement of long-term interest rates is associated with movements of the term premiums. Regarding the co-movement with long-term rates in the United States, the data show that a considerable part of this co-movement occurs through the co-movement with the U.S. term premium.

IMPACT OF THE U.S. TERM PREMIUM ON SMALL AND OPEN ECONOMIES

Empirical Model

We follow the approach of Fornero, Montero, and Yany (2015) to compute the IRFs to a 50 basis point U.S. term premium shock in small and open economies. The empirical model is a SVAR with two blocks: a first block composed of foreign variables and a second block composed of the domestic variables of a small and open economy. We assume block exogeneity for the foreign block, such that changes in domestic variables do not affect the responses of foreign variables. Using the notation of Arias, Rubio-Ramirez, and Waggoner (2014), the model can be written as:

$$[y_t^{*'} \ y_t'] \begin{bmatrix} A_{01} & A_{02} \\ 0 & A_{04} \end{bmatrix} = \sum_{i=1}^{p} [y_{t-i}^{*'} \ y_{t-i}'] \begin{bmatrix} A_{l1} & A_{l2} \\ 0 & A_{l4} \end{bmatrix} + c + [\varepsilon_t^{*'} \ \varepsilon_t'], \qquad (5.2)$$

where $Y_t' = [y_t^{*'} \ y_t']$ denotes an $n \times 1$ vector of endogenous variables of the small open economy, y_t^* denotes an $n^* \times 1$ vector of endogenous variables of the foreign block, and p is the lag length of the model. The zero blocks in the system reflect the block exogeneity assumption, and A_l is the matrix of structural parameters to be estimated, with A_0 invertible. The vector c is a vector of parameters and the model is defined for $1 \leq t \leq T$, where T is the sample size. The vectors ε_t and ε_t^* are Gaussian, with mean zero and variance-covariance matrix I_{n+n^*}, corresponding to the $(n + n^*) \times (n + n^*)$ identity matrix.

The model can be compactly written as:

$$Y_t' A_0 = X_t' A_+ + \varepsilon_t', \qquad (5.3)$$

where $Y_t' = [y_t^{*'} \ y_t']$, $X_t' = [Y_{t-1}' \ldots Y_{t-p}' \ 1]$. The reduced-form model can be written as:

$$Y_t' = X_t' B + u_t', \qquad (5.4)$$

where $B = A_+ A_0^{-1}$, $u_t' = \varepsilon_t' A_0^{-1}$ and $E[u_t u_t'] = \Sigma = (A_0 A_0')^{-1}$. Structural shocks and parameters are identified and estimated using an identification procedure that we describe briefly in the following subsection.

Identification Scheme

We use the "agnostic" procedure introduced in Uhlig (2005) and recently developed by Arias, Rubio-Ramirez, and Waggoner (2014). Under this approach, structural identification is achieved by imposing sign and zero restrictions directly on the IRFs of the model, and the estimation is done in a Bayesian framework. In this chapter we use the methodology of Fornero, Montero, and Yany (2015), which is an extension of Arias, Rubio-Ramirez, and Waggoner (2014) with the addition of a foreign exogenous block into the model.[3] The identification algorithm can be briefly summarized as follows:

- Draw $(B; \Sigma)$ from the posterior of the reduced-form parameters;
- Generate $(A_0^*; A_+^*)$ by using a mapping between the reduced-form and the structural parameters;[4]
- Draw an orthogonal matrix Q such that $(A_0^* Q; A_+^* Q)$ satisfies the zero restrictions;[5]
- Keep the draw if sign restrictions are satisfied;
- Repeat the previous steps until the desired number of simulations is reached;
- Compute the median for the full set of IRFs that satisfy the restrictions.

Data and Restrictions

As mentioned earlier, we independently estimate the SVAR model for nine economies: Australia, Canada, Chile, Colombia, Korea, Mexico, South Africa, Switzerland, and Thailand. All these countries are small open economies, such that foreign business cycles—characterized here by U.S. data—can be considered exogenous. We use official monthly data covering the period from January 2003 to March 2015. To facilitate the comparison across countries, for all reported countries we choose one lag in the VAR model and we add a constant as a deterministic trend.

The endogenous domestic block includes the following set of variables: (1) the output gap, measured as the Christiano-Fitzgerald filtered business cycle of the monthly index of production (in logs); (2) the annual Consumer Price Index (CPI) inflation rate; (3) the risk-neutral interest rate; (4) the 10-year term premium rate; and (5) the nominal exchange rate (in logs).

The exogenous foreign block includes (1) the U.S. output gap, measured as the Christiano-Fitzgerald filtered business cycle of the U.S. industrial production index; (2) the U.S. annual CPI inflation rate; (3) the U.S. risk-neutral interest rate; (4) the U.S. 10-year term premium rate; (5) a real commodity price index (in logs); (6) the CBOE Volatility Index (VIX, in logs); and (7) the 10-year–1-year yield spread. Details of variables, transformations, and sources are provided in Appendix 5.1.

---

[3] A full description of the methodology is beyond the scope of this chapter. See Arias, Rubio-Ramirez, and Waggoner (2014) and Fornero, Montero, and Yany (2015) for a more detailed description.

[4] The mapping between structural and reduced-form parameters can be implemented by using a function $h()$ such that $h(X)' h(X) = X$, i.e., Cholesky decomposition: $(A_0^*; A_+^*) = (h(\Sigma)^{-1}; Bh(\Sigma)^{-1})$.

[5] Using the QR decomposition ($X = QR$), which holds for any $n \times n$ random matrix on which each element is $i.i.d.$ from a $N(0,1)$.

TABLE 5.3

Sign and Zero Restrictions Imposed on the Impulse Response Functions in the Structural Vector Autoregression Model

	Model 1		Model 2	
Variable	$t=0$	$t>1$	$t=0$	$t>1$
Foreign Block				
U.S. output gap	0	?	0	?
U.S. annual inflation rate	0	?	0	?
U.S. risk-neutral rate	?	?	?	?
U.S. term premium	+	+5	+	+5
U.S. 10-year versus 1-year spread	+	+5	+	+5
Log real commodity price	?	?	?	?
Log VIX	?	?	?	?
Domestic Block				
Output gap	0	?	0	?
Annual inflation rate	0	?	0	?
Risk-neutral rate	?	?	?	?
Term premium	?	?	+	+5
Log nominal exchange rate	?	?	?	?

Source: Authors' compilation.
Note: +N indicates a positive sign restriction for N months, 0 indicates a zero restriction; ? indicates that no restriction was imposed on the variable.

In Table 5.3 we summarize the sign and zero restrictions imposed on the IRFs, which are quite standard and based on economic theory. We compute the IRFs of two different exercises ("Model 1" and "Model 2"). In both exercises, we choose a U.S. term premium shock that is positive for at least six months. The shock does not have contemporary effects on output gaps or annual inflation rates in either country. Also, in both identification schemes the shock has a positive impact on the interest rate spread for at least six months. However, in Model 2 we add a positive sign restriction for six months on the domestic term premium. We add this restriction to the domestic block for robustness and to help identify the shock's transmission in the small open economy.

RESULTS

Tables 5.4 to 5.7 show the median impulse responses of the foreign and domestic variables to an increase of 50 basis points in the U.S. term premium for the nine selected countries under both identification schemes (Models 1 and 2). We divide these countries into three categories: advanced economies (Australia, Canada, and Switzerland), Latin American countries (Chile, Colombia, and Mexico), and the others (Korea, South Africa, and Thailand) in order to identify regional cross-country patterns and differences across emerging market and advanced economies.

Table 5.4 shows the responses of the foreign variables in Model 1. The results suggest that the U.S. term premium shock is quite persistent, with a half-life of

TABLE 5.4

Monthly Impulse Response Functions of Foreign Variables to a U.S. Term Premium Shock of 50 Basis Points: Exercise with Model 1

(Mean and standard deviation across countries)

	Log VIX (%)		U.S. Output Gap (basis points)		U.S. Annual Inflation (basis points)		U.S. Term Premium (basis points)		U.S. Risk-Neutral Rate (basis points)		Log Real Commodity Price (%)	
$t = 0$	4.4	(1.6)	0.0	(0.0)	0.0	(0.0)	50.0	(0.0)	−13.2	(1.3)	−0.1	(0.4)
$t = 1$	6.2	(1.4)	0.0	(1.1)	4.8	(0.6)	46.2	(0.5)	−14.5	(1.1)	0.5	(0.3)
$t = 6$	10.5	(0.5)	−16.5	(3.2)	6.6	(2.2)	30.8	(0.9)	−22.0	(0.9)	0.8	(0.5)
$t = 12$	8.4	(0.4)	−41.5	(3.8)	−7.8	(2.2)	20.7	(0.7)	−26.6	(1.3)	−0.3	(0.5)
$t = 24$	1.8	(0.2)	−52.9	(3.3)	−16.8	(0.8)	9.8	(0.4)	−19.9	(1.4)	−1.5	(0.3)
$t = 36$	−0.8	(0.1)	−34.9	(2.1)	−8.4	(0.9)	3.8	(0.4)	−7.9	(1.0)	−1.6	(0.2)

Source: Authors' calculations.
Note: The variable Log Real Commodity Price in the exogenous block varies across countries, so the impulse responses of exogenous block variables are not the same in each estimate. The table shows the average estimate across countries. The corresponding standard deviation is in parentheses. VIX = Chicago Board Options Exchange Volatility Index.

approximately 10 months. The estimated shock generates a persistent contraction of the U.S. output gap, with a decrease of 41 basis points on average after 12 months. In line with the contractionary effects of the shock on activity, the U.S risk-neutral rate—which represents the expected path of future short-term rates—decreases on average by 15 basis points on impact, and by 26 basis points after one year. Moreover, the shock causes a rise in volatility—measured here as the log of the VIX index—of 10 percent above its steady-state level after six months and 8 percent after one year. Finally, real commodity prices do not show important responses to the shock, decreasing by only 1.5 percent after one year.

Table 5.5 reports the impulse responses for the term premium in panel 1 and of the log nominal exchange rate in panel 2, under the identifying assumptions of Model 1. The SVAR estimates suggest a clear pass-through from U.S. to local term premiums, which increase in most cases between 10 and 30 basis points in the first six months. In most of the analyzed countries, the size of the response of local term premiums is less than 50 basis points, implying a pass-through coefficient that is smaller than 1. The magnitude of responses varies across country groups, with an average of 14 basis points in advanced economies, and 43 basis points in Latin American countries. In particular, Chile and Mexico have similar and strong responses, with a peak of almost 30 basis points after six months, and approximately 20 basis points after one year, respectively. In contrast, advanced economies have weaker and less persistent responses, with the local term premiums rising less than 20 basis points in Canada and only about 10 basis points in Australia and Switzerland. On the other hand, the nominal exchange rate depreciates between 1 and 2 percent in most countries. In particular, the exchange rate in Latin American countries depreciates 1 percent on impact and returns to its initial level after one year.

TABLE 5.5

Monthly Impulse Response Functions to a U.S. Term Premium Shock of 50 Basis Points: Exercise with Model 1

	Australia	Switzerland	Canada	Chile	Colombia	Mexico	Korea	Thailand	South Africa	Advanced Economies	Latin America
1. Term Premium (basis points)											
t = 0	7.3	9	15.8	15	31.6	11.5	−0.2	3	15.8	10.7	19.3
t = 1	11.1	12.4	17.4	21	40.3	20.2	5.5	4.8	17.4	13.6	27.1
t = 6	14.1	12.2	16.4	29.4	69.6	29.7	11.4	12.3	16.4	14.2	42.9
t = 12	4	10.4	9.2	22.2	73.5	17.3	8.4	9.3	9.2	7.9	37.7
t = 24	−6.9	8.5	−0.3	0.7	69.3	1.9	6.2	2	−0.3	0.4	23.9
t = 36	−6.1	4.9	−2.2	−1.1	57.4	2.4	3.2	1.3	−2.2	−1.1	19.6
2. Log Nominal Exchange Rate (percent)											
t = 0	1.5	0.5	0.2	0.9	0.9	0.9	1.1	−0.2	0.2	0.7	0.9
t = 1	2	0.6	−0.1	0.9	0.9	1	1.5	−0.2	−0.1	0.9	1
t = 6	0.9	0.3	−0.6	1.3	0.9	0.3	2	0.3	−0.6	0.2	0.9
t = 12	−0.2	0.2	−1	0.8	0.3	−0.6	2.2	0.7	−1	−0.3	0.1
t = 24	−0.6	0.4	−1.2	0.1	0.5	0	1.8	0.7	−1.2	−0.5	0.2
t = 36	−0.2	0.5	−0.5	1.1	2.3	1	1	0.4	−0.5	−0.1	1.4
3. Output Gap (basis points)											
t = 0	0	0	0	0	0	0	0	0	0	0	0
t = 1	4.7	−0.6	8.7	−3.6	12.3	−2.4	−0.3	−36.2	8.7	4.3	2.1
t = 6	8.3	−4.6	6.6	−20.7	7.6	−24.7	−27.6	−142.5	6.6	3.4	−12.6
t = 12	0.3	−14.7	−29.3	−35.6	−72.7	−45.5	−47	−150.2	−29.3	−14.6	−51.3
t = 24	−16.4	−23.1	−62.9	−31.8	−166.1	−46.4	−19.9	−81.6	−62.9	−34.1	−81.4
t = 36	−17.1	−15.8	−55.7	−21.2	−53.9	−24.2	11.8	−48.6	−55.7	−29.6	−33.1

(continued)

TABLE 5.5 (continued)

Monthly Impulse Response Functions to a U.S. Term Premium Shock of 50 Basis Points: Exercise with Model 1

	Australia	Switzerland	Canada	Chile	Colombia	Mexico	Korea	Thailand	South Africa	Advanced Economies	Latin America
4. Annual inflation (basis points)											
$t=0$	0	0	0	0	0	0	0	0	0	0	0
$t=1$	3.8	9.9	6.9	11.3	1.9	11.2	15.4	0	6.9	6.9	8.1
$t=6$	24.4	19.4	14.2	42.1	20.4	30.7	41	-2.1	14.2	19.4	31.1
$t=12$	18	5.8	3	19.4	13.5	23.9	25.1	-12.2	3	8.9	18.9
$t=24$	-8.6	-6.1	-11.3	-40.8	-31.6	2.6	-2.4	-14.1	-11.3	-8.7	-23.3
$t=36$	-9.3	-4	-9.1	-34	-20.6	-2.2	-3.1	-9.8	-9.1	-7.4	-19
5. Risk-Neutral Rate (basis points)											
$t=0$	7.4	4.9	-5.3	-5.8	-3.2	5.1	5.7	-5.6	-5.3	2.3	-1.3
$t=1$	13.2	9.8	-1.8	-6.6	0.2	10.2	6.5	-5	-1.8	7	1.3
$t=6$	10.7	4.8	1.8	-6.5	-1.5	18.5	5.5	-10	1.8	5.8	3.5
$t=12$	1.5	-8.6	-3.2	-3.9	-21.4	12.4	-2.1	-12.2	-3.2	-3.4	-4.3
$t=24$	-1	-17.8	-8.2	-2	-74	-0.6	-13	-9.6	-8.2	-9	-25.5
$t=36$	-0.1	-9	-6.1	-2.9	-64.7	-0.9	-11.8	-4.6	-6.1	-5.1	-22.9

Source: Authors' calculations.
Note: The last two columns show the average estimate across countries.

TABLE 5.6

Monthly Impulse Response Functions of Foreign Variables to a U.S. Term Premium Shock of 50 Basis Points: Exercise with Model 2
(Mean and standard deviation across countries)

	Log VIX (%)		U.S. Output Gap (basis points)		U.S. Annual Inflation (basis points)		U.S. Term Premium (basis points)		U.S. Risk-Neutral Rate (basis points)		Log Real Commodity Price (%)	
t = 0	3.9	(3.3)	0.0	(0.0)	0.0	(0.0)	50.0	(0.0)	−10.1	(3.9)	0.6	(0.9)
t = 1	6.0	(2.8)	0.8	(2.3)	5.9	(1.6)	46.2	(0.4)	−11.5	(3.7)	1.1	(1.0)
t = 6	10.7	(0.8)	−13.1	(7.2)	9.8	(5.7)	31.1	(0.9)	−19.9	(2.9)	1.5	(1.0)
t = 12	9.0	(0.7)	−39.2	(7.4)	−5.8	(4.6)	21.1	(0.7)	−25.6	(2.3)	0.4	(0.9)
t = 24	2.5	(0.5)	−54.2	(4.0)	−15.9	(1.0)	10.7	(0.7)	−20.9	(1.8)	−1.0	(0.5)
t = 36	−0.3	(0.3)	−38.3	(2.9)	−8.9	(0.9)	4.6	(0.5)	−9.5	(2.0)	−1.1	(0.3)

Source: Authors' calculations.
Note: The table shows the average estimate across countries. The corresponding standard deviation is in parentheses. The variable *Log Real Commodity Price* varies across countries, so its response is not the same in each estimate. VIX = Chicago Board Options Exchange Volatility Index.

Domestic annual inflation (Table 5.5, panel 4) increases in most of the analyzed countries, in line with the nominal depreciation of local currencies. The results suggest a stronger and more persistent response in Latin American countries compared with advanced economies, with annual inflation increasing on average by 31 basis points after six months and 19 basis points after one year. In contrast, in advanced economies the response is on average 19 basis points after six months and only 9 basis points after one year. Regarding domestic activity, Table 5.5 (panel 3) shows the responses of the output gap in Model 1. The increase in the U.S. term premium is undoubtedly contractionary: after one year, the output gap decreases more than 30 basis points in most of the analyzed countries. The response is stronger in Latin American countries, where the output gap decreases 51 basis points on average after one year. In particular, in Chile and Mexico, the response is persistent after two years, with a decrease in the output gap of more than 30 basis points. In advanced economies, the responses are clearly weaker: the output gap diminishes only 15 basis points on average after one year. In the rest of the countries, the results are quite similar to those for Latin America, with the exception of Thailand.

How do central banks respond following a shock to the U.S. term premium? Table 5.5 (panel 5) reports the movement in risk-neutral interest rates. Across countries, responses are quite heterogeneous. On impact, some countries (Australia, Mexico, and Switzerland) show a rise in the expected monetary policy rate, while others show a reduction in it (Canada, Chile, Colombia, and South Africa). This heterogeneity might reflect the existence of monetary policy stability trade-offs. While some countries are expected to try to mitigate the contractionary effects on activity, others are expected to increase the policy rate to reduce inflation. For instance, Chile and Mexico show different responses of the risk-neutral rate, even though most of the other variables in the estimated model (output gap, annual inflation, and the term premium) react similarly.

So far we have discussed the effects of a U.S. term premium shock without imposing any sign restriction on the domestic term premium (Model 1). As mentioned earlier, we conduct a second exercise (Model 2) imposing a positive sign restriction on the domestic term premium for six months to facilitate the transmission of the shock to the domestic block. Results of this estimation are provided in Tables 5.6 and 5.7. In general, the responses are qualitatively comparable with the previous exercise: (1) contractionary effects on the output gap; (2) inflationary effects on local consumer prices; and (3) a persistent pass-through to domestic term premiums. However, with these additional restrictions, the pass-through to local financial conditions is clearly larger. Figure 5.3 displays the responses after one year of long-term interest rates and term premiums in Models 1 and 2. Long-term interest rates are, by definition, the sum of the term premium and the risk-neutral rate. According to the results reported in Figure 5.3, the U.S. term premium shock generates an increase in long-term interest rates and term premiums. This effect is larger in Latin American economies, which are situated in the upper-right corner of both panels of the figure. However, the impact on local term premiums and long-term interest rates are stronger when imposing sign and zero restrictions on the domestic block. For instance, in Chile and Mexico, the pass-through to long-term interest rates is almost twice as high in Model 2 as in Model 1. Finally, our results are broadly consistent with the recent results of Miyajima, Mohanty, and Yetman (2014), who analyzed the spillovers of unconventional monetary policy to Asian economies in the period from January 2003 to December 2007.

CONCLUSIONS

This chapter has studied the macroeconomic effects of the global financial cycle on small and open economies and the monetary policy implications of financial shocks. To tackle this issue, we conducted an estimation of a SVAR model with sign and zero restrictions for several countries following the methodology of Arias, Rubio-Ramirez, and Waggoner (2014). We included U.S. and domestic variables in each model and computed the impulse responses of the local variables to a U.S. term premium shock. Several findings emerge from this analysis:

- A clear pass-through to local financial conditions, with a rise in domestic long-term interest rates and term premiums;
- An increase in domestic inflation and contractionary impact on activity;
- As a consequence, we observe heterogeneity across monetary policy responses that might reflect the existence of monetary policy trade-offs;
- These effects are stronger in Latin American countries.

From a general perspective, the results indicate that the global financial cycle has significant effects on small open economies, especially in Latin American

TABLE 5.7

Monthly Impulse Response Functions to a U.S. Term Premium Shock of 50 Basis Points: Exercise with Model 2

	Australia	Switzerland	Canada	Chile	Colombia	Mexico	Korea	Thailand	South Africa	Advanced Economies	Latin America
1. Term Premium (basis points)											
t = 0	15.4	20.1	12.7	40.1	105.6	26.2	18.8	28.1	51.2	16.1	57.3
t = 1	19.5	19.9	16.4	41.5	109.5	34.8	22	29.5	46.6	18.6	61.9
t = 6	21.6	17.2	14	41.6	106.7	40.2	18.2	25.1	33.8	17.6	62.8
t = 12	9.9	9.5	11.1	27.4	91.7	25.6	9.8	13.9	24.8	10.2	48.2
t = 24	−5.2	−1.6	9.4	1.3	75	2.4	6.3	0.4	17.9	0.9	26.2
t = 36	−6.5	−3.2	5.2	−0.6	62	1.4	4.2	1.9	8.2	−1.5	21
2. Log Nominal Exchange Rate (percent)											
t = 0	0.3	0.3	0.9	1.1	1.9	1.8	1.7	−0.3	3	0.5	1.6
t = 1	0.3	0.1	1.3	1.1	1.7	1.9	1.6	−0.2	2.2	0.6	1.6
t = 6	−0.3	−0.9	1.2	1.5	1.1	0.6	1.8	0.6	−0.2	0	1.1
t = 12	−0.7	−1.3	0.6	0.7	0.1	−1	2.1	1.1	−2	−0.5	−0.1
t = 24	−0.8	−1.5	0.5	−0.1	0.1	−0.7	1.9	0.4	−1.8	−0.6	−0.3
t = 36	−0.4	−0.8	0.6	0.8	2.6	0.9	1.4	0.2	−1.7	−0.2	1.4
3. Output Gap (basis points)											
t = 0	0	0	0	0	0	0	0	0	0	0	0
t = 1	6.4	9.7	−0.2	−2.2	12.6	−2	3	−10.7	−5.8	5.3	2.8
t = 6	17.2	9.6	−6.1	−15.2	7.7	−25.6	−16.6	−18.3	−28.7	6.9	−11
t = 12	10.9	−25.5	−16.4	−29.6	−85.3	−52	−42.5	−17.2	−35.8	−10.3	−55.6
t = 24	−1.1	−70.6	−23.6	−31.6	−187	−48.5	−21.8	−34	−51.3	−31.8	−89
t = 36	−6.9	−58.4	−16.3	−22.4	−45.9	−22.1	8.8	−30.5	−61.3	−27.2	−30.1

(continued)

TABLE 5.7 *(continued)*

Monthly Impulse Response Functions to a U.S. Term Premium Shock of 50 Basis Points: Exercise with Model 2

	Australia	Switzerland	Canada	Chile	Colombia	Mexico	Korea	Thailand	South Africa	Advanced Economies	Latin America
					4. Annual Inflation (basis points)						
t = 0	0	0	0	0	0	0	0	0	0	0	0
t = 1	6.7	7.3	8.2	7.7	5	10.9	17.6	2.4	12.1	7.4	7.9
t = 6	33.5	17.7	17.7	32.2	23.5	34.6	48.3	12.7	43.1	23	30.1
t = 12	28.8	5.2	6.4	16.7	12.8	28.2	33	12.3	19.9	13.5	19.3
t = 24	-1.6	-11.4	-5.2	-34.5	-37.2	-0.7	2.1	-5.5	-52.7	-6.1	-24.1
t = 36	-7.6	-10.5	-3.9	-34.8	-23.2	-4.3	-1.1	-10.5	-57.7	-7.3	-20.8
					5. Risk-Neutral Rate (basis points)						
t = 0	15.1	-5	-2.3	-9.5	-48.8	13.8	10.7	-6.7	-9	2.6	-14.8
t = 1	18.5	-1.5	2.1	-8	-42.4	18.9	12	-7.9	-0.4	6.4	-10.5
t = 6	12.8	2.4	0.9	-2.9	-25.9	26.5	13.1	-10.6	4.1	5.4	-0.8
t = 12	2.7	-2.8	-9.8	0	-34.3	20.2	5.9	-9.2	-4.8	-3.3	-4.7
t = 24	-0.8	-9.1	-17.2	-0.6	-85.9	0.9	-9	-8.1	-12.3	-9.1	-28.5
t = 36	-0.5	-6.8	-8.2	-2.5	-68.6	-1.1	-11.1	-5.5	-9.6	-5.2	-24.1

Source: Authors' calculations.
Note: The last two columns show the average estimate across countries.

Figure 5.3. Responses of Domestic Term Premium and Implied 10-Year Interest Rate after One Year to a U.S. Term Premium Shock of 50 Basis Points
(Basis points)

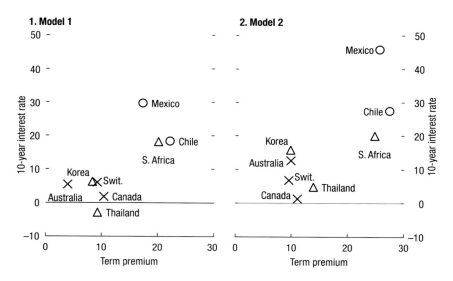

Source: Authors' calculations.
Note: Developed countries are indicated with an x, Latin American countries with circles, and the rest with triangles. Colombia is excluded from the figure because it is situated in the upper-right corner.
S. Africa = South Africa; Swit. = Switzerland.

countries. In this context, central banks face monetary policy trade-offs that involve mitigating high inflation rates in countries with output deceleration. This issue will be crucial in the months ahead as the United States continues to normalize its monetary policy.

APPENDIX 5.1. DATA AND TERM PREMIUM ESTIMATION

Data

We use official monthly data for each country on short- and long-term yields, production, the nominal exchange rate, and the annual inflation rate.

The output gap is measured as the Christiano-Fitzgerald filter (18–96; full sample and asymmetric; removing linear trends) of the monthly industrial production index. For Chile, we use the monthly economic activity index. We use the 12-month percentage change of the CPI as a proxy for annual inflation. Industrial production indexes, short- and long-term yields, CPIs, and the VIX are from Bloomberg L.P. and Organisation for Economic Co-operation and

Development databases. The real commodity price index is computed with data taken from the IMF's *International Financial Statistics*, and is deflated using the U.S. Producer Price Index.

Term Premium Estimation

Affine Model of the Term Structure

The decomposition of long-term yields into a risk-neutral rate and a term premium has been widely studied in the literature in the last two decades. A recent and popular tool has been the estimation of affine models of the term structure of yields (Ang and Piazzesi 2003; Adrian, Crump, and Moench 2013; Bauer, Rudebusch, and Wu 2014; Blake, Rule, and Rummel 2015). In this chapter, we decompose the 10-year yield for different countries following the approach of Ceballos and Romero (2015), who estimate affine models for several countries using the methodology of Adrian and others (2013), which we describe briefly in this appendix. First, we suppose that the term structure depends on its K principal components X_t, which evolve according to a VAR of order 1:

$$X_{t+1} = \mu + \phi X_t + v_{t+1}, \tag{5.5}$$

with $v_t \sim N(0, \Sigma)$. The short-term interest rate r_t is assumed to depend on the principal components of the term structure and is modeled as an affine function:[6]

$$r_t = \delta_0 + \delta_1 X_t. \tag{5.6}$$

Second, we denote P_t^n the price in period t of an n-period zero coupon bond. Using the assumption of no arbitrage (Ang and Piazzesi 2003), bond prices satisfy the following recursive dynamic:

$$P_t^n = E_t[M_{t+1} P_{t+1}^{n-1}], \tag{5.7}$$

where M_{t+1} is the stochastic discount factor, which in turn is assumed to be exponentially affine:

$$M_{t+1} = \exp\left(-\tfrac{1}{2}\lambda_t' \lambda_t - r_t - \lambda_t' \Sigma^{-1/2} v_{t+1}\right). \tag{5.8}$$

The parameter λ_t is the market price of risk, which is also assumed to evolve according to an affine process with respect to the principal components of the term structure:

$$\lambda_t = \lambda_0 + \lambda_1 X_t. \tag{5.9}$$

Using the assumptions above, one can deduce the following model-implied yield:[7]

---

[6] We use the three-month yield as a proxy for the short-term interest rate.

[7] See Ang and Piazzesi (2003) or Adrian, Crump, and Moench (2013) for a detailed computation of these equations.

$$P_t^n = \exp(A_n + B_n X_t), \tag{5.10}$$

where A_n and B_n satisfy the following recursive process:

$$\begin{cases} A_{n+1} = A_n + B_n(\mu - \Sigma\lambda_0) + \frac{1}{2}B_n'\Sigma\Sigma'B_n - \delta_0 \\ B_{n+1}' = B_n'(\phi - \Sigma\lambda_1) - \delta_1' \end{cases}, \tag{5.11}$$

with $A_1 = -\delta_0$ and $B_1 = -\delta_1$. With this, one can compute forecasts of bond prices P_t^n and deduce the associated yield y_t^n, defined by:

$$y_t^n = \frac{-\log(P_t^n)}{n}. \tag{5.12}$$

Finally, to compute the risk-neutral rate, we set the market price of risk to zero (i.e., $\lambda_0 = \lambda_1 = 0$, so that $\lambda_t = 0 \,\forall t$):

$$\begin{cases} A_{n+1} = A_n + B_n\mu + \frac{1}{2}B_n'\Sigma\Sigma'B_n - \delta_0 \\ B_{n+1}' = B_n'\phi - \delta_1' \end{cases}. \tag{5.13}$$

Thus, the term premium can be computed as a residual of the model-implied yield y_t^n and the estimated risk-neutral rate.

Model Estimation

The parameters $\{\mu, \phi, \Sigma, \delta_0, \delta_1\}$ are estimated independently by ordinary least squares (OLS) on the equations where they are defined. To estimate $\{\lambda_0, \lambda_1\}$, first we denote rx_t, the log excess holding return on a bond maturing in n periods:

$$rx_{t+1}^{n-1} = \ln(P_{t+1}^{n-1}) - \ln(P_t^n) - r_t. \tag{5.14}$$

It can be shown that rx_t satisfies the following equation:

$$rx_{t+1}^{n-1} = \beta^{n-1}(\lambda_0 + \lambda_1 X_t) - \frac{1}{2}(\beta^{n-1'}\Sigma\beta^{n-1} + \sigma^2) + \beta^{n-1'}v_{t+1} + e_{t+1}^{n-1}, \tag{5.15}$$

$\forall t = 1, \ldots, T; \forall n = 1, \ldots, N$, where e_{t+1}^{n-1} is a return pricing error identically distributed with variance σ^2 and

$$\beta^{n-1} = \text{Cov}(rx_{t+1}^{n-1}, v_{t+1}')\Sigma^{-1}. \tag{5.16}$$

The system can be stacked and compactly rewritten as:

$$rx = \beta'(\lambda_0 1_T' + \lambda_1 X_-) - \frac{1}{2}(B^*\text{vec}(\Sigma) + \sigma^2 1_N) 1_T' + \beta' V + E, \tag{5.17}$$

where rx is a $N \times T$ matrix of excess returns, $\beta = [\beta^1, \beta^2, \ldots, \beta^N]$, 1_T and 1_N are $T \times 1$ and $N \times 1$ vectors of ones, $X_- = [X_0, X_1, \ldots, X_{T-1}]$, $B^* = [\text{vec}(\beta^1, \beta^{1'}), \ldots, \text{vec}(\beta^n, \beta^{n'})]$, and V and E are matrices of errors.

With this, the parameters can be estimated with the following three-step methodology:

1. Estimate $\{\mu, \phi, \Sigma, \delta_0, \delta_1\}$ independently by OLS on the equations where these parameters are defined.

2. Estimate the following equation of excess returns by OLS:

$$rx = a1'_T + \beta' V + cX_- + E, \quad (5.18)$$

and deduce $\hat{B}^*$ and $\hat{\sigma}^2 = tr(\hat{E}\hat{E}')/NT$.

3. Compute $\{\lambda_0, \lambda_1\}$ using the following estimators:

$$\begin{cases} \hat{\lambda}_0 = (\hat{\beta}\hat{\beta}')^{-1}\hat{\beta}\left(\hat{a} + \frac{1}{2}\left(\hat{B}^* \text{vec}(\hat{\Sigma}) + \hat{\sigma}^2 1'_N\right)\right) \\ \hat{\lambda}_1 = (\hat{\beta}\hat{\beta}')^{-1}\hat{\beta}\hat{c} \end{cases}. \quad (5.19)$$

REFERENCES

Adrian, T., R. K. Crump, and E. Moench. 2013. "Pricing the Term Structure with Linear Regressions." *Journal of Financial Economics* 110(1): 110–38.

Ang, A., and M. Piazzesi. 2003. "A No-Arbitrage Vector Autoregression of Term Structure Dynamics with Macroeconomic and Latent Variables." *Journal of Monetary Economics* 50(4): 745–87.

Arias, J. E., J. F. Rubio-Ramirez, and D. F. Waggoner. 2014. "Inference Based on SVARs Identified with Sign and Zero Restrictions: Theory and Applications." International Finance Discussion Paper 1100, Board of Governors of the Federal Reserve System.

Bauer, M. D., G. D. Rudebusch, and J. C. Wu. 2014. "Term Premia and Inflation Uncertainty: Empirical Evidence from an International Panel Dataset: Comment." *American Economic Review* 104(1): 323–37.

Bernanke, B. 2013. "The Past and Future of Monetary Policy." Speech at the Annual Monetary and Macroeconomics Conference, San Francisco Federal Reserve, March 1.

Blake, A. P., G. R. Rule, and O. J. Rummel. 2015. "Inflation Targeting and Term Premia Estimates for Latin America." *Latin American Economic Review* 24(1): 1–21.

Canova, F. 2005 "The Transmission of U.S. Shocks to Latin Data." *Journal of Applied Econometrics* 20: 229–51.

Ceballos, L., A. Naudon, and D. Romero. 2015. "Nominal Term Structure and Term Premia: Evidence from Chile." Working Paper 752, Central Bank of Chile, Santiago.

Ceballos, L., and D. Romero. 2015. "Decomposing Long-Term Interest Rates: An International Comparison." Working Paper 767, Central Bank of Chile, Santiago.

Fornero, J., R. Montero, and A. Yany. 2015. "Reassessing the Effects of Foreign Monetary Policy on Output: New Evidence from Structural and Agnostic Identification Procedures." Central Bank of Chile, Santiago. Unpublished.

Gagnon, J., M. Raskin, J. Remache, and B. Sack. 2011. "The Financial Market Effects of the Federal Reserve's Large-Scale Asset Purchases." *International Journal of Central Banking* 7(1): 3–43.

Joslin, S., M. Priebsch, and K. J. Singleton. 2014. "Risk Premiums in Dynamic Term Structure Models with Unspanned Macro Risks." *Journal of Finance* 69(3): 1197–233.

Mackowiak, B. 2007. "External Shocks, US Monetary Policy and Macroeconomic Fluctuations in Emerging Markets." *Journal of Monetary Economics* 54(8): 2512–20.

Miyajima, K., M. Mohanty, and T. Chan. 2012. "Emerging Market Local Currency Bonds: Diversification and Stability." BIS Working Paper 391, Bank for International Settlements, Basel.

Miyajima, K., M. Mohanty, and J. Yetman. 2014. "Spillovers of US Unconventional Monetary Policy to Asia: The Role of Long-Term Interest Rates." BIS Working Paper 478, Bank for International Settlements, Basel.

Rey, H. 2013. "Dilemma Not Trilemma: The Global Financial Cycle and Monetary Policy Independence." Proceedings from the Federal Reserve Bank of Kansas City Economic Policy Symposium, Jackson Hole, Wyoming, August 22–24.

Turner, P. 2014. "The Global Long-Term Interest Rate, Financial Risks and Policy Choices in EMEs." BIS Working Paper 441, Bank for International Settlements, Basel.

Uhlig, H. 2005. "What Are the Effects of Monetary Policy on Output? Results from an Agnostic Identification Procedure." *Journal of Monetary Economics* 52(2): 381–419.

Wright, J. H. 2011. "Term Premia and Inflation Uncertainty: Empirical Evidence from an International Panel Dataset." *American Economic Review* 101(4): 1514–34.

CHAPTER 6

Forward Guidance and Prudence in Conducting Monetary Policy

JULIÁN ANDRÉS PARRA POLANÍA, CENTRAL BANK OF COLOMBIA

Over the past 25 years, there have been fundamental changes in the conduct of monetary policy. Many of them are related to the adoption of inflation-targeting frameworks and the increase in central bank communication with the public. Important discussions have taken place during these years, ranging from the desirability of low and stable inflation to the inclusion of financial stability as an explicit objective of central banks.

In recent years the global financial crisis gave rise to new challenges and debates. Although Latin America was not strongly affected by the crisis, it is no stranger to these debates. Some of them are relevant for the conduct of monetary policy under any circumstances, and others can teach us much about the use, costs, and benefits of resorting to unconventional policies in future crises.

The staff of the Central Bank of Colombia (Banco de la República) has closely followed many of these debates and has provided insights on some of them from its perspective. This chapter summarizes the analysis of two topics related to the conduct of monetary policy: forward guidance and dealing with uncertainty.

The term "forward guidance" as used here mainly refers to a policy strategy through which the central bank makes a promise about future levels of the monetary policy rate. The interest in forward guidance arose from the fact that several central banks in advanced economies (e.g., the Bank of Canada, the Bank of England, and the U.S. Federal Reserve) during the global financial crisis resorted to different unconventional policies—one of which was to commit to keep the interest rate low in the future so as to stimulate the economy through the effect on market expectations. The first part of this chapter uses a very simple framework to analyze some basic features of forward guidance in order to understand how useful this strategy can be during a crisis and whether it is worth pursuing during normal times. This will help us understand how useful the strategy could be for Latin America, since it is not going through a crisis.

The author would like to thank Deniz Igan, Hernando Vargas, Krishna Srinivasan, Hamid Faruqee, Yan Carrière-Swallow, participants at the August mid-point seminar at the IMF, and participants at the session on Challenges of Latin American Central Banks at the 2015 meeting of the Latin American and Caribbean Economic Association for their comments.

Since forward guidance has been widely analyzed in recent years, additional results and more technical details can be found in the previous literature. For instance, Eggertsson and Woodford (2003) show that, in theory, credibly committing to a low future policy rate is the optimal policy in a zero-lower-bound situation. However, empirically, there are mixed results on the effectiveness of forward guidance, as discussed in the next section. This chapter focuses on unconditional promises that are the common feature of time-based forward guidance, although recent literature (Boneva, Harrison, and Waldron 2015; Florez-Jimenez and Parra Polanía 2016) has argued in favor of the superiority of state-contingent forward guidance (i.e., announcing the economic conditions under which the central bank will deviate from the promised rate). This chapter also works under the assumption of perfect credibility; however, imperfectly credible promises have been considered (Bodenstein, Hebdon, and Nunes 2012). For a survey of theory versus practice of forward guidance, we refer the reader to Moessner, Jansen, and de Haan (2015).

Regarding the second topic of uncertainty and monetary policy, the Colombian central bank's interest came from observing an increase in the volatility of some components of the country's GDP, which gave rise to the idea that it could be related to an increase in the volatility of the measurement error. We studied the effects of uncertainty on optimal decision making from two different perspectives, the "standard" one, where the policymaker minimizes the expected loss; and the "prudent" one, where the policymaker minimizes the maximum possible loss across all potential scenarios as a way to avoid huge losses in the worst-case scenarios.

As in the case of forward guidance, additional results and more technical details can be found in the previous literature on policymaking under uncertainty from a robust control perspective. The robustness/prudence criterion has been recently considered for the design of optimal policies under uncertainty, and it is widely discussed in Hansen and Sargent (2008) and Barlevy (2009). Two recent examples of the analysis of monetary policy from the robust control perspective are Tillmann (2014) and Gerke and Hammermann (forthcoming). The former studies uncertainty about potential output and finds that robustness strengthens the case for appointing a conservative central banker. The latter analyzes monetary policy with imperfect interest rate pass-through and uncertainty about the model specification. They find that the aggressiveness or cautiousness of the robust optimal policy response depends on the source of the shock.

The next sections of this chapter provide details about the analysis of forward guidance and then prudence. These sections draw on the analysis of Florez-Jimenez and Parra Polanía (2016) on forward guidance and Parra Polanía and Vargas (2014) on prudence. Further analysis and technical details can be found in those studies.

FORWARD GUIDANCE

Following Campbell and others (2012), this section starts by distinguishing two types of forward guidance: Delphic and Odyssean. The former refers to the central bank making public its own forecast on the likely path of future policy rates. This can be an effective communication tool, because it provides added information to market participants. The latter refers to the policy strategy of announcing and committing to, rather than just forecasting, a specific path of future rates. This distinction is relevant because while the main purpose of Delphic forward guidance is to communicate the central bank's economic outlook, and, in that sense, is primarily an act of transparency, Odyssean forward guidance mostly intends to stimulate the economy by communicating a temporary change in the approach to the conduct of monetary policy.

To see the difference, consider the following examples. First, think of a central bank releasing a policy rate forecast (Delphic forward guidance) below the one expected by the market. The market might become more pessimistic (or less optimistic) about the future, since the forecast is communicating that the central bank thinks additional stimulus will be required. If, instead, the central bank promises a policy rate below the one initially expected (Odyssean forward guidance), as long as communication is clear, the market might become more optimistic (or less pessimistic) about the future, as the central bank is committing to keep the policy rate low even after the time when the economy requires a higher rate. In this case, the market understands that such action is not required to stimulate the economy in the future but to stimulate the economy today via expectations.

Odyssean forward guidance may face several problems, including, inter alia, lack of credibility and lack of clarity. With regard to the former, the announcement of a low future policy rate has to be credible so as to stimulate the economy through the effect on the market's expectations. However, in order to live up to the promise, the monetary policymaker has to sacrifice flexibility, particularly, the possibility to respond to inflationary pressures in the future. Then the question arises why the central bank would assume the cost of fulfilling a promise whose benefits are already realized. Reputation could be a possible answer.

With regard to clarity, Odyssean forward guidance may be ineffective or even harmful to the economy if it is not clearly understood by the markets. For instance, the markets might interpret the announcement of a low future policy rate as a downward revision of the economic outlook (a projection rather than a promise).

Empirical assessments of the effectiveness of forward guidance as an alternative policy have produced mixed results. This may be due to the imperfect credibility of forward guidance and the ambiguity of the announcements (i.e., it is not crystal clear whether the announcements are projections or promises). For instance, while Campbell and others (2012) find that the markets impute Delphic content to policy announcements—that is, forward guidance is perceived as the release of central bank projections—Raskin (2013) and Femia, Friedman, and Sack (2013) find evidence that forward guidance leads to a change in the perception of the Federal Open Market Committee's reaction function, and is therefore perceived as containing information about changes in the conduct of policy.

Under the assumption that Odyssean forward guidance is crystal clear and fully credible, let us now illustrate, in a two-period model, the following three results:

1. Forward guidance can improve welfare when the economy faces zero lower bound events;
2. However, even under such conditions (i.e., the promise is crystal clear and fully credible), unconditional commitment to future policy rates is better than discretion only in the most severe zero lower bound situations;
3. Therefore, Odyssean forward guidance does not improve welfare if the economy is not under a zero lower bound event.

The analysis corresponds to the case of unconditional promises, which is the common feature of "time-based" guidance (i.e., the central bank sets a date after which the current policy stance will change). Florez-Jimenez and Parra Polanía (2016) provide details in the case of "state-contingent" guidance (i.e., the central bank announces the economic conditions under which the policy stance will change and, in this sense, the promise has an escape clause).[1]

The model consists of three equations; namely the loss function:

$$L_t = \pi_t^2 + \lambda y_t^2, \quad (6.1)$$

the Phillips curve:

$$\pi_t = \beta E_t \pi_{t+1} + \kappa y_t, \quad (6.2)$$

and the investment/saving (IS) curve:

$$y_t = E_t y_{t+1} - \sigma(i_t - E_t \pi_{t+1}) + d_t, \quad (6.3)$$

where π_t is inflation, y_t is the output gap, E_t is the expectations operator conditional on information available at time t, $\beta \in (0,1)$ is the discount factor, λ, σ, and κ are positive constants, i_t is the nominal interest rate, and d_t is the demand shock, which we assume is independently distributed over time. All variables are expressed as deviations from the steady state.

The central bank minimizes the loss function with respect to the interest rate. Since there are no lagged variables in the equations and shocks are uncorrelated, $E_t y_{t+1} = E_t \pi_{t+1} = 0$, and the solution is simple: $i_t^* = (1/\sigma) d_t$ for every t. In this case the loss for every period t is $L_t = 0$.

Now, assume there is a lower bound for the nominal interest rate such that a required condition for the interest rate is $i_t \geq i_{min}$ ($i_{min} < 0$).[2] As a result, if the demand shock in period t is negative and less than a specific value (σi_{min}), the

---

[1] In the case of state-contingent forward guidance, the (conditional) promise is welfare improving and better than discretion for any zero lower bound event. It remains the conclusion that forward guidance is not welfare improving if the economy is not under a zero lower bound event.

[2] This does not mean the interest rate can be negative. Since all variables in the model are expressed as deviations from the steady state, this condition implies that the lower bound is below the steady-state value of the interest rate. For instance, if the steady state is 3 percent and the lower bound for the rate is 0 percent, then $i_{min} = -3$ percent.

central bank is not able to set the interest rate at its optimal level (since $i_t^* < i_{min}$), that is, the economy faces a zero lower bound situation. Also assume that in period $t+1$ the economy is expected to recover and the demand shock is expected to be positive (and hence no zero lower bound event is expected to occur in $t+1$).

If, under the above circumstances, the central bank acts discretionarily, $i_t = i_{min}$ and $i_{t+1} = (1/\sigma) d_{t+1}$, the loss in period t is[3]

$$L_t^D = \sigma^2(\kappa^2 + \lambda)(i_t^* - i_{min})^2, \tag{6.4}$$

and the expected loss for $t+1$ is zero. The higher the deviation of the optimal rate (with respect to the interest rate lower bound) the higher the loss in period t.

The central bank can alleviate the loss in period t (through the expectations channel) by committing to a future policy rate lower than the expected optimal rate, and therefore at the cost of increasing the expected loss of period $t+1$. The central bank promises, in t, an interest rate for period $t+1$ ($i_{t+1|t}$) in order to minimize the expected discounted loss, that is, $L_t^{FG} + \beta E_t L_{t+1}^{FG}$. The solution to this problem yields

$$i_{t+1|t} = \left(\frac{1}{\sigma}\right) E_t d_{t+1} - a(i_{min} - i_t^*), \tag{6.5}$$

where

$$a \equiv \frac{(\sigma\kappa + 1)(\kappa^2 + \lambda) + \kappa^2\beta}{(\kappa^2 + \lambda)[(\sigma\kappa + 1)^2 + \beta] + \kappa^2\beta[2(\sigma\kappa + 1) + \beta]} \in (0,1).$$

The economy is stimulated in t, via expectations, by promising a future policy rate below the value that would be expected under discretion. The higher the deviation of the interest rate lower bound from the optimal rate, the lower the promised interest rate.

Using equations (6.1)–(6.3) and (6.5) we obtain:

$$L_t^{FG} + \beta E_t L_{t+1}^{FG} = \beta(\kappa^2 + \lambda)\,\mathrm{VAR}_t[d_{t+1}] + \frac{\beta a \sigma^2[(\kappa^2 + \lambda)^2 + \kappa^2\beta\lambda]}{(\sigma\kappa + 1)(\kappa^2 + \lambda) + \kappa^2\beta}(i_t^* - i_{min})^2, \tag{6.6}$$

where $\mathrm{VAR}_t[d_{t+1}]$ is the conditional variance of d_{t+1}. Comparing equation (6.4) to (6.6), it can be verified that

$$L_t^{FG} + \beta E_t L_{t+1}^{FG} < L_t^D \text{ if, and only if, } d_t < \sigma(i_{min} - \sqrt{\omega}), \tag{6.7}$$

where

$$\omega \equiv \frac{\beta(\kappa^2 + \lambda)\,\mathrm{VAR}_t[d_{t+1}]}{a\sigma^2[(\sigma\kappa + 1)(\kappa^2 + \lambda) + \kappa^2\beta]}.$$

From equation (6.7) we can see that under certain conditions forward guidance can improve welfare (with respect to discretion) when the economy faces a zero lower bound situation. Those conditions imply that the demand shock has

---

[3] We use the superscript D to refer to the discretionary case and to compare this case to that of forward guidance.

to be negative and large enough to make forward guidance preferable to discretion.[4] In those cases where the economy faces a zero lower bound situation but the negative demand shock is not very large ($\sigma\left(i_{min} - \sqrt{\omega}\right) < d_t < \sigma i_{min}$), the central bank prefers to act discretionarily rather than making an unconditional promise.

At the moment when this topic was analyzed, Colombia did not face a zero lower bound situation. The policy rate was 3.25 percent, so it was possible to make further reductions. However, we also wanted to know if forward guidance could be a useful alternative strategy for normal times. From the above results, the answer is no. Forward guidance stimulates the economy today at the cost of deviating from the optimal action tomorrow. The cost can be high, which is why even under a moderate zero lower bound situation, it is not good to resort to forward guidance. In normal times, if the economy requires further stimulus, the best choice is to reduce the current policy rate. If the central bank is still able to reduce the current policy rate to respond to current shocks, it has no incentives to stimulate the economy by making a promise that will tie its hands in responding to future shocks. Furthermore, why would the market believe the central bank will set the future policy rate below its optimal value when, at the same time, it is not willing to further reduce it today?

Notice, however, that the aforementioned conclusion refers to Odyssean forward guidance. As noted earlier, the purpose of Delphic forward guidance is mostly related to transparency, and therefore its effects may be substantially different.[5] By providing forward guidance, the central bank may reveal some private information to the markets, and this in turn may help reduce uncertainty, which could positively affect the economy. Since reducing uncertainty can be relevant both in crisis and normal times, Delphic forward guidance could be helpful at any moment. However, as explained above, if the purpose is to provide further stimulus to the economy, Delphic forward guidance may not always be the best tool, particularly if private information is revealing a negative economic outlook.

From the theoretical point of view here described, since sacrificing flexibility is costly, promises on the future interest rate path seem to be useful in crisis periods only (especially if accompanied by an escape clause), while Delphic forward guidance can be mainly used during normal times.[6] In practice, however, language is tricky, and communication problems may make it difficult to distinguish clearly between a promise and a forecast, although this may also be a consequence of the central bank incentives to communicate strategically.

---

[4]For the benchmark in Florez-Jimenez and Parra Polanía (2016), unconditional or time-based forward guidance is better than discretion only in the most extreme 16 percent of zero lower bound situations. Feroli and others (2016) also highlight the fact that time-based forward guidance should be used only in very unusual circumstances.

[5]Empirical examples of Delphic forward guidance can be found in the Czech Republic, New Zealand, Norway, or Sweden.

[6]Using a New Keynesian model, Fujiwara and Waki (2016) argue, however, that Delphic forward guidance can be undesirable, because revealing the central bank's private information about future shocks may increase the volatility of inflation expectations.

Finally, it should be noted that the analysis here is based on a simple model. Further analysis is required to incorporate other elements, such as financial risks related to the increased predictability of a very low rate for long periods.

PRUDENCE

In 2013, when the Colombian statistics office revealed the figure for the country's economic growth in the third quarter of 2012, it was surprising both for the market and for the central bank. Specifically, the figure for the growth of civil works was unexpectedly low. Although this component is characterized by high volatility, at that particular moment there was some evidence that it had become more volatile in recent quarters.

Higher volatility of an estimated variable can be attributed to an increase in the volatility of the actual variable or an increase in the volatility of its measurement error. One of the questions we tried to answer with regard to this matter was how monetary policy should react to higher volatility in the measurement error in an indicator of aggregate economic activity.

To answer that question, we analyzed the problem from two different perspectives, according to the objective of the monetary policymaker. From the first perspective, from which we derive the "standard" policy, the central bank minimizes its expected loss function. From the second perspective, from which we derive the "prudent" policy, the central bank minimizes the maximum possible loss across all potential scenarios.

The latter perspective has been well received in the economic literature.[7] This is because, on the one hand, it represents an alternative way to explore the design of optimal policies under conditions of uncertainty, particularly when the decision makers do not know the probabilities of all relevant scenarios (and therefore *cannot* calculate the expected loss). On the other hand, this perspective is seen as a prudent approach because it avoids large losses in all possible events, regardless of how likely they are. An intuitive example is provided by Feldstein (2003), who writes that a "prudent" man is the one who carries an umbrella even when the weather forecast says the probability of rain is low, because the small inconvenience of doing so protects him from the larger trouble of being caught in a downpour.

Using a stylized model in which the output gap is measured with error (i.e., there is a noisy signal of the demand shock), we obtain the following results:

1. As is common, both the standard and the prudent central bank reduces (increases) the policy rate when it receives a signal of a negative (positive) demand shock. However, the prudent central bank reduces (increases) the interest rate more than the standard one.
2. If the volatility of the measurement error increases, the standard central bank attenuates its response to the signal. The reaction of the prudent central bank

---

[7]As mentioned in the introduction, more details on this approach can be found in Hansen and Sargent (2008) and Barlevy (2009).

is the same if its risk aversion is low to moderate, or the opposite (i.e., its response is stronger) if its risk aversion is high enough.

We also analyze numerical results for the same model but with forward-looking expectations and find that result (2) is robust to this change. But result (1) changes: in this case the prudent central bank is less aggressive than the standard one in responding to the shock signal.

We set up a stylized model that incorporates two particular features: first, some degree of persistence for the output gap, and second, a monetary policy lag such that it affects output more rapidly than inflation.

The model consists of three equations, namely, the loss function:

$$L_t = \pi_t^2 + \lambda y_t^2, \tag{6.8}$$

the Phillips curve:

$$\pi_t = \eta E_{t-1} \pi_t + \kappa y_{t-1}, \tag{6.9}$$

and the IS curve,

$$y_t = \rho y_{t-1} - \sigma(i_{t-1} - E_{t-1} \pi_t) + d_t, \tag{6.10}$$

where π_t is inflation, y_t is the output gap, E_t is the expectations operator conditional on information available at time t, $\eta \in (0,1)$, λ, σ, and κ are positive constants, i_t is the nominal interest rate, and d_t is the demand shock, which we assume is independently and normally distributed over time, $d_t \sim N(0, \text{VAR}_{d,t})$, where $\text{VAR}_{d,t}$ is the variance of d_t.

There is a statistics office that releases a provisional estimate of the output gap every period for that same period ($\hat{y}_t$), and the final estimate of the same variable for the previous period (y_{t-1}). The former estimate contains a measurement error (i.e., $\hat{y}_t \equiv y_t + \varepsilon_t$, $\varepsilon_t \sim N(0, \text{VAR}_{e,t})$) and the latter estimate contains no error.

Neither the central bank nor private agents have private information. The timing for any period s is as follows: (1) the statistics office releases $\hat{y}_s$ and y_{s-1}; (2) private agents form rational expectations; (3) the central bank picks i_s; and (4) shocks (d_s, ε_s) realize but they are unobserved.

Standard Perspective

To solve the above setup from the standard perspective, we can model uncertainty as a signal extraction problem (Harvey and de Rossi 2006) in which economic agents construct a signal of the demand shock (in period $t-1$) using the available information: $\hat{d}_{t-1} \equiv \hat{y}_{t-1} - \rho y_{t-2} + \sigma(i_{t-2} - E_{t-2} \pi_{t-1})$, and therefore, from equation (6.10) and the definition of $\hat{y}_t$: $\hat{d}_{t-1} = d_{t-1} + \varepsilon_{t-1}$, $\hat{d}_{t-1}$ is a noisy signal of the demand shock and the corresponding forecast is:

$$E_{t-1}\left[d_{t-1} \big| \hat{d}_{t-1}\right] = \gamma \hat{d}_{t-1},$$

where $\gamma \equiv \text{VAR}_{d,t} / (\text{VAR}_{d,t} + \text{VAR}_{e,t})$. The higher the relative amount of noise $\text{VAR}_{e,t} / \text{VAR}_{d,t}$, the lower the weight given to the signal.

It can be shown that, given that expectations are rational, minimizing the expected loss implies:[8]

$$i^*_{t-1} = \left(\frac{\kappa}{1-\eta} + \frac{\rho}{\sigma}\right) E_{t-1} y_{t-1},$$

and $E_{t-1} y_{t-1} = \rho y_{t-2} - \sigma(i_{t-2} - E_{t-2}\pi_{t-1}) + \gamma \hat{d}_{t-1}$. Due to the uncertainty about the exact value of the output gap, the central bank needs to estimate its value, which in turn involves the past output gap (due to output persistence), the lagged real interest rate (due to the monetary policy lag), and the signal of the demand shock.

The above result, in turn, implies that

$$\frac{\partial i^*_{t-1}}{\partial \hat{d}_{t-1}} = \left(\frac{\kappa}{1-\eta} + \frac{\rho}{\sigma}\right)\gamma > 0,$$

that is, a higher demand-shock signal increases the policy response. Since the weight γ depends on the measurement error volatility ($\text{VAR}_{\varepsilon,t}$), we can also obtain

$$\partial \frac{\partial i^*_{t-1}/\partial \hat{d}_{t-1}}{\partial \text{VAR}_{\varepsilon,t}} = \left(\frac{\kappa}{1-\eta} + \frac{\rho}{\sigma}\right)\frac{\partial \gamma}{\partial \text{VAR}_{\varepsilon,t}} < 0,$$

that is, an increase in the measurement error volatility implies a higher proportion of noise in the signal, and therefore the central bank's optimal response to changes in the signal is mitigated.

Prudence

For this approach, following the previous literature (van der Ploeg 2009), we assume that the central bank plays a min-max game where the measurement error is externally set with the purpose of maximizing the loss taking account of the central bank's action. In this case the objective function (also known as the "stress function") of the central bank includes its degree of prudence:

$$\Gamma_t = \pi_t^2 + \lambda y_t^2 - \frac{\theta}{\text{VAR}_{\varepsilon,t}}\varepsilon_{t-1}^2,$$

where $\theta > 0$ is inversely related to the central bank's risk aversion, and the last term in the objective function incorporates the fact that there is a finite level of prudence, and therefore measurement errors cannot inflict infinite losses on the central bank.

It can be shown that, given the measurement error process and the expectations of private agents, the optimal response of the central bank is:[9]

$$i^*_{t-1} = \left(\frac{\kappa}{1-\eta}b_1 + \frac{\rho}{\sigma}b_2\right)E_{t-1} y_{t-1} + \frac{\rho}{\sigma}b_2(1-\gamma)\hat{d}_{t-1},$$

---

[8] From the standard perspective, it can be seen that the solution to the one-period problem is equal to that for the multiple-period problem. See Parra Polanía and Vargas (2014, footnote 5). This is no longer true for the case of forward-looking expectations.

[9] In this case the model is solved for an infinite-horizon scenario. See Parra Polanía and Vargas (2014).

where

$$b_1 = 1 + \frac{\eta \rho \kappa}{\sigma(\theta/\text{VAR}_{e,t} - \kappa^2)} > 1$$

and

$$b_2 = \frac{\theta/\text{VAR}_{e,t}}{\theta/\text{VAR}_{e,t} - \kappa^2} > 1.$$

From the above equation,

$$\frac{\partial i_{t-1}^*}{\partial \hat{d}_{t-1}} = \frac{\kappa}{1-\eta} b_1 \gamma + \frac{\rho}{\sigma} b_2 > 0.$$

As in the standard case, a higher demand-shock signal increases the policy response of the central bank. However, since $b_1 > 1$ and $b_2 > 1$, the response of the prudent central bank to changes in the signal is greater than that of the standard one. If risk aversion of the central bank were nil ($\theta/\text{VAR}_{e,t} \to \infty$), there would be no difference between the standard and the prudent response. However, the presence of risk aversion makes the prudent central bank less willing to mitigate its response to the signal.

Also, as

$$\partial \frac{\partial i_{t-1}^*/\partial \hat{d}_{t-1}}{\partial \text{VAR}_{e,t}} = \frac{\kappa}{1-\eta} b_1 \frac{\partial \gamma}{\partial \text{VAR}_{e,t}} + \frac{\rho \kappa^2 \theta}{\sigma (\text{VAR}_{e,t})^2} \frac{1 - \eta(1-\gamma)}{(\theta/\text{VAR}_{e,t} - \kappa^2)^2(1-\eta)},$$

when the measurement error volatility increases, there are two opposite effects on the optimal policy response. On the one hand, there is a reduction on the signal's weight in agents' expectations and, through this channel, it is less relevant for the central bank. On the other hand, it increases the central bank's relative prudence, as can be seen in the objective function. As a result, the total effect can be negative (as in the standard case) or positive, that is, the central bank responds more strongly to the signal when there is a perceived increase in the measurement error volatility. The latter occurs only when the central bank's risk aversion is very high.

We also can change the Phillips curve (to $\pi_t = \eta E_t \pi_{t+1} + \kappa y_{t-1}$) in order to incorporate forward-looking expectations. In this case we derive conclusions from numerical solutions for a specific set of parameters (Parra Polanía and Vargas 2014). We find that, as in the original model, when the measurement error volatility increases, the effect on the change of the policy rate can be positive or negative. However, while in the original model we find that it is always the case that the prudent central bank reacts more aggressively to a higher demand-shock signal, in the model with forward-looking expectations, the prudent central bank reacts less aggressively to it. The influence of forward-looking expectations on the transmission mechanism reduces the damage measurement errors can cause.

CONCLUSIONS

This chapter has summarized some insights from the perspective of the staff of the Central Bank of Colombia on two topics related to monetary policy: forward guidance (in its Odyssean version, that is, committing to future policy rates) and policy prudence under uncertainty.

The chapter has argued that unconditional (or time-based) forward guidance improves welfare only in the most severe zero lower bound events (despite the fact that it is assumed to be fully credible and clear). As a corollary, forward guidance should not be used as a strategy in normal times.

With regard to dealing with uncertainty from a robust control or prudent perspective, the chapter has argued that a prudent central bank reacts (changing the policy rate) more aggressively to a demand shock signal than a standard central bank. However, the opposite happens when the market's expectations are forward-looking: robustness or prudence does not always imply a stronger response in the face of uncertainty.

The chapter has also maintained that when the volatility of measurement errors (of the demand shock) increases, the standard central bank attenuates its response to the signal. The reaction of the prudent central bank is similar, if its risk aversion is relatively low, or the opposite (i.e., its response is stronger) if its risk aversion is high enough.

REFERENCES

Barlevy, G. 2009. "Policymaking under Uncertainty: Gradualism and Robustness." *Journal of Economic Perspectives* 23(3): 38–55.

Bodenstein, M., J. Hebden, and R. Nunes. 2012. "Imperfect Credibility and the Zero Lower Bound." *Journal of Monetary Economics* 59(2): 135–49.

Boneva, L., R. Harrison, and M. Waldron. 2015. "Threshold-Based Forward Guidance: Hedging the Zero Bound." Working Paper 561, Bank of England, London.

Campbell, J., C. Evans, J. Fisher, and A. Justiniano. 2012. "Macroeconomic Effects of FOMC Forward Guidance." *Brookings Papers on Economic Activity* 44(1): 1–80.

Eggertsson, G., and M. Woodford. 2003. "The Zero Bound on Interest Rates and Optimal Monetary Policy." *Brookings Papers on Economic Activity* 34(1): 139–235.

Feldstein, M. 2003. "Monetary Policy in an Uncertain Environment." NBER Working Paper 9969, National Bureau of Economic Research, Cambridge, Massachusetts.

Femia, K., S. Friedman, and B. Sack. 2013. "The Effects of Policy Guidance on Perceptions of the Fed's Reaction Function." Staff Report 652, Federal Reserve Bank of New York.

Feroli, M., D. Greenlaw, P. Hooper, F. Mishkin, and A. Sufi. 2016. "Language after Liftoff: Fed Communication away from the Zero Lower Bound." Paper presented at the 2016 U.S. Monetary Policy Forum, University of Chicago Booth School of Business conference, February 2016.

Florez-Jimenez, M. L., and J. Parra Polanía. 2016. "Forward Guidance with an Escape Clause: When Half a Promise Is Better Than a Full One." *Applied Economics* 48(15): 1372–81.

Fujiwara, I., and Y. Waki. 2016. "Private News and Monetary Policy: Forward Guidance or the Expected Virtue of Ignorance." Discussion Paper 16027, Research Institute of Economy, Trade and Industry (RIETI), Tokyo.

Gerke, R., and F. Hammermann. Forthcoming. "Robust Monetary Policy in a New Keynesian Model with Imperfect Interest Rate Pass-Through." *Macroeconomic Dynamics*.

Hansen, L. P., and T. J. Sargent. 2008. *Robustness*. Princeton, New Jersey: Princeton University Press.

Harvey, A., and G. de Rossi. 2006. "Signal Extraction." In *Palgrave Handbook of Econometrics* Vol. 1, edited by T. C. Mills and K. Patterson. London: Palgrave MacMillan.

Moessner, R., D.-J. Jansen, and J. de Haan. 2015. "Communication about Future Policy Rates in Theory and Practice: A Survey." Working Paper 475, De Nederlandsche Bank, Amsterdam.

Parra Polanía, J., and C. Vargas. 2014. "Changes in GDP's Measurement Error Volatility and Response of the Monetary Policy Rate: Two Approaches." *Ensayos sobre Política Económica* 32(75): 41–47.

Raskin, M. D. 2013. "The Effects of the Federal Reserve's Date-Based Forward Guidance." Finance and Economics Discussion Series, Working Paper 2013-37, Board of Governors of the Federal Reserve, Washington, DC.

Tillmann, P. 2014. "Robust Monetary Policy, Optimal Delegation, and Misspecified Potential Output." *Economics Letters* 123(2): 244–47.

van der Ploeg, F. 2009. "Prudent Monetary Policy and Prediction of the Output Gap." *Journal of Macroeconomics* 31(2): 217–30.

PART III

Macroprudential Policies and Monetary Frameworks

CHAPTER 7

Financial Stability Objectives: Drivers of Gains from Coordinating Monetary and Macroprudential Policies

JESSICA ROLDÁN-PEÑA (CENTRAL BANK OF MEXICO), MAURICIO TORRES-FERRO (CENTRAL BANK OF MEXICO), AND ALBERTO TORRES (MINISTRY OF FINANCE OF MEXICO)

This chapter studies the trade-offs that can arise between inflation-targeting and financial stability objectives. We use a simple framework to conduct macroeconomic policy analysis under two strategies that aim to attain both objectives: monetary policy leaning against the wind and policy coordination between monetary and macroprudential instruments. The chapter identifies cases in which the trade-offs between policy objectives create scope for improving macroeconomic performance when monetary and macroprudential policies are coordinated. These improvements are larger when financial shocks are the main driver of macroeconomic fluctuations. The findings further emphasize the importance of assessing the relative effectiveness and interactions of different policies that policymakers have at their disposal to help guide the economy.

The 2008–09 financial crisis shook the global economic landscape in a significant way. The need to take immediate actions to solve time-pressing problems left policymakers—especially central bankers in both advanced and emerging market economies—with the difficult task of restoring or maintaining macroeconomic and financial stability without much guidance on how to do so. Indeed, the existing macroeconomic policy toolkit was generally inadequate to address the challenges that arose, while the effectiveness and externalities of unconventional

---

This chapter is related to previous work done by Roldán-Peña, Sámano, and Torres (2014). We are grateful for Ana Aguilar's support throughout the completion of this project. We thank Giovanni Dell'Ariccia and participants of the Midpoint Seminar at the IMF and the 2015 LACEA Meetings for their comments. We also thank María Diego and Carlos Zarazúa for helpful suggestions. Finally, we thank Cid Rodriguez for providing excellent econometric assistance. The views presented here are exclusively of the authors and do not necessarily reflect those of Banco de México or Secretaría de Hacienda y Crédito Público.

tools remained largely unknown.[1] The aftermath of the crisis inevitably led to a rethinking of the conduct of macroeconomic policy in general, and monetary policy in particular.[2] One of the main challenges for central bankers in the years ahead will be to advance their understanding of how their respective financial systems work in order to modify and adapt their macroeconomic policy frameworks.

Without a doubt, two issues that have received the most attention in reexamining the conduct of macroeconomic policy are the recognition that (1) price stability does not necessarily imply financial stability and that (2) a broader perspective in prudential supervision and regulation is needed to prevent the accumulation of financial imbalances. With regard to the latter issue, a new field of macroeconomic policy, namely macroprudential policy, emerged in recognition of the fact that regulatory policy focused on individual institutions was ill-equipped to prevent the buildup of macro-financial and systemic risks. Nevertheless, given the inherent links between the real and financial sectors of the economy and the feedback loops between monetary and macroprudential policies, some basic questions arose. Should monetary policy be responsible for attaining financial stability objectives in addition to price stability objectives? In other words, should monetary policy lean against the wind? Alternatively, should macroprudential policy be tasked with pursuing financial stability objectives? And if so, what should be its relation with monetary policy?[3]

This chapter examines the trade-offs that arise between the pursuit of price stability objectives through a flexible inflation-targeting regime and financial stability objectives. To do so, we estimate a standard, reduced-form, and small open economy model (commonly used to conduct monetary policy analysis in emerging markets), which we extend to consider a stylized financial sector. Within this framework, we study the performance of the model economy under different policy strategies. Specifically, two cases are examined: (1) a leaning-against-the-wind case in which monetary policy sets the short-term nominal interest rate in order to attain certain predetermined financial stability objectives, in addition to price stability, in the context of a flexible inflation-targeting

---

[1] Some notable exceptions, however, can be found in emerging market economies that experienced financial crises during the 1980s and 1990s.

[2] See Blanchard, Dell'Ariccia, and Mauro (2010, 2013), Borio (2011), and Mishkin (2011).

[3] The question on whether monetary policy should lean against the wind is not new. The possible dangers associated with asset-price bubbles had already been pointed out before the crisis by economists such as Cecchetti and others (2000), Borio and Lowe (2002) and Borio, English, and Filardo (2003). They argued that central banks should at times lean against the financial wind by raising interest rates to stop bubbles from getting out of hand. In their view, raising interest rates to slow a bubble's growth would produce better outcomes because it would either prevent the bubble or result in a less severe bursting of it, with far less damage to the economy. A contrasting dominant view argued that monetary policy should not try to lean against asset-price bubbles, but rather just clean up after they burst, since monetary policy was, at best, ineffective in dealing with such bubbles (Mishkin 2011).

regime;[4] and (2) a coordination case in which both monetary and macroprudential policies jointly set their instruments in order to attain both objectives. Additionally, we also consider as a benchmark the "prior to crisis" case in which monetary policy actions focused only on price stability objectives. Following the literature, we relate traditional inflation-targeting objectives to a particular specification of the monetary policy's loss function, defined in terms of macroeconomic variables. Likewise, we associate financial stability objectives with a loss function that considers the stabilization of financial variables. To assess each case's relative effectiveness to attain its policy objectives, we examine the model's transmission mechanism and policy implications. Therefore, we compare the volatility that each case entails for a set of relevant macroeconomic and financial variables.

The purpose of this work is twofold: first, to provide a simplified framework within which to account for the trade-offs that arise when an inflation-targeting central bank also pursues financial stability objectives; and, second, to identify cases where these trade-offs allow for improvements in macroeconomic performance under coordination of monetary and macroprudential policies.

The results suggest that including financial stability considerations as an additional objective of monetary policy indeed reduces the volatility of financial variables. However, this improvement comes at the expense of increasing the volatility of macroeconomic variables. This cost is present regardless of the type of shocks that affect the economy but tends to increase when fluctuations are driven by financial shocks. These results provide evidence that supports the views of those who do not favor leaning against the wind because of the costly trade-offs involved and advocate for the use of macroprudential policy to address financial stability objectives.[5]

When identifying the cases where there is an improvement in macroeconomic performance owing to a coordination of monetary and macroprudential policies, our findings emphasize the importance of assessing the relative effectiveness and interactions of the different instruments/policies that policymakers have at their disposal. Our framework features room for gains from coordination, even when macroeconomic shocks are the only type of shocks affecting the economy, either when monetary policy is not an effective tool to address vulnerabilities in the financial sector or when it conflicts with macroprudential policy. In other words,

---

[4] Woodford (2012) argues that it is possible to incorporate financial stability considerations into a model in a way that it represents a natural extension of "flexible inflation targeting." We associate the leaning-against-the wind case examined in this chapter with his definition of flexible inflation targeting.

[5] See Williams (2014). For Borio (2014), attaining monetary and financial stability simultaneously calls for monetary policy that leans more deliberately against booms and eases less aggressively during busts, within a context where all macroeconomic policies play a mutually supportive role. In this respect, Svensson (2014) argues that monetary and macroprudential instruments and policies vary greatly from country to country, such that each economy must be scrutinized before judging whether there is a case for leaning against the wind.

we are referring to cases where one approach responds in a countercyclical way and the other in a procyclical way.

This chapter relates to a growing literature that explores the interaction between monetary and macroprudential policy (Angelini, Neri, and Panetta 2014; Angeloni and Faia 2013; Beau, Clerc, and Mojon 2012; De Paoli and Paustian 2013; Kannan, Rabanal, and Scott 2012; and Lambertini, Mendicino, and Punzi 2013). Our exercise follows closely the approach in Angelini, Neri, and Panetta (2014), who study the benefit of the interaction between capital requirements and monetary policy in a dynamic general equilibrium model featuring a banking sector. They find that an overall improvement in economic stability is attained when monetary and macroprudential policies are coordinated in the presence of financial shocks. Unlike previous studies, which consider a Taylor-type rule to account for monetary policy actions and distinguish between cooperative and noncooperative interactions between monetary and macroprudential policies, we consider optimal policy rules and assume that when monetary and macroprudential policies coexist they do so under a coordination scheme. Although the results of both approaches are similar, our model is much simpler. This allows us to focus on the broad intuition rather than on specific channels driving our results. Hence, our main contribution is to provide a common ground for thinking about the interaction between optimal monetary and macroprudential policies, even in cases when country-specific circumstances call for specific ways to model an economy.

The next section outlines the different policy strategies considered to examine the trade-offs between inflation-targeting and financial stability objectives. The chapter then describes the model, presents the main results, provides a sensitivity analysis, and concludes.

POLICY STRATEGIES

There are two possible policy objectives: one that is associated with standard inflation targeting, and another that adds a financial stability goal. These goals can be attained by using at most two policy instruments: the short-term nominal interest rate, i_t, the instrument of monetary policy (henceforth the policy rate); and the coverage ratio, crr_t, defined as the ratio of loan-loss reserves to nonperforming loans that banks are required to bear, which serves as the instrument for macroprudential policy.[6] We study the following policy strategies throughout the analysis:

1. A *benchmark* case in which monetary policy is guided by a flexible inflation-targeting regime and as such, it sets the policy rate aiming at stabilizing inflation around its target, the output gap, and changes in the policy rate.

---

[6]More details about the coverage ratio and the rationale for its role as a macroprudential policy instrument are provided in the next section of this chapter.

Hence, the monetary policy's optimization problem is to set i_t to minimize the following loss function:

$$L^{benchmark} = \sigma_\pi \left(\pi_t - \pi^*\right)^2 + \sigma_x x_t^2 + \sigma_{\Delta i} \left(i_t - i_{t-1}\right)^2, \tag{7.1}$$

where σ_π, σ_x, and $\sigma_{\Delta i}$ represent the monetary authority's relative preferences for stabilizing deviations of inflation from its target, $\left(\pi_t - \pi^*\right)$; the output gap, x_t; and changes in the reference rate, $\left(i_t - i_{t-1}\right)$, subject to the dynamics of the economy.[7]

2. A *leaning against the wind* case considers that monetary policy aims to stabilize both the traditional objectives of inflation-targeting and financial stability objectives by setting the optimal level of its policy rate. The monetary policy's optimization problem in this case is to set i_t to minimize the following loss function:

$$L^{LAW} = L^{benchmark} + \sigma_{spread}\left(spread_t - spread^*\right)^2 + \sigma_{crgap} crgap_t^2, \tag{7.2}$$

where σ_{spread} and σ_{crgap} represent the monetary authority's relative preferences for stabilizing the credit spread, denoted by *spread*, around its long-term average and the credit-to-GDP gap, *crgap*, respectively. These variables will be further explained when we describe the model.[8]

3. The *monetary and macroprudential policies coordination* case considers that monetary and macroprudential policies aim to attain inflation-targeting and financial stability objectives by setting their respective policy instruments—namely, the policy rate and the coverage ratio. These two instruments are jointly and optimally set in order to minimize the following loss function:

$$L^{coord} = L^{benchmark} + \sigma_{spread}\left(spread_t - spread^*\right)^2 + \sigma_{crgap} crgap_t^2 + \sigma_{\Delta crr}\left(crr_t - crr_{t-1}\right)^2, \tag{7.3}$$

---

[7] Woodford (2003) shows that a loss function determined by inflation deviations from its target and the output gap can be justified as a quadratic approximation to the goal of maximizing the representative agent's utility in a simple version of a New Keynesian model. As estimated central bank reaction functions also incorporate some degree of partial-adjustment dynamics of the interest rate itself, the last term in equation (7.1) ensures that movements in the policy rate are not excessively volatile.

In a micro-founded model, σ_π and σ_x are functions of deep parameters of the economy and reflect the degree by which distortions affect economic welfare. A framework characterized by the use of a semistructural model, like ours, is not able to trace down the effects of deep parameters on economic welfare. Instead we assume that these weights characterize policymakers' preferences, which ultimately should be associated with the deep parameters of the economy. Angelini, Neri, and Panetta (2014), who analyze the interaction between monetary and macroprudential policies, use loss functions like the ones described in this work.

[8] Cúrdia and Woodford (2009) show that a loss function with the usual inflation and output gap stabilization goals and other terms that represent the welfare consequences implied by financial frictions and/or the loss in resources incurred by the financial intermediary sector, can be justified as a quadratic approximation to the goal of maximizing the average expected utility of households.

where $\sigma_{\Delta crr}$ represents the relative preference for stabilizing changes in the macroprudential instrument.[9]

When considering the coexistence of monetary and macroprudential policies, we restrict our analysis to the case where both of them interact in a coordinated manner. This assumption allows for acknowledging an important result found in the literature, namely, the fact that since both policy instruments work less than perfectly, one cannot ignore the limitations of the other and, hence, should account for its effects on the economy (Blanchard, Dell'Ariccia, and Mauro 2013). According to De Paoli and Paustian (2013), this way of interaction between monetary and macroprudential policies is consistent with a first-best solution.

THE MODEL

A growing literature emphasizing the role of macro-financial linkages in macroeconomic models for monetary policy analysis has emerged in recent years.[10] Most of these models build on the work developed by Bernanke, Gertler, and Gilchrist (1999) and Iacoviello (2005) that introduce endogenous financial frictions—which arise due to the presence of agency costs (à la Bernanke and Gertler 1986) or the lack of financial-contract enforceability (à la Kiyotaki and Moore 1997)—into general equilibrium frameworks with real and nominal rigidities. In general, these types of models focus on understanding factors affecting the demand for credit that tend to propagate and amplify the transmission of shocks through a "financial accelerator" mechanism, leaving no relevant role for financial intermediaries to play. In response to this, macroeconomic models emphasizing the role of credit supply factors (e.g., the market structure of the banking system, the rate-setting strategy of banks, the role of banks' balance sheet composition and management, etc.) in the transmission of macroeconomic and financial shocks have also been developed.[11] Despite these contributions, no canonical framework is yet available within which to study the relationship between financial frictions, financial intermediation, and macroeconomic activity and its implications both for monetary and macroprudential policies.[12]

---

[9] Angelini, Neri, and Panetta (2014) propose a loss function in the same spirit as the one proposed here when studying the interaction between monetary and macroprudential policies in the case of cooperation. The last term in equation (7.3) represents policymakers' concern with the variability of the macroprudential policy instrument.

[10] Vlcek and Scott (2012) provide an extensive survey of models featuring financial frictions and/or financial intermediation in use by central banks.

[11] See Andrés and Arce (2012), Cúrdia and Woodford (2011), Gerali and others (2010), Gertler and Karadi (2011), and Meh and Moran (2010).

[12] In this respect, Galati and Moessner (2013, 854) point out that "[w]hile the literature on monetary policy has provided a common conceptual framework over the past two or three decades, research on macroprudential policy is still in its infancy and appears far from being able to provide an analytical underpinning for policy frameworks. . . . [This may be due to, among other reasons, the fact that] we lack a thorough understanding and established models of the interaction between the financial system and the macroeconomy."

Given this lack of consensus, we use a simple model that accounts for the interaction between a standard macroeconomic setup and some financial variables as the basis for our analysis. Specifically, we follow the approach taken by Sámano (2011), who augments a reduced-form New Keynesian small and open economy model, that is, the *macroeconomic block*, by appending a macroeconometric financial sector or *financial block*. This approach allows for the introduction of macro-financial linkages into an otherwise standard macroeconomic model—commonly used to analyze monetary policy in emerging markets—to study the propagation of macroeconomic shocks into the financial sector and vice versa. Admittedly, the nature of this framework has limitations, including: (1) the lack of micro foundations, which makes the model sensitive to the Lucas critique and inadequate for welfare analysis; (2) it is based on a representative agent setup, leaving out specific wedges that arise due to heterogeneity among agents and that characterize models where financial frictions are present; and (3) it is a linearized representation around the steady state of the economy. As a result, the model does not capture potential nonlinear effects of sufficiently large shocks capable of producing financial instability, and thus only features macroeconomic fluctuations under "normal times" (i.e., it is not a model where financial crises occur). Regardless, we consider it useful to provide guidelines about relevant trade-offs between policy objectives.

Macroeconomic Block

The structure of the macroeconomic block is characterized by aggregate supply and demand relationships that include the effect of economic openness (via the impact of the real exchange rate and foreign output, inflation, and interest rates on domestic activity and inflation):

$$\pi_t^{core} = a_1 E_t[\pi_{t+1}^{core}] + a_2 x_{t-1} + a_3 (\Delta e_{t-1} + \pi_{t-1}^f) + a_4 \pi_{t-1}^{core} + \varepsilon_t^{core}, \quad (7.4)$$

$$x_t = b_1 E_t[x_{t+1}] - b_2(i_{t-1} - E_{t-1}[\pi_t]) + b_3 x_{t-1}^f + b_4 rer_{t-1} + b_5 x_{t-1} - b_6 spread_{t-1} + \varepsilon_t^x, \quad (7.5)$$

$$rer_t = c_1 rer_{t-1} + c_2 (E_t[rer_{t+1}] + (r_t^f - r_t)) + \varepsilon_t^{rer}. \quad (7.6)$$

Equation (7.4) is a hybrid Phillips curve that explains core inflation as a linear combination of expected and lagged inflation (with E_t representing the time-t rational expectations operator), the output gap and changes in the nominal exchange rate, $\Delta e \equiv \Delta rer + \pi - \pi^f$, and foreign inflation, π^f.[13] Equation (7.5) is a hybrid investment-saving (IS) curve that establishes that the output gap depends on its expected and lagged values, the real ex-ante interest rate, $i - E[\pi]$, (with the policy rate set according to the different cases under analysis, described in the previous section), the real exchange rate, *rer*, and the credit spread, *spread*. The

---

[13] One can further consider that firms' costs, and thus their price-setting behavior, are affected by credit market conditions. We leave this consideration for future work.

latter variable, not present in the standard New Keynesian model, arises with the introduction of financial considerations into the model. It accounts for the distortions on the allocation of expenditures imposed by the presence of financial frictions and/or financial intermediation.[14] The spread, for which we provide further details later, is what drives the feedback mechanism between the financial sector and the rest of the economy. Lastly, equation (7.6) models the real exchange rate dynamics imposing uncovered interest rate parity.

The set of exogenous variables of the macroeconomic block include noncore inflation (recall that the loss functions in the previous section are defined in terms of the deviations of headline inflation from its target), foreign output, inflation, and interest rates. Noncore inflation is assumed to follow an autoregressive process of order 1, while foreign variables are modeled using a vector autoregressive model of order 2.

Financial Block

A financial block (sketched in Figure 7.1) is appended to the rest of the economy in order to capture, in a stylized fashion, the credit channel of monetary policy. Specifically, we consider a financial sector, characterized by the existence of banks, in charge of intermediating resources among borrowers and lenders. This intermediation is done at a cost, represented by the credit spread. We further capture vulnerabilities in the financial sector by introducing credit dynamics into the model.[15]

We assume that there is an intermediation technology that transforms real deposits into real loans subject to costs associated with loan monitoring activities. These costs are related to the presence of some financial friction on the demand side of credit, which gives rise to an external financing premium imposed on borrowers, as in Cúrdia and Woodford (2009). Following Gerali and others (2010), banks devote some of their resources to managing their balance sheets and/or to fulfilling costs associated with regulatory requirements. We also assume that banks enjoy some degree of market power due to the presence of monopolistic competition. This allows banks to charge a markup over the policy rate—that is, the relevant rate at which banks intermediate resources in the interbank market absent other intermediation costs—when setting loan (or active) rates, on the one hand, and a markdown with respect to the policy rate when setting deposit (or passive) rates, on the other.

The active interest rate, i_t^{loan}, whose dynamics evolve as follows,

$$i_t^{loan} = \beta_1 i_t + \beta_2 delinq_t + \beta_3 crr_t + \varepsilon_t^{i^{loan}}, \qquad (7.7)$$

---

[14]Alternatively, credit volumes or lending standards could have been used instead of the credit spread. However, according to Sámano (2011), preliminary evidence for the case of Mexico points out that credit volumes do not Granger-cause the output gap. Furthermore, for the case of Mexico, lending standards are available for a very short period, making it highly imprecise to perform statistical inference with the latter variable.

[15]According to Dell'Ariccia and others (2014), who analyze the characteristics of financial booms that end up in busts or crises, credit growth can be a powerful predictor of financial crises.

Figure 7.1. Model Mechanism

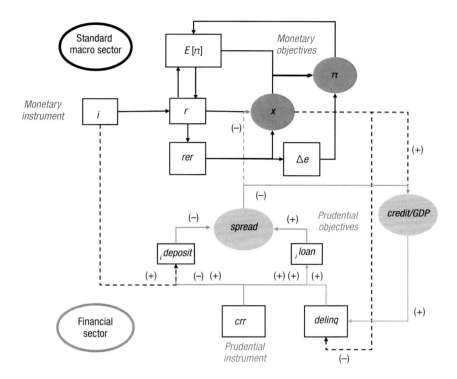

Source: Authors' representation.

is directly affected by monetary policy, with $\beta_1 (< 1)$ representing a limited pass-through from policy rates to active rates that arise from market power. It is also affected by a finance premium channel, *delinq*, to be defined momentarily, and the potential macroprudential policy tool or costs associated with the management of the bank's balance sheet, *crr*. For the passive rate we assume a similar structure:

$$i_t^{\text{deposit}} = \gamma_1 i_t + \gamma_2 delinq_t + \gamma_3 crr_t + \varepsilon_t^{\text{deposit}}, \tag{7.8}$$

where γ_1 determines the pass-through of the policy rate to funding costs that arise from banks' market power on deposit markets. Thus, the credit spread is given by the following expression:

$$spread_t = i_t^{\text{loan}} - i_t^{\text{deposit}}. \tag{7.9}$$

We capture the buildup of risks in the financial sector through the evolution of the credit-to-GDP gap, which is positively related to economic activity (i.e., credit booms generally start after periods of rapid economic growth), and negatively related to the credit spread. The latter relationship lets us account for the linkage between financial conditions and credit booms:[16]

$$crgap_t = \delta_1 crgap_{t-1} + \delta_2 x_{t-1} - \delta_3 spread_t + \varepsilon_t^{crgap}. \tag{7.10}$$

The delinquency index, *delinq*, is assumed to depend on economic activity, the credit-to-GDP gap, and its own lagged value:

$$delinq_t = \eta_1 delinq_{t-1} - \eta_2 x_t + \eta_3 crgap_{t-1} + \varepsilon_t^{delinq}. \tag{7.11}$$

The rationale behind this specification is, on one hand, that episodes of economic expansion lead to a reduction in nonperforming loans as debtors' defaults decline. On the other hand, an accelerated credit expansion, captured by a positive credit-to-GDP gap, may lead to vulnerabilities via a reduction in the quality of new loans as a result of looser lending standards during credit booms. This eventually translates into an increase of the delinquency index.

The coverage ratio rule, *crr*, has two possible interpretations depending on the policy strategy being considered. In the benchmark case and the leaning against the wind case, where macroprudential policy is not present, it is interpreted as a cost associated with banks' balance sheet management. In these cases, we simply assume that it follows an autoregressive process of order 1:

$$crr_t = \mu_1 crr_{t-1} + \varepsilon_t^{crr}. \tag{7.12}$$

The second interpretation of *crr* is that of a regulatory requirement imposed by the macroprudential authority. This interpretation becomes relevant when we analyze the case in which monetary and macroprudential policies coordinate. In this case, *crr* is defined as follows:

$$crr_t = \operatorname{argmin}\{L^{coord}\}, \tag{7.13}$$

subject to the rest of the economy.

This ratio should be understood as a dynamic-provisioning-type instrument that reduces the procyclicality of the financial system by forcing banks to build a buffer against losses when the financial cycle is booming and allows for a softer landing when it goes bust. Banks are forced to put aside resources to account for the possible losses incurred as credit quality deteriorates. Hence, the adoption of dynamic provisioning typically pursues three objectives: (1) to allow during good times for the buildup of reserves that would serve as a buffer in bad times; (2) to smooth credit growth over the business cycle; and (3) to shield the real economy from shocks originated in the financial sector.

The financial block is hence represented by equations (7.7) to (7.10), where the delinquency rate and the coverage ratio evolve according to equations (7.11) and (7.12) or (7.13), respectively.

---

[16]Drehmann and Juselius (2013) find that the credit-to-GDP gap is a good early warning indicator of banking crises.

Model Estimation

For illustrative purposes, we estimate the proposed model for the Mexican economy. The data set used in the estimation includes core and noncore inflation, the policy rate, the output gap, the real exchange rate, and the nominal exchange rate. The macroeconomic block includes the U.S. output gap, inflation, and policy rate. For the financial block: the nominal implicit loan rate for new loans, a delinquency index for aggregate credit, the average cost of bank term-deposits, financing to the nonfinancial private sector, and the measure of the coverage ratio. All data are at quarterly frequency.[17] We estimate equations (7.4) to (7.12) using the generalized method of moments and ordinary least squares. Our sample ranges from the first quarter of 2001 to the fourth quarter of 2014. All coefficients are summarized in Table 7.1.

RESULTS

Trade-offs between inflation-targeting and financial stability objectives arise when growing financial risks warrant a higher interest rate than the one necessary to tame inflation. In contrast, no trade-offs arise when higher interest rates due to an expansion of economic activity are also sufficient to contain financial stability risks. This section examines the trade-offs between policy objectives that result from the policy arrangements described in the previous section using our estimated model for the Mexican economy. To do so, we examine the model's transmission mechanism and policy implications under each case. In particular, we assess the cases' relative effectiveness in attaining their policy objectives (inflation targeting in the benchmark case and inflation targeting and financial stability in the leaning-against-the-wind and coordination cases) by comparing the volatility that

---

[17]Inflation is calculated as the quarter-over-quarter percent change of the corresponding index. The nominal interest rate is the short-term interbank funding rate. The output gap is estimated with a tail-corrected Hodrick-Prescott filter over real GDP. For the real exchange rate, we consider a bilateral index between Mexico and the United States constructed by Banco de México; the change in nominal exchange rate is thus the quarter-over-quarter percent change in the bilateral nominal rate. The lending spread corresponds to the difference between the implicit rate and the average cost of bank term deposits. The delinquency index is an adjusted index constructed by Banco de México, consisting of the sum of overdue loans and loans written off in the prior 12 months divided by total loans plus loans written off in the last 12 months. For the credit-to-GDP gap we filter the ratio of total financing from commercial banks to the nonfinancial private sector over GDP, using a Hodrick-Prescott filter with a smoothing parameter of 400,000. Finally, the variable capturing the coverage ratio rule (*crr*) is the ratio of loan-loss reserves to nonperforming loans for the Mexican banking system. Notice that to account for the *crr* we consider a realized measure of the ratio of loan-loss reserves to nonperforming loans as opposed to a legal actual requirement (the Mexican banking regulation does not include a dynamic provisioning requirement; instead it considers an expected loss approach consistent with the Basel III framework). The source of all data is Banco de México, Comisión Nacional Bancaria y de Valores, and Instituto Nacional de Estadística y Geografía.

TABLE 7.1

Estimation Results

Equation	Coefficient	i = 1	i = 2	i = 3	i = 4	i = 5	i = 6	Adj. R^2	J-stat.
(7.4) Phillips curve	a_i	0.621**	0.019**	0.005*	0.249**			0.70	0.53
(7.5) Investment-savings equation	b_i	0.508**	0.136**	0.198**	1.823**	0.184**		0.90	0.99
(7.6) Real exchange rate	c_i	0.308**	0.674**				0.046**	0.79	0.66
(7.7) Active rate	β_i	0.625**	0.043**	0.114*				0.53	0.99
(7.8) Passive rate	γ_i	0.778**	0.017**	0.364**				0.95	0.92
(7.10) Credit gap	δ_i	0.875**	0.708**	0.35				0.91	
(7.11) Delinquency index	η_i	0.750**	0.109**	0.052**				0.96	

Source: Authors' estimates.

Note: Equations (7.4) to (7.8) are estimated by the generalized method of moments. Equations (7.10) and (7.11) are estimated by ordinary least squares. As mentioned previously, it is difficult to pin down a precise estimate for δ_3. Therefore, we calibrate it so that the credit spread influences the credit-to-GDP gap by as much as half of its influence on the output gap. ** and * represent the 5 and 10 percent levels of significance, respectively.

each of them entails for a set of relevant macroeconomic and financial variables.[18] We conduct this analysis for two economic environments: one in which the economy is only affected by macroeconomic shocks, and another in which the economy is only affected by financial shocks.[19]

The general procedure used consists in feeding the model with 1,000 draws of shocks and simulating it 10,000 times to obtain the model's invariant distribution. The variances of the relevant variables and the values of the loss functions are then compared across cases and economic environments. To derive optimal policy rules for each case, we need to choose specific weights for the "preference parameters" in the loss functions (i.e., to assign values for σ_i, for all i in equations (7.1), (7.2), and (7.3)).[20] Unlike micro-founded models that assign welfare-based weights, our choice is arbitrary. In particular, we set all weights equal to 1 so that, in principle, the results are not distorted by a given preference for stabilizing one particular variable over another.

Macroeconomic Shocks

Table 7.2 shows our results when the economy is affected only by macroeconomic shocks. A monetary policy response that leans against the wind is effective in reducing fluctuations in financial variables, and even in output, relative to the case where monetary policy has traditional objectives (labeled "Benchmark" in the table). Intuitively, in the former case, monetary policy recognizes the effect that movements in the policy rate entail for the financial sector and internalizes this when setting the rate. As a result, the volatility of the policy rate is also reduced. However, this improvement does not come without a cost. A less reactive interest rate also entails somewhat larger inflation fluctuations. In particular, for the estimated version of our model and the specific "preference parameters" that we consider, the differences between the model dynamics in the two cases are relatively small: output and financial variables are between 8 and 6 percent less volatile, while inflation volatility increases by only 3 percent.

When comparing the model dynamics where monetary and macroprudential policies coordinate (labeled "Monetary and Macroprudential Coordination") vis-à-vis those where monetary policy leans against the wind, we observe a further reduction in the volatility of output and of financial variables but no relative gains in terms of inflation volatility. Smets (2014) points out that incorporating financial considerations into the central bank's objectives may lead to an inflationary bias problem, since monetary policy is kept looser than necessary for price

---

[18] For all cases presented below, each of the terms in the loss function is weighed out by the inverse of the variance of the corresponding historical series from 2001 to 2014.

[19] Evidently, the overall effectiveness of each particular policy strategy is a combination of its effectiveness in both environments and depends on the relative importance of macroeconomic versus financial shocks in the economy. However, separating the studied effects by type of shock makes it easier to understand the sources of the results.

[20] Optimal policy rules are calculated following Söderlind (1999).

TABLE 7.2

Simulation Results: Macro Shocks					
	Benchmark	Leans against the Wind	Monetary and Macroprudential Coordination	Relative Gains	
	(a)	(b)	(c)	(a)/(b)	(b)/(c)
L_π	0.201	0.207	0.207	0.972	0.999
L_x	4.770	4.391	4.313	1.086	1.018
$L_{\Delta i}$	54.300	50.079	50.007	1.084	1.001
L_{spread}	2.713	2.578	2.097	1.053	1.229
L_{crgap}	20.657	19.355	17.948	1.067	1.078
$L_{\Delta crr}$			0.015		

Source: Authors' estimates.

stability. As will be discussed when we perform our sensitivity analysis, this lack of improvement can be related to the relative ability of both the monetary and the macroprudential policy instruments to affect the financial sector's spread in a significant way.

Figures 7.2 and 7.3 depict the model's response to a positive demand shock and a positive cost-push shock, respectively. In the first case, inflationary pressures call for a restrictive monetary policy reaction. The policy rate increases to raise the real interest rate and moderate the increased economic activity. In the second case, inflation expectations increase mechanically due to the increase in inflation, which calls for a mild increase in the policy rate. Although these responses are the same in all cases, notice that the increase in the policy rate in the benchmark case slightly exceeds that in the other two. This confirms the intuition described above. When internalizing the effect of movements in the policy rate on the stabilization of the financial sector, monetary policy's responses are toned down. This policy reaction comes along with a tepid increase in the coverage ratio—the macroprudential instrument—in the coordination case. Notice, however, that the difference in the response of all variables across cases is negligible, as expected from the magnitudes of the changes in volatilities previously described.

Financial Shocks

Table 7.3 shows our results when the economy is only affected by financial shocks. In particular, we examine two shocks: (1) a shock to credit spreads due to changes in the loan rate, which can be interpreted as a reduction in the risk premium, and (2) a shock to the credit-to-GDP gap, which will allow us to analyze the policy response to an exogenous buildup of financial imbalances.

A monetary policy that leans against the wind implies larger volatility for both inflation and output relative to one with only traditional objectives. The reason why output volatility increases when the economy faces financial shocks is that, in this environment, the policy rate aims at stabilizing the financial sector not only through its effect on economic activity but also through its effect on the

Figure 7.2. Impulse Response to a One Standard Deviation Demand Shock
(Percentage points from steady state)

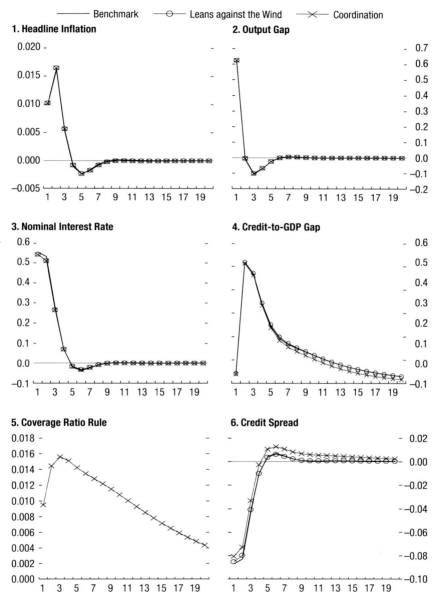

Source: Authors' estimates.

Figure 7.3. Impulse Response to a One Standard Deviation Push Shock
(Percentage points from steady state)

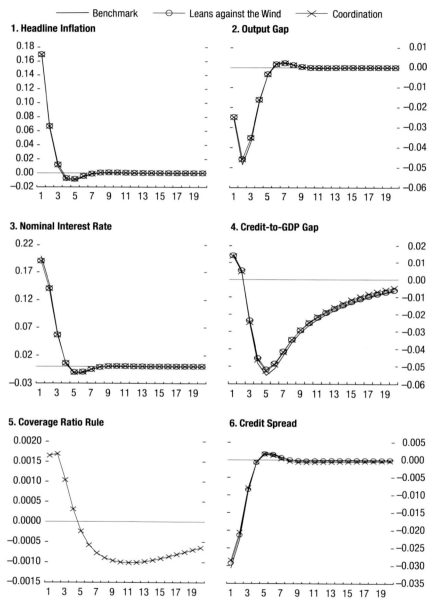

Source: Authors' estimates.

TABLE 7.3

Simulation Results: Financial Shocks					
	Benchmark	Leans against the Wind	Monetary and Macroprudential Coordination	Relative Gains	
	(a)	(b)	(c)	(a)/(b)	(b)/(c)
L_π	0.001	0.002	0.002	0.713	1.108
L_x	0.408	0.448	0.399	0.910	1.122
$L_{\Delta i}$	10.290	10.244	9.745	1.004	1.051
L_{spread}	2.202	2.130	1.699	1.034	1.254
L_{crgap}	5.223	5.591	4.181	0.934	1.337
$L_{\Delta crr}$			0.011		

Source: Authors' estimates.

credit channel (i.e., the credit spread). Inflation volatility is affected in a twofold manner. First, when monetary policy has an additional objective, the room for maneuver to temper the volatility of more variables declines, and this in turn affects inflation expectations. Second, larger output volatility necessarily translates into more inflation volatility. Additionally, this increase in output volatility translates into larger fluctuations in the credit-to-GDP gap, which leaves the monetary policy instrument at odds when trying to stabilize both objectives. In particular, for the case that we analyze, inflation and output volatility increase by 38 and 9 percent, respectively, while the credit-to-GDP gap increases by nearly 7 percent. The credit spread is less volatile by about 3 percent.

To further understand these responses, we examine the model dynamics when the economy is affected by a reduction in the risk premium that decreases the loan rate, which fuels economic activity through lower credit spreads (Figure 7.4). In the benchmark case, the responses of variables are straightforward. A decrease in credit spreads increases output and inflation. The improvement in economic activity initially translates into a lower delinquency index (i.e., a decrease in nonperforming loans), but the higher credit-to-GDP gap eventually offsets this effect, leading to a higher delinquency index. Monetary policy response is countercyclical in order to moderate economic activity and inflation. When monetary policy leans against the wind, the policy rate is set so as to contain the initial decrease in the credit spread through the credit channel. Since in our baseline estimation monetary policy has a negative net effect on credit spreads, the policy rate is set in a procyclical manner, which implies a reduction in the rate. This response amplifies the mechanism described in the benchmark case and leads to even higher levels of the credit-to-GDP gap and the delinquency index.

Figure 7.5 illustrates the model's response to an increase in the credit-to-GDP gap. In the benchmark case, this shock implies higher levels for the delinquency index, which leads to an increase in credit spreads due to an upward adjustment in the loan rate. The policy reaction is merely to tone down output and inflation. On the other hand, a monetary policy that leans against the wind counteracts the effect on the credit-to-GDP gap through lower economic activity, which implies a higher level for the policy interest rate and thus a decrease in inflation.

Figure 7.4 Impulse Response to a One Standard Deviation Spread Shock
(Percentage points from steady state)

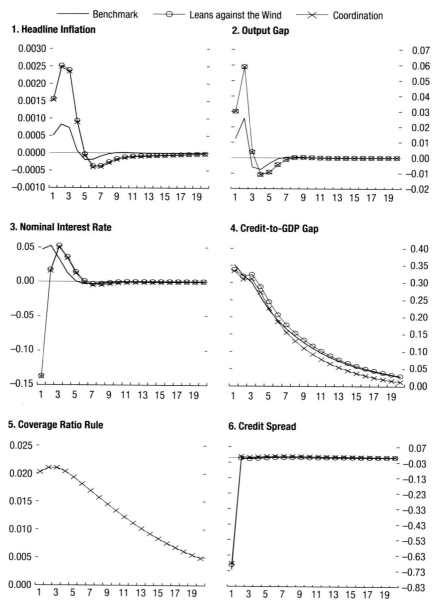

Source: Authors' estimates.

Figure 7.5 Impulse Response to a One Standard Deviation Credit-to-GDP Gap Shock
(Percentage points from steady state)

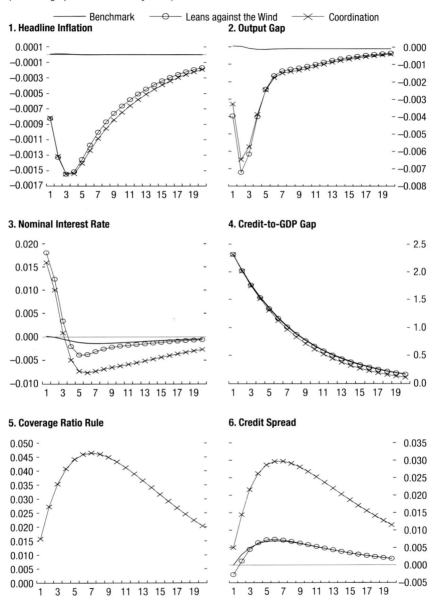

Source: Authors' estimates.

After examining monetary policy responses to financial shocks, one can easily understand why macroeconomic variables become more volatile when monetary policy has to lean against the wind. In our model, the policy rate goes above and beyond what would be required in the absence of financial stability objectives, in order to affect credit and the credit spreads. These dynamics suggest that the increase in the volatility of macroeconomic variables in our simulation exercise depends on the relative strength of the credit channel, that is, the effect of the policy rate on credit spreads, and on the feedback of output fluctuations into the financial sector. We will return to this point in the next section.

Table 7.3 also shows the results of the model's dynamics when both monetary and macroprudential policies coordinate. Coordination of the two instruments leads to a subtle improvement in the effectiveness of monetary and macroprudential policies to attain price and financial stability relative to the case in which monetary policy leans against the wind. These results are illustrated in Figures 7.4 and 7.5 as well, where it can be seen that the introduction of a macroprudential policy tool (*crr*) entails more favorable dynamics for financial variables under the shocks described above and hence less distortions in traditional objectives.

To sum up, this chapter has presented several main findings. First, adding a financial stability objective to monetary policy reduces the volatility of some financial variables. However, this improvement with respect to financial stability may come at the expense of increasing the volatility of macroeconomic variables. Second, this cost is present regardless of the type of shocks that affect the economy, but tends to increase when fluctuations are driven by financial shocks. This is probably what critics of monetary policy leaning against the wind had in mind prior to the 2008–09 financial crisis when they argued that the costs of such a strategy would likely be high (see Mishkin 2011 and references therein). Third, regardless of the type of shocks hitting the economy, we observe modest gains from coordination between monetary and macroprudential policies to achieve macroeconomic stability relative to having monetary policy leaning against the wind in our estimated model for the Mexican economy. Moreover, as can be seen in Tables 7.2 and 7.3, despite the observed reductions in volatility of most variables, inflation volatility remains high relative to the benchmark case.[21] The next section will shed light on the properties of the model driving this last result.

SENSITIVITY ANALYSIS

The results presented above are particular to the estimated model for the Mexican economy and hence cannot be generalized (i.e., it may be the case that country-specific aspects of the transmission of shocks in the Mexican economy are the main drivers of our results). In what follows, we assess the robustness of our

---

[21]According to these findings, and given that the size of gains from coordination for other variables is relatively small, the risk that financial stability considerations undermine the credibility of the central bank's price stability mandate might eventually generate further welfare losses.

findings. We mainly focus on identifying the reasons behind the lack of significant improvement in macroeconomic performance under coordination of monetary and macroprudential policies relative to monetary policy leaning against the wind. Specifically, we explore the importance of the ability of monetary and macroprudential instruments to affect financial variables through changes in credit spreads.

Ability of Monetary and Macroprudential Instruments to Affect Financial Variables

There is no doubt that the effectiveness of any policy strategy to attain its objective(s) should rest on the ability of the corresponding instrument to affect the economy in the desired way. In our model, this ability is given by the magnitude of the pass-through of the policy rate to loan and deposit rates—and thus its overall effect on credit spreads—and by the effect of the coverage ratio on the loan rate.

Let us first analyze the sensibility of our results to monetary policy's effectiveness to affect credit spreads. To do so, recall equations (7.7) and (7.8) that account for the effect of the policy rate on credit spreads. By substituting (7.7) and (7.8) into (7.9) we obtain the following:

$$spread_t = (\beta_1 - \gamma_1) i_t + (\beta_2 - \gamma_2) delinq_t + (\beta_3 - \gamma_3) crr_t + \varepsilon_t^{loan} - \varepsilon_t^{deposit},$$

with β_1 denoting the pass-through of the policy rate to the loan rate, γ_1 to the deposit rate, and $(\beta_1 - \gamma_1)$ its "net effect."

Table 7.4 illustrates the losses in terms of volatility of our baseline model relative to others with different values for this "net effect" when the economy is affected by financial shocks. First, notice that an economy is better off with a net effect equal to 0, when the loan and deposit rates are equally affected by movements in the policy rate. In such a case, changes in credit spreads are not directly obtained through movements in loan and/or deposit rates but rather through the effect that the policy rate has on other macroeconomic variables such as the output gap. For positive values of the net effect—which can be associated with a countercyclical effect of monetary policy on the financial sector—losses begin to increase, but not by as much as for negative values of the net effect, where losses can more than double.

We now focus on the case where the impact of macroprudential effectiveness on credit spreads is changed—that is, when we vary β_3 in equation (7.7). Table 7.5 illustrates the losses in terms of volatility of our baseline model relative to others with different values for this parameter, when the economy is affected by financial shocks. The larger the impact of macroprudential policy on credit spreads, the greater the gains of coordination versus leaning against the wind. Results are straightforward, as in this framework the transmission mechanism of macroprudential policy is quite simple. Figure 7.6 summarizes the results presented above and shows that our framework features room for gains from coordination between monetary and macroprudential policies, either when monetary policy is not an effective tool for the financial sector or when it enters into clear conflict with macroprudential policy. This result emphasizes the importance of assessing the relative effectiveness of the different tools that policymakers have at

TABLE 7.4

Simulation Results: Monetary Policy, Net Effect

	Negative Net Effect			Positive Net Effect			Zero Net Effect		
	Leans against the Wind (b)	Monetary and Macroprudential Coordination (c)	Relative Gains (b)/(c)	Leans against the Wind (b)	Monetary and Macroprudential Coordination (c)	Relative Gains (b)/(c)	Leans against the Wind (b)	Monetary and Macroprudential Coordination (c)	Relative Gains (b)/(c)
L_π	0.021	0.016	1.370	0.015	0.011	1.317	0.001	0.001	1.086
L_x	1.341	1.115	1.202	0.940	0.816	1.152	0.391	0.349	1.122
L_u	11.376	10.172	1.118	6.861	6.570	1.044	9.402	9.024	1.042
L_{spread}	15.683	9.850	1.592	10.409	7.608	1.368	0.735	0.714	1.029
L_{cspp}	46.507	27.126	1.714	15.214	9.565	1.591	1.360	1.198	1.136
$L_{\Delta crr}$		0.171			0.082			0.001	

Source: Authors' estimates.

TABLE 7.5

Simulation Results: Macroprudential Policy, β_3

	$\beta_3 = 0$			$\beta_3 = 0.5$			$\beta_3 = 0.8$		
	Leans against the Wind (b)	Monetary and Macroprudential Coordination (c)	Relative Gains (b/c)	Leans against the Wind (b)	Monetary and Macroprudential Coordination (c)	Relative Gains (b/c)	Leans against the Wind (b)	Monetary and Macroprudential Coordination (c)	Relative Gains (b/c)
L_π	0.002	0.002	1.099	0.002	0.002	1.208	0.002	0.002	1.287
L_x	0.469	0.419	1.119	0.469	0.410	1.144	0.469	0.404	1.162
$L_{\Delta i}$	10.357	9.875	1.049	10.357	9.655	1.073	10.357	9.526	1.087
L_{spread}	2.647	2.225	1.190	2.647	1.497	1.768	2.647	1.167	2.268
L_{crgap}	6.949	5.515	1.260	6.949	3.748	1.854	6.949	3.022	2.300
$L_{\Delta crr}$		0.010			0.029			0.034	

Source: Authors' estimates.

Figure 7.6. Gains from Policy Instruments, L^{LAW}/L^{Coord} (Financial Shocks)

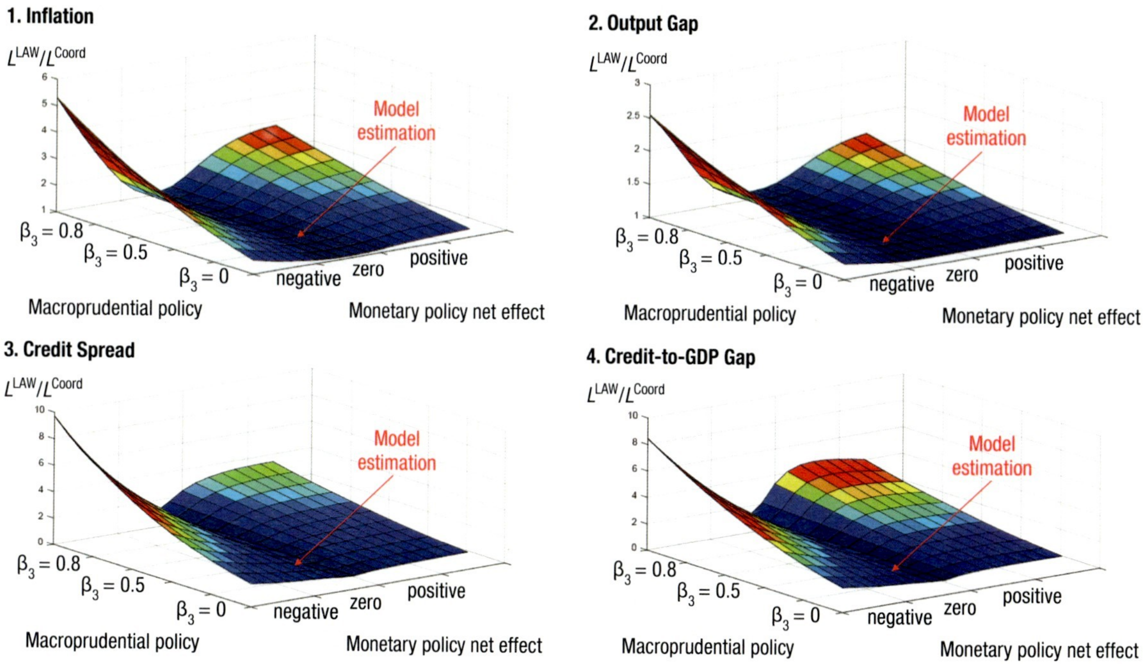

1. Inflation
2. Output Gap
3. Credit Spread
4. Credit-to-GDP Gap

Source: Authors' estimates.

their disposal to achieve policy objectives, as well as the interactions among these tools. The room for improvement is larger when the shocks affecting the economy come from the financial sector.

CONCLUSIONS

Despite the simplicity of the framework used in this chapter, our findings highlight some important aspects regarding how the interlinkages between the real and financial sectors determine the appropriate policy responses to shocks. In particular, our results suggest that the trade-offs to attain price and financial stability objectives increase in the presence of financial shocks.

The decision whether to use monetary policy as the main tool to counter the financial cycle by leaning against the wind versus using coordinated monetary and macroprudential policies to do so is ultimately a decision between having one versus two instruments to attain two different but inherently interconnected policy objectives. The fact that under a given situation (i.e., under the presence of financial shocks) there is a trade-off between inflation-targeting and financial stability objectives opens up the possibility to improve macroeconomic performance with coordinated monetary and macroprudential policies. The main result of this chapter is that the magnitude of these benefits depends on a wide range of determinants such as the effectiveness of policy instruments to affect credit spreads in the economy.

This result highlights the importance of further research on at least two fronts. The first is the price-setting behavior of banks. In particular, understanding the main determinants of profit margins in the banking system is of vital importance. The second is how the characteristics of the financial system shape the amplification and persistence of financial shocks to the economy. Within this task lies the need to understand the effect of having a particular degree of financial penetration in the economy, and detecting and assessing the importance of the financial frictions that account for the transmission of financial shocks.

A deeper understanding of these topics will lead to developing larger, more complex, and more wide-ranging country-specific macroeconomic models that allow for capturing the main features of the economies which policymakers attempt to influence.

REFERENCES

Andrés, J., and O. Arce. 2012. "Banking Competition, Housing Prices and Macroeconomic Stability." *Economic Journal* 122(565): 1346–72.

Angelini, P., S. Neri, and F. Panetta. 2014. "The Interaction between Capital Requirements and Monetary Policy." *Journal of Money, Credit and Banking* 46(6): 1073–112.

Angeloni, I., and E. Faia. 2013. "Capital Regulation and Monetary Policy with Fragile Banks." *Journal of Monetary Economics* 60(3): 311–24.

Beau, D., L. Clerc, and B. Mojon. 2012. "Macro-prudential Policy and the Conduct of Monetary Policy." Working Paper 390, Banque de France, Paris.

Bernanke, B., and M. Gertler. 1986. "Agency Costs, Collateral, and Business Fluctuations." NBER Working Paper 2015, National Bureau of Economic Research, Cambridge, Massachusetts.

———, and S. Gilchrist. 1999. "The Financial Accelerator in a Quantitative Business Cycle Framework." In *Handbook of Macroeconomics*, Volume 1, edited by J. B. Taylor and M. Woodford. Amsterdam: North-Holland.

Blanchard, O., G. Dell'Ariccia, and P. Mauro. 2010. "Rethinking Macroeconomic Policy." IMF Staff Position Note 2010/03, International Monetary Fund, Washington, DC.

———. 2013. "Rethinking Macro Policy II; Getting Granular." IMF Staff Discussion Note 13/003, International Monetary Fund, Washington, DC.

Borio, C. 2011. "Rediscovering the Macroeconomic Roots of Financial Stability Policy: Journey, Challenges and a Way Forward." BIS Working Paper 354, Bank for International Settlements, Basel.

———. 2014. "Monetary Policy and Financial Stability: What Role in Prevention and Recovery?" BIS Working Paper 440, Bank for International Settlements, Basel.

———, and P. Lowe. 2002. "Asset Prices, Financial and Monetary Stability: Exploring the Nexus." BIS Working Paper 114, Bank for International Settlements, Basel.

Borio, C., W. English, and A. Filardo. 2003. "A Tale of Two Perspectives: Old or New Challenges for Monetary Policy?" BIS Working Paper 127, Bank for International Settlements, Basel.

Cecchetti, S., H. Genberg, J. Lipsky, and S. Wadhwani. 2000. "Asset Prices and Central Bank Policy." Geneva Reports on the World Economy No. 2 (July). Centre for Economic Policy Research, London.

Cúrdia, V., and M. Woodford. 2009. "Credit Spreads and Monetary Policy." NBER Working Paper 15289, National Bureau of Economic Research, Cambridge, Massachusetts.

———. 2011. "The Central-Bank Balance Sheet as an Instrument of Monetary Policy." *Journal of Monetary Economics* 58(1): 54–79.

De Paoli, B., and M. Paustian. 2013. "Coordinating Monetary and Macro-prudential Policies." Staff Report 653, Federal Reserve Bank of New York.

Dell'Ariccia, G., D. Igan, L. Laeven, and H. Tong. 2014. "Policies for Macro-financial Stability: Dealing with Credit Booms and Busts." In *Financial Crises: Causes, Consequences, and Policy Responses*, edited by S. Claessens, A. Kose, L. Laeven, and F. Valencia. Washington, DC: International Monetary Fund.

Drehmann, M., and M. Juselius. 2013. "Evaluating Early Warning Indicators of Banking Crises: Satisfying Policy Requirements." BIS Working Paper 421, Bank for International Settlements, Basel.

Galati, G., and R. Moessner. 2013. "Macroprudential Policy: A Literature Review." *Journal of Economic Surveys* 27(5): 846–78.

Gerali, A., S. Neri, L. Sessa, and F. M. Signoretti. 2010. "Credit and Banking in a DSGE Model of the Euro Area." *Journal of Money, Credit and Banking* 42(s1): 107–41.

Gertler, M., and P. Karadi. 2011. "A Model of Unconventional Monetary Policy." *Journal of Monetary Economics* 58(1): 17–34.

Iacoviello, M. 2005. "House Prices, Borrowing Constraints, and Monetary Policy in the Business Cycle." *American Economic Review* 95(3): 739–64.

Kannan, P., P. Rabanal, and A. M. Scott. 2012. "Monetary and Macroprudential Policy Rules in a Model with House Price Booms." *B.E. Journal of Macroeconomics* 12(1): 1–44.

Kiyotaki, N., and J. Moore. 1997. "Credit Cycles." *Journal of Political Economy* 105(2): 211–48.

Lambertini, L., C. Mendicino, and M. T. Punzi. 2013. "Leaning against Boom–Bust Cycles in Credit and Housing Prices." *Journal of Economic Dynamics and Control* 37(8): 1500–22.

Meh, C. A., and K. Moran. 2010. "The Role of Bank Capital in the Propagation of Shocks." *Journal of Economic Dynamics and Control* 34(3): 555–76.

Mishkin, F. S. 2011. "Monetary Policy Strategy: Lessons from the Crisis." NBER Working Paper, National Bureau of Economic Research, Cambridge, Massachusetts.

Roldán-Peña, J., D. Sámano, and A. Torres. 2014. "Monetary and Macro Prudential Policies: Interaction and Complementarity." Banco de México, Mexico City. Unpublished.

Sámano, D. 2011. "In the Quest for Macroprudential Policy Tools." Working Paper 2011-17, Banco de México, Mexico City.

Smets, F. 2014. "Financial Stability and Monetary Policy: How Closely Interlinked?" *International Journal of Central Banking* 10(2): 263–300.

Söderlind, P. 1999. "Solution and Estimation of RE Macro Models with Optimal Policy." *European Economic Review* 43(4–6): 813–23.

Svensson, L. E. O. 2014. "Inflation Targeting and Leaning against the Wind." *International Journal of Central Banking* 10(2): 103–14.

Vlcek, J., and R. Scott. 2012. "Macrofinancial Modeling at Central Banks; Recent Developments and Future Directions." IMF Working Paper 12/21, International Monetary Fund, Washington, DC.

Williams, J. C. 2014. "Financial Stability and Monetary Policy: Happy Marriage or Untenable Union?" *FRBSF Economic Letter* 2014-17 (June 9).

Woodford, M. 2003. *Interest and Prices: Foundations of a Theory of Monetary Policy*. Princeton, New Jersey: Princeton University Press.

———. 2012. "Inflation-Targeting and Financial Stability." NBER Working Paper 17967, National Bureau of Economic Research, Cambridge, Massachusetts.

CHAPTER 8

A Brazilian Perspective on Macroprudential and Monetary Policy Interaction

FABIA A. DE CARVALHO AND MARCOS R. DE CASTRO, CENTRAL BANK OF BRAZIL

This chapter examines the interaction between monetary and macroprudential policy in Brazil under both normative and positive perspectives. The chapter investigates optimal combinations of simple and implementable macroprudential and monetary policy rules that react to the financial cycle, based on a dynamic stochastic general equilibrium (DSGE) model built to reproduce Brazilian particularities and estimated with Bayesian techniques using data spanning the inflation-targeting period. The chapter also looks at whether recent macroprudential policy announcements in Brazil that targeted credit variables had important spillover effects on variables targeted by monetary policy. To this end, we use a daily panel of private inflation forecasts surveyed by the central bank. We also investigate the impact of announcements of macroprudential policy changes on the gap between inflation forecasts and the inflation target. Finally, the chapter presents an overview of the difficulties facing macroprudential policy in Brazil after the global financial crisis and discusses a few important future challenges.

The Latin American region sailed well through the years immediately following the collapse of Lehman Brothers in the United States. With several recurrent sovereign debt and systemic banking crisis episodes behind it, the region had shifted from procyclical to countercyclical fiscal and monetary policies by the late 1990s. This helped the region build solid macroeconomic fundamentals (Végh and Vuletin 2013) and sound and resilient financial systems, giving room to maneuver throughout the initial phases of the global financial crisis.

To alleviate risks of financial instability, owing to either a liquidity crunch or a worsening of external accounts, Latin American countries pursued different

---

The authors are grateful to Eduardo Lima, Laura Kodres, Solange Gouvea, Hamid Faruqee, Alfredo Cuevas, Jorge Roldós, Marcello Estevão, Alberto Torres, Troy Matheson, David Einhorn and the participants at the IMF's midpoint seminar on "The Future of Central Banking in Latin America" for helpful comments and discussions.

combinations of macroeconomic and macroprudential policy responses. This included measures to stimulate domestic demand by boosting bank loan origination, in some cases using public banks, to avoid a credit crunch. In addition, with abundant international liquidity associated with a balance of risks shifting favorably toward emerging markets, the region received significant inflows of foreign capital, which also helped fuel credit expansion.[1]

More recently, plummeting commodity prices and economic slowdown in major trading partners, such as China, have been a drag on the region's growth, particularly in the context of fiscal buffers being practically exhausted. Increased household indebtedness, deteriorating labor market prospects, and worsening credit conditions have become important challenges from both macroeconomic and macroprudential policy perspectives. In some instances, financial and macroeconomic cycles have been synchronous, and macroprudential policy has worked favorably towards meeting macroeconomic policy goals. However, at other times, macroprudential policy decisions might have had undesired spillovers from a macroeconomic policy perspective.

This chapter contributes to the ongoing debate by exploring two issues related to the interaction between macroprudential and monetary policy, taking Brazil as the central case. First, from a normative perspective, given the frequent and varied use of macroprudential instruments in the country even prior to the financial crisis, we seek an optimal combination of macroprudential and monetary policy, using the DSGE model in Carvalho and Castro (2015), which was carefully customized to represent essential features of the Brazilian banking system.[2] Second, we take the analysis further by comparing the optimal set of policies with narrower subsets of policies that can be more easily implemented in a timely manner.

With respect to the first task, the optimal monetary and macroprudential policy mix for Brazil is still an unexplored issue. This chapter tries to answer the question by finding the optimal combination of sets of macroprudential and monetary policies that may react to a credit gap, given ample evidence that this indicator is a good, if not the best, early warning indicator of financial crisis (see Silva, Sales, and Gaglianone 2012 for the Brazilian case and Taylor 2015 and Drehman and Tsatsaronis 2014 for cross-country studies). Basel III also recommends the use of the credit gap to justify changes in the countercyclical capital buffer.

In order to find the optimal policy combinations, we follow the method proposed by Schmitt-Grohé and Uribe (2007), and focus on simple and implementable

---

[1] Jácome, Nier, and Imam (2012) thoroughly discuss the measures implemented in the region.

[2] Our approach of using a realistic model of the Brazilian economy, estimated with actual data, adds robustness to the results. De Fiore and Tristani (2013), for instance, recognize that their numerical findings of optimal rules are illustrative and the quantitative features derived from them should be validated through more complex models.

policy rules.³ We also investigate the properties of more easily implementable rules given the Brazilian regulatory framework.

Several studies have investigated the optimality of monetary policy reacting to financial conditions. Some have found that alternative monetary policy rules that react to financial variables have negligible stabilization gains when compared with strict inflation targeting or traditional Taylor rules (Bernanke and Gertler 2001; Faia and Monacelli 2007; Gilchrist and Leahy 2002; Iacoviello 2005). Other studies find that it can be welfare improving to let monetary policy react to financial variables (Angeloni and Faia 2013; Benigno and others 2011; Cúrdia and Woodford 2010; De Fiori and Tristani 2013; Fendoğlu 2014; Kannan, Rabanal, and Scott 2012). These studies are heterogeneous with respect to the model structure, financial frictions, financial targets,⁴ and parameterization. The conclusions might be model dependent, and, for a particular model, they can also be sensitive to the parameterization. They are also highly sensitive to the set of disturbances allowed in the model.⁵

This study distinguishes itself from others in a number of aspects. First, we include a varied and practical set of macroprudential policy instruments interacting with monetary policy, while most of the literature focuses only on monetary policy as the single instrument to stabilize multiple targets, including financial conditions.⁶ Second, our model is of a small and open economy with foreign trade and financial flows, while most of the literature focuses on closed

---

³Ramsey-type optimal policy analysis requires an arbitrary weight of each class of agents in the model. Lambertini, Mendicino, and Punzi (2013) find an important role for heterogeneity with respect to classes of agents in determining welfare implications. They cannot find a uniform ranking of policy frameworks for both classes of agents in their model. In addition, rules that deviate from the optimal in individual terms have important welfare effects for only one class of agent, the borrower, which is more directly affected by the financial constraint.

⁴In Faia and Monacelli (2007) monetary policy faces a trade-off between stabilizing consumer inflation or asset prices. In Angeloni and Faia (2013), financial targets are asset prices or bank leverage. In Fendoğlu (2014), financial targets are asset prices or credit spreads. They study optimal policy with costly-state verification–type financial frictions, but focus on monetary policy rules. In Kannan, Rabanal, and Scott (2012), the financial friction occurs in housing loans, but the external finance premium is assumed, rather than obtained from first-order conditions. Monetary policy is allowed to react to credit growth.

⁵Brzoza-Brzezina and Kolasa (2013) provide an extensive analysis of model-implied differences in responses of the main economic variables by examining credit constraint and external finance premium financial accelerators vis-à-vis a standard New Keynesian model. For a detailed description of the impact of the set of disturbances allowed in a particular model on optimal policy rules, see Lambertini, Mendicino, and Punzi (2013).

⁶Some exceptions that introduce a second policy instrument are Benigno and others (2011) and Cesa-Bianchi and Rebucci (2015), who study the interaction of monetary policy with macroprudential policy when borrowing constraints bind; Angeloni and Faia (2013), who introduce a countercyclical capital rule that interacts with monetary policy; and Lambertini, Mendicino, and Punzi (2013), who study the optimality of countercyclical loan-to-value ratio caps in a model based on Iacoviello and Neri (2010), focused on the mortgage market.

economies.[7] Third, our model has features that are necessary to reproduce the main aspects of the Brazilian credit market, such as heavy regulation of housing loans and savings deposits and a consumer credit segment in which credit originations are strongly based on households' future labor income, yet facing significant default ratios. Conducting optimal policy analysis in models intended for practical use at central banks is a strikingly different approach compared to what has been usually adopted in the literature. The preferred choice of prototype models in this literature is most likely due to the dimension of practical models and the challenges faced in their estimation.

We find that certain combinations of reserve requirements and risk weights can result in losses that are very close to the optimum, involving a more complete combination of instruments, including the Basel III countercyclical capital buffer. The more restricted combination of instruments also results in dynamic responses very close to the optimal rules. Given the fact that changes to reserve requirements and risk weights are more easily implementable, the finding gives support to the Central Bank of Brazil's extensive use of reserve requirements and risk weights to affect credit, and the stability of the overall capital requirement ratio to date.

With respect to the second task, although most of the literature is concerned with the issue of whether monetary policy should react to financial variables, the reverse argument has not been explored. Given the possible lack of synchronization of macroprudential and monetary policy in some recent episodes in Brazil, it is important to investigate whether macroprudential policy announcements can potentially affect the anchoring of inflation expectations. To this end, we use a panel of private inflation forecasts surveyed on a daily basis by the Central Bank of Brazil's Investor Relations Office to estimate the impact of some macroprudential policy events—which explicitly targeted the credit market—on the formation of inflation expectations. We draw on the work of Carvalho and Minella (2012) to find a representative expectations formation rule, but we augment it with the investigated events in addition to some other necessary controls.

Among 14 events analyzed in our study, we find a subset of 6 events that suggest that macroprudential policy announcements affected the gap between inflation expectations and the inflation target. In 4 of these events, the impact was in the direction of widening the gap. When we group the events that were expected to increase credit into two different sets, one when monetary policy was contractionary and the other when monetary policy was expansionary, we find that the former had a positive significant impact on inflation expectations, while the latter was not significant. This can be interpreted as evidence that when

---

[7]An exception is Benigno and others (2011), but the financial frictions they incorporate are significantly different from ours. They assume that there are eventually binding collateral constraints with a reduced set of nominal rigidities and that borrowing occurs in foreign currency, while our financial frictions in the borrowing side of the model come from costly-state verification, with bank borrowing carried out in domestic currency. Notice that our model has other important frictions that constrain banks' balance sheet locations and have real effects.

macroprudential policy announcements are not synchronized with monetary policy, the anchoring of inflation expectations can be difficult.

The next section of this chapter describes how Brazil managed to build a solid financial system after a banking crisis. The chapter then reviews the main macroprudential measures implemented in Brazil in the aftermath of the financial crisis and during the postcrisis period. We present the optimal policy exercise using the DSGE model that was tailored to the Brazilian economy and then empirically investigate the impact of macroprudential policy announcements on monetary policy credibility before presenting the chapter's conclusions.

THE BRAZILIAN BANKING CRISIS AND BANK REGULATORY REFORM

The last episode of a banking crisis in Brazil immediately followed the implementation of the inflation stabilization plan—the *Real* Plan—in 1994 (Reinhart and Rogoff 2011). At that time, inflation stabilization had eliminated an important source of bank revenues and exposed banks' practices to vulnerabilities that could undermine financial stability. To address these risks, in the first years of the inflation stabilization period the government implemented two major bank restructuring programs: the Program of Incentives to Restructure and Strengthen the National Financial System (PROER) and the Program of Incentives to Reduce the State-Level Public Sector in Bank Activity (PROES).

Local government banks had had a long history of impaired credit portfolios, with high default rates, posing systemic risks to the financial system and feeding fiscal imbalances. PROES addressed these problems through either the privatization of public banks or the transformation of public commercial banks into development banks, which were prohibited from extending loans to their public controllers. The Fiscal Responsibility Law, enacted in 2001, outlawed credit operations between public banks and their public controllers, further enhancing fiscal discipline.

PROER was a milestone in the regulatory framework of the Brazilian financial system. One of the pillars of this program was the enhanced framework under which the central bank—which is also the regulatory and supervisory authority—was authorized to intervene in troubled financial institutions. The program also included a number of other important measures, including a deposit-insurance facility.

In addition to these major restructuring programs, Brazil adopted best practices with respect to its bank regulatory and supervisory framework by adhering to the first Basel Accord in 1994 and adopting a strict regulatory and supervisory stance thereafter.[8] Basel III capital regulations were first published in March 2013 and their phasing in started within a few months, in October. The Basel Committee on Banking Supervision performed its last assessment of Basel

---

[8] Agénor and Silva (2013) have qualified Brazil's bank supervisory environment as "strong, sophisticated and intrusive" with a "robust regulatory environment," which differentiates the country from other middle-income countries.

III regulations in Brazil in December 2013 and found that the country was compliant with the terms of the agreement. Brazil's financial regulatory and supervisory framework ranks favorably among those evaluated by the Financial Stability Board (FSB), while it was ranked first in the IMF's 2012 assessment of countries' compliance with Basel principles. The Brazilian financial system is well capitalized and shows comfortable levels of liquidity indicators, with a Basel index of 16.7, a provisions-to-capital ratio, net of delinquencies, of 11 percent, and a net-assets-to-short-term-liabilities ratio of about 200.[9]

OVERVIEW OF MONETARY AND MACROPRUDENTIAL POLICY IN BRAZIL AFTER THE FINANCIAL CRISIS

Brazilian banks were not exposed to subprime loans or troubled assets during the global financial crisis. Hence, the crisis affected the Brazilian financial system mostly through the liquidity channel.[10] However, uncertainties with respect to the viability of small banks that were negatively affected by the shortage of foreign credit lines caused a temporary disruption in interbank liquidity provision, particularly for smaller banks.

To even out liquidity positions in the interbank market, the Brazilian central bank implemented unconventional changes in reserve requirement regulations. These instruments were important to give the central bank room to maneuver in moments of distress.

On another front, policy measures were adopted to reduce the volatility caused by strong international liquidity inflows into the country, a response to quantitative-easing programs and unconventional policies adopted by central banks in major advanced economies. Some of those measures aimed to reduce the incentives for foreign investors to invest in short-term assets, while others called for stricter requirements on banks' foreign exchange exposure.

Signs of a possible credit crunch led to a set of regulatory relief measures, triggering intervention by public banks in the credit market mainly through looser credit origination conditions. The strong response of public banks changed the composition of credit in the system and fueled an important acceleration of consumer indebtedness, to a point where the country ranked sixth in the world in terms of household debt service and principal payments to income.[11] More recently, household indebtedness with respect to housing loans shows signs of moderation, while indebtedness with respect to other credit segments is clearly decelerating (Figure 8.1).

To date, the evolution of consumer indebtedness has not posed a large threat to financial stability, given relatively low levels of credit to GDP, but looser terms of credit origination have contributed to vulnerabilities in some market segments.

---

[9]Data from the IMF's Financial Soundness Indicator database (http://fsi.imf.org/Default.aspx).

[10]Silva and Harris (2012) provide an extensive report on the measures adopted in Brazil to fight the global financial crisis.

[11]IMF, Financial Soundness Indicators database.

Figure 8.1. Household Indebtedness and Income Commitment in Brazil
(Percent)

1. Household Indebtedness

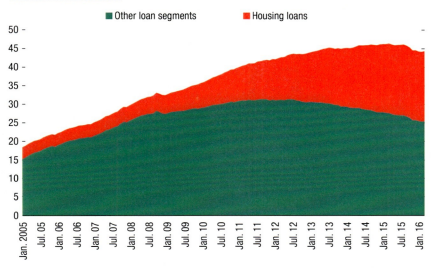

2. Household Income Commitment

Source: Central Bank of Brazil.

Figure 8.2. Evolution of Banks' Regional Presence in Brazil

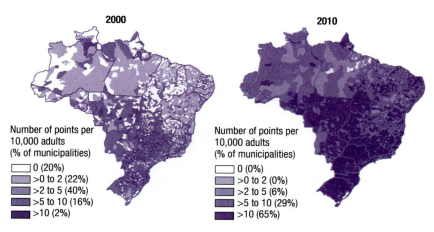

Source: Central Bank of Brazil.
Note: Points refer to bank counters, branches, or correspondents.

The regulatory policy response to this was either specific to identified vulnerabilities in certain markets or of a more general nature. For instance, the implementation of risk-weight factors directly related to the maturity and loan-to-value of credit operations proved effective in constraining their impact on specific targets. Martins and Schechtman (2013) and Afanasieff and others (2015) provide evidence supporting the precision of the measures adopted in 2010 for auto loans. In some instances, the direction of macroprudential measures was in line with the monetary stance of the economy.

An important challenge facing both the regulatory and the monetary authorities has been the fast and intense financial deepening process that Brazil has undergone over recent years. Figure 8.2 shows the evolution of banks' regional presence in Brazil, and Figure 8.3 shows the migration of social classes over the years. Financial inclusion has been the result of technological and regulatory improvements in the financial system, income distribution policies, public banks' credit origination policies, and a stable macroeconomic environment.

Sahay and others (2015) find a positive relationship between the pace of financial deepening and the risk of crisis and macroeconomic instability, conditional on the efficiency of a financial system's regulation and supervision. To avoid these risks, the Brazilian central bank has closely monitored the financial deepening process and the quality of credit origination so that credit growth and income commitment are kept within sustainable boundaries. Essential to this task is the Credit Bureau, created in 1997 and restructured in 2008, which collects detailed information on each and every credit origination in the banking system above R$1,000 (about US$300). Such transactions currently account for 99 percent of the entire credit portfolio of the Brazilian financial system. The Credit Bureau is

Figure 8.3. Social Mobility in Brazil

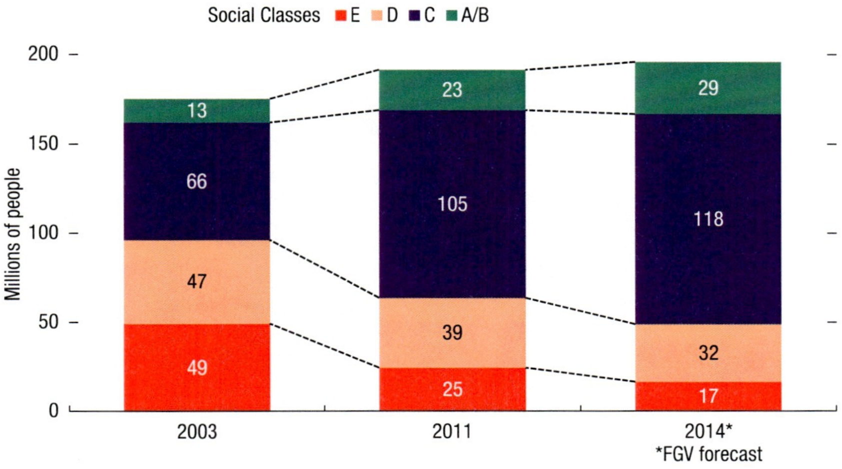

	2003	2011	2014*
A/B	13	23	29
C	66	105	118
D	47	39	32
E	49	25	17

(Millions of people)

*FGV forecast

Source: Central Bank of Brazil, Fundação Getulio Vargas (FGV).

managed by the central bank, and the information available is processed and analyzed on a daily basis not only by the supervisory and regulatory departments of the central bank, but also by economic departments, constituting an important input for a broad set of policy decisions.

Other important risk-mitigating measures have been put in place, including: the approval of the Credit Default Law in 2005;[12] improvements in the Deposit Guarantee Fund (including the introduction of a similar fund for cooperative credit unions that target low-income borrowers); enactment of a law that approved the creation of a positive borrowers' record (in addition to credit registries); and a derivatives exposure registry (CED).

The central bank's capacity to monitor the Brazilian financial system is in many respects unique in the world. Not only is it comprehensive in terms of banks' operations, portfolios, and exposures, it also responds in a timely manner and is appropriately designed to monitor and detect inconsistencies in the wide range of information given to the central bank. Table 8.1 offers a glimpse at the dimension of database monitoring at the Central Bank of Brazil.

Another factor that has limited the impact of higher default rates of low-income borrowers to the rest of the financial system is the fact that these

---

[12]Ponticelli and Alencar (2013) show that the Credit Default Law allowed for a significant increase in the probability of collateral recovery in the case of liquidation of a borrowing firm. It also had significantly positive effects on loan originations to companies in the transformation industry (which was the only industry examined in the study). The law generated an overall impact in the form of lower lending rates, longer maturities, and lower collateral requirements. The effects were more noticeable in regions where judges are quicker to analyze these cases.

TABLE 8.1

Database Monitoring at the Central Bank	
Assets and securities markets	• Data sources: SELIC, CETIP, BM&F BOVESPA, Brazilian Payments System, and all financial institutions • Processes 40 million registers per day • Processes over 900 documents per month • Produces daily macro- and microprudential analysis on liquidity and market risks of the financial system • Monitors the market for public bonds and the behavior of bank funding daily • Releases information on the Central Bank of Brazil's website

Credit operations	• Data sources: Monthly information from financial institutions
	   ○ 480 million operations
	   ○ Credit operations outstanding of 75 million clients
	   ○ Each operation has 36 information fields
	• Produces monthly micro- and macroprudential analysis on credit risks of the financial system
	• Manages the Credit Bureau System and publishes information for the public and for financial institutions on credit operations
	• Releases information on the Central Bank of Brazil's website

Purchasing consortium groups	• Information on 13.7 million quotas, distributed among 21,000 groups • Data on 9 million quotas with past-due earnings • 880 million data registers received on a quarterly basis and 60,000 received on a monthly basis • Produces individual and aggregate quarterly analysis on the purchasing consortium segment • Releases information on the Central Bank of Brazil's website

Foreign exchange operations	• Foreign exchange system:
	   ○ 207 authorized financial institutions
	   ○ 7.8 million operations per year
	• 31,000 operations per day
	• Central bank receives additional 25.5 million operations per year via monthly files
	• Produces daily microprudential analysis on foreign exchange operations carried out by financial institutions
	• Monitors foreign inflows and the foreign exchange flow daily
	• Releases information on the Central Bank of Brazil's website

Accounting information	• Receives 1,136 bank financial statements on a monthly basis and 2,267 limit statements (600,000 monthly registers) • Receives over 7,300 documents on a quarterly basis (2.2 million quarterly registers) • Produces monthly macro- and microprudential analysis on the financial-economic situation of the financial institutions • Monitors the adherence of financial institutions to regulatory operational limits monthly • Releases information on the Central Bank of Brazil's website

Others	• Other sources of information:
	   ○ Regulators
	   ○ Deposit guarantee fund
	   ○ Custody chambers
	   ○ Registry chambers
	   ○ External auditors
	   ○ Rating agencies
	   ○ International organizations—Financial Stability Board
	   ○ Government databases
	   ○ Private databases—SERASA
	   ○ Institutions that are not regulated by the Central Bank of Brazil

Source: Central Bank of Brazil.

loans have been mostly originated by a public bank (Caixa Econômica Federal) as part of a wider policy of social inclusion.[13]

INTERACTION BETWEEN MONETARY AND MACROPRUDENTIAL POLICY

Monetary and financial stability are the core missions of the Central Bank of Brazil. The Monetary Policy Committee (COPOM) was created by the central bank in 1996 with the purpose of setting the monetary policy stance,[14] and since 1999 its decisions must be directed toward achieving the inflation targets set by the National Monetary Council.[15]

The Financial Stability Committee (COMEF) was created by the central bank in 2011 to set directives and guidelines for central bank conduct in order to preserve financial stability, assess systemic risk, and carry out macroprudential oversight.[16] Although COMEF's guidelines are enforced, the board of governors is not constrained by the meeting days of COMEF or COPOM to set the central bank's policy instruments (with the exception of the monetary policy interest rate). In addition, both COPOM and COMEF comprise the same members, the Central Bank of Brazil's board of governors. Board members have restated that each committee's objectives and decisions are independent. However, communication, which is seen as essential to avoid misperceptions that could undermine policy effectiveness, remains a challenge.

There are pros and cons in having supervision and financial regulation within the central bank. For instance, the IMF (2013) considers this double assignment a vulnerability of the overall Brazilian regulatory and supervisory framework, as it brings time consistency issues and communication challenges.

However, as also stated in the IMF report, there are several benefits from this arrangement, such as having macroprudential policy decisions drawing on central bank expertise in financial and macroeconomic analyses and data availability, which facilitates the analysis of the side effects of each policy. The report also mentions the benefits of better shielding macroprudential policy from political influence compared to when this function is assigned to a separate regulatory body.

---

[13]This could increase the procyclicality of housing loans because the fiscal stance of the economy could play an important role in the capacity to originate new loans.

[14]Central Bank of Brazil Circular #2698 of June 20, 1996 created both the COPOM and its monetary policy instrument, the rediscount (TBC) rate, which was the official monetary policy instrument until 1999, when it was informally replaced by the base (SELIC) rate. Circular #2966 of February 8, 2000 formalized the SELIC rate as the central bank's monetary policy instrument.

[15]The National Monetary Council is composed of the Minister of Finance, Minister of Planning and Budget, and the Governor of the Central Bank of Brazil.

[16]Central Bank of Brazil Portaria #65180 of May 18, 2011 created COMEF. The central bank's *portarias* are legal instruments issued by the central bank governor. *Circulares* must be approved by the central bank's board of directors.

In addition to continuously improving the regulatory and supervisory stance of the Brazilian financial system, the central bank has actively used a variety of instruments to try to influence the financial cycle, with either narrow or broader purposes. Important policy choices for these purposes have been risk-weight factors, reserve requirements, and taxation of foreign capital inflows; overall capital requirement ratios have remained unchanged since the implementation of Basel I. In most instances, communication of the targeted impact of policy decisions has not been detailed and the macroprudential policy decision framework remains highly discretionary.

During the inflation-targeting period, monetary policy has followed the traditional inflation-targeting framework, with the (SELIC) interest rate being the central policy instrument. Very rarely were reserve requirements explicitly used to reinforce the monetary policy stance.[17] Their use has been associated mostly with macroprudential purposes, and only occasionally have they been used to attain other goals, such as draining liquidity from the large inflows of foreign capital, or in times of distress in government bonds issuances.

National Monetary Council Resolution #4193 of March 1, 2013 instituted the additional conservation and countercyclical bank capital requirement to come into effect in 2016. According to Central Bank of Brazil Comunicado #20615 of February 17, 2011, the countercyclical capital requirement will be activated in case of excessive credit growth that potentially builds up systemic risk. Any changes in the countercyclical capital requirement should be announced one year in advance. So far, the decision framework for the activation of this instrument is still work in progress.

Given that currently available policy instruments have been used to affect the financial cycle, and a new instrument is soon to be implemented, several questions arise. How should these instruments interact? How strongly should they respond to the financial cycle? Should all of them be used for the same purpose? In addition, given the unsettled debate on whether monetary policy should be concerned with financial stability, what would be the recommendation for Brazil?

Our contribution to the normative perspective of macroprudential regulation in Brazil is to use a model that was built and estimated for Brazil to find an optimal combination of macroprudential and monetary policies that are allowed to react to the financial cycle, which in this study is represented by the credit gap. We focus on the (wide) set of macroprudential instruments that have been more intensely used in Brazil to influence credit markets, especially after the financial crisis, namely reserve requirements on time, savings, and demand deposits and risk-weight factors on consumer, commercial, and housing loans, in addition to the new countercyclical capital buffer and monetary policy.

---

[17] For a more detailed overview of reserve requirements in the pre-global-crisis period, see Carvalho and Azevedo (2008).

OPTIMAL POLICY

To search for the optimal monetary and macroprudential policy combination, we use the DSGE model with financial frictions developed by Carvalho and Castro (2015), which incorporates the main features of the Brazilian credit market, including the heavily regulated housing loan market. This model was estimated with Brazilian data spanning the inflation-targeting regime. The model was carefully built to allow for relevant policy analysis at the Central Bank of Brazil and was shown to fit the empirical behavior of several key policy variables.

Consumer loan origination in the model is dependent on lenders' expectations with respect to borrowers' capacity to pay loans with future labor income, with endogenous default. This has been an important feature of the Brazilian credit market. Housing loans use houses as collateral, but indebtedness in this market affects borrowers' available income, affecting their decisions with respect to consumer credit. Housing loan payments have seniority over consumer loans, which explains the very low default rates compared with the consumer credit segment observed in the data. Commercial credit takes capital as collateral and also faces endogenous default.

In addition to financial frictions that aim to represent the Brazilian credit market, the model also incorporates important features regarding Brazil's connection with the rest of the world. The model includes all major balance of payment accounts, with special attention to foreign direct investment (FDI), which has been the most important source through which foreign capital has accumulated in the country. The interaction of FDI with the financial system is indirect. The recipients of FDI flows are entrepreneurs who also fund their projects with bank loans.

The real sector of the economy is modeled in line with the standard DSGE literature. Households are distributed in groups of savers and borrowers, both supplying labor to a continuum of labor unions that operate under monopolistic competition, and consuming goods and housing. Savers have a wider array of possible investment opportunities and are more patient than borrowers, who take out risky loans for consumption and housing. Entrepreneurs manage productive capital. Domestic producers combine capital and labor to produce intermediate goods that will be combined with imported intermediate goods to produce final goods for consumption (private and public), investment, and exports. Price frictions are introduced in both domestic and imported intermediate goods. The model also incorporates capital and housing investment producers. Exporting firms face adjustment costs on quantum changes and take working capital loans from domestic banks. Figure 8.4 shows the structure of the real economy.

The financial sector is composed of a retail money market fund that takes deposits from savers and issues foreign debt to invest in banks' time deposits and government bonds. The banking conglomerate is composed of a continuum of competitive banks that get funding from deposit branches and extend credit to households, entrepreneurs, and export firms through their lending branches. They optimally choose their balance sheet composition, subject to regulatory requirements and several frictions intended to replicate banks' incentives to deal with regulatory constraints. They can accumulate capital by retaining profits, the

Figure 8.4. The Real Sector of the Carvalho and Castro (2015) Open-Economy Dynamic Stochastic General Equilibrium Model with Financial Frictions for Brazil

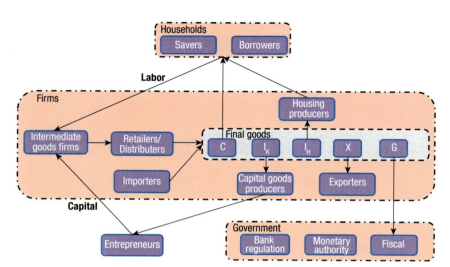

choice variable in the intertemporal dynamic optimization problem of the bank. Figure 8.5 shows the financial structure of the model.

The model has the following macroprudential instruments: reserve requirements on demand, savings and time deposits, risk weights on consumer, commercial and housing loans, tax on credit, and standard minimum capital requirement ratios. Reserve requirements on demand deposits are not remunerated, whereas the other types of reserve requirements are remunerated at exactly the same rate that accrues on bank deposits. In the benchmark (estimated) model, neither macroprudential policies nor monetary policy respond to the credit cycle.

One advantage of analyzing the interaction between monetary and macroprudential policies using DSGE models is that these models can account for the side effects that the use of one policy tool has on the targets of the others.

We use the model to seek an optimal combination of macroprudential and monetary policy rules that may react to the credit gap. For each of the exercises we perform, the optimal policies are obtained by minimizing a loss function composed of the volatility of output, inflation, the policy interest rate, and total credit.[18] The weights on output, inflation, and interest rate volatility in this loss function are obtained in such a way that the minimization of a loss function composed of only these three variables would result in an optimal monetary

---

[18]Credit in the model is composed of consumer, housing, and commercial credit. For all of these credit segments, the model allows for endogenous default due to imperfect monitoring. Consumer credit is extended based on borrowers' future labor income, net of payments related to housing loans. Housing loans are subject to loan-to-value (LTV) constraints that constrain borrowers' available income. Commercial loans are taken by the entrepreneurs and are subject to LTV constraints.

Figure 8.5. The Financial Flows in the Carvalho and Castro (2015) Open-Economy Dynamic Stochastic General Equilibrium Model with Financial Frictions for Brazil

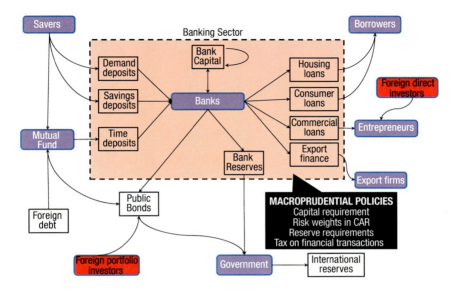

policy rule in the benchmark model, in which the policies do not directly respond to the credit gap. The weight attributed to credit is arbitrary.[19]

Optimization takes into account all sources of fluctuation in the model, an approach that is also adopted by Lambertini, Mendicino, and Punzi (2013). Since the model is estimated, the influence of each shock on the optimal solution will rely on realistic values of the stochastic processes governing the shocks. Several studies address the optimal responses to a few selected shocks, but given the fact that in practice considerable judgment is required to assess the real-time source of a shock driving economic variables, it is equally important to find an optimal rule that could be transparent to and predictable for the public.

The optimal simple monetary and macroprudential policies are allowed to react to the credit gap. Monetary policy follows an augmented, forward looking, Taylor-type rule:

$$R_t = R_{t-1}^\rho \left(R \left(\frac{\pi_{t+3}}{\bar{\pi}_t} \right)^{\gamma_\pi} \left(\frac{y_t}{y} \right)^{\gamma_y} \right)^{1-\rho} \left(\frac{b_{E,t} + b_{C,t} + b_{H,t}}{b_{E,ss} + b_{C,ss} + b_{H,ss}} \right)^\chi \exp(\varepsilon_{R,t}), \qquad (8.1)$$

where $\bar{\pi}_t$ is the nonzero inflation target, y_t is GDP detrended by permanent technology and population growth shocks, $b_{E,t}$, $b_{C,t}$, and $b_{H,t}$ are commercial, consumer, and housing credit gaps from the stationary trend driven by permanent

---

[19] We show below some sensitivity analysis on the impact of different weights on the credit gap in the loss function.

technology and population growth shocks, all variables indexed as "ss" represent steady-state values, y is steady-state detrended GDP, R is the steady-state interest rate, and $\varepsilon_{R,t}$ is a white noise shock.

The capital requirement ratio is augmented with the countercyclical capital buffer:

$$\Gamma_{K,t} = \bar{\Gamma}_{K,t} \Gamma_{CC,t}, \tag{8.2}$$

where the traditional component is centered on the current required ratio (11 percent):

$$\ln\left(\frac{\Gamma_{K,t}}{0.11}\right) = \rho_\Gamma \ln\left(\frac{\Gamma_{K,t-1}}{0.11}\right) + \varepsilon_{\Gamma,t}, \tag{8.3}$$

and the countercyclical capital buffer follows:

$$\ln(\Gamma_{CC,t}) = \rho_{cc} \ln(\Gamma_{CC,t-1}) + (1 - \rho_{cc})\gamma_{CC}\left(\ln\left(\frac{b_{E,t} + b_{C,t} + b_{H,t}}{b_{E,ss} + b_{C,ss} + b_{H,ss}}\right)\right) + \varepsilon_{CC,t}, \tag{8.4}$$

where the steady state value of $\Gamma_{CC,t}$ is 1.

Reserve requirement ratios on demand, savings, and time deposits react to the total credit gap according to the following policy rules:

$$\tau_{D,t} = \rho_D \tau_{D,t-1} + (1 - \rho_D)\tau_{D,SS} + \gamma_D\left(\ln\left(\frac{b_{E,t} + b_{C,t} + b_{H,t}}{b_{E,ss} + b_{C,ss} + b_{H,ss}}\right)\right) + \varepsilon_{D,t}, \tag{8.5}$$

$$\tau_{S,t} = \rho_S \tau_{S,t-1} + (1 - \rho_S)\tau_{S,SS} + \gamma_S\left(\ln\left(\frac{b_{E,t} + b_{C,t} + b_{H,t}}{b_{E,ss} + b_{C,ss} + b_{H,ss}}\right)\right) + \varepsilon_{S,t}, \tag{8.6}$$

$$\tau_{T,t} = \rho_T \tau_{T,t-1} + (1 - \rho_T)\tau_{T,SS} + \gamma_T\left(\ln\left(\frac{b_{E,t} + b_{C,t} + b_{H,t}}{b_{E,ss} + b_{C,ss} + b_{H,ss}}\right)\right) + \varepsilon_{T,t}, \tag{8.7}$$

where $\tau_{D,t}$, $\tau_{S,t}$, and $\tau_{T,t}$ are reserve requirement ratios on demand, savings, and time deposits, $\varepsilon_{D,t}$, $\varepsilon_{S,t}$, and $\varepsilon_{T,t}$ are white noise shocks, and all variables indexed as "ss" represent steady-state values.

Actual capital adequacy is calculated as the ratio of bank capital to risk-weighted assets:

$$CAR_t = \frac{K_{B,t}}{RWA_t}, \tag{8.8}$$

and risk-weighted assets are computed according to

$$RWA_t = \varsigma_{E,t} b_{E,t} + \varsigma_{C,t} b_{C,t} + \varsigma_{H,t} b_{H,t} + \varsigma_{B,t} b_t + v_t, \tag{8.9}$$

where $\varsigma_{E,t}$, $\varsigma_{C,t}$, and $\varsigma_{H,t}$ are risk-weight factors on commercial, consumer, and housing loans, $\varsigma_{B,t}$ is the risk-weight factor on banks' portfolios of liquid assets, which in the model is composed of risk-free public bonds, and hence $\varsigma_{B,t} = 0$. The last term, v_t, is an AR(1) process to account for the share of Brazilian financial system assets that are not formally included in the model.

Risk-weight factors are allowed to react to their specific credit segments, since Carvalho and Castro (2015) show that these instruments have a primary impact on their specific credit segments.[20] They can be expressed according to the following policy rules:

$$\varsigma_{E,t} = \rho_E \varsigma_{E,t-1} + (1-\rho_E)\varsigma_{E,SS} + \gamma_E\left(\ln\left(\frac{b_{E,t}}{b_{E,SS}}\right)\right) + \varepsilon_{E,t}, \quad (8.10)$$

$$\varsigma_{C,t} = \rho_C \varsigma_{C,t-1} + (1-\rho_C)\varsigma_{C,SS} + \gamma_C\left(\ln\left(\frac{b_{C,t}}{b_{C,SS}}\right)\right) + \varepsilon_{C,t}, \quad (8.11)$$

$$\varsigma_{H,t} = \rho_H \varsigma_{H,t-1} + (1-\rho_H)\varsigma_{H,SS} + \gamma_H\left(\ln\left(\frac{b_{H,t}}{b_{H,SS}}\right)\right) + \varepsilon_{H,t}, \quad (8.12)$$

where $\varepsilon_{E,t}$, $\varepsilon_{C,t}$, and $\varepsilon_{H,t}$ are white noise shocks.

We follow Schmitt-Grohé and Uribe (2007) and focus on simple and implementable policy rules. We find the optimal coefficients $\{\rho, \rho_{CC}, \rho_D, \rho_S, \rho_T, \rho_E, \rho_C, \rho_H, \gamma_\pi, \gamma_y, \chi, \gamma_{CC}, \gamma_D, \gamma_S, \gamma_T, \gamma_E, \gamma_B, \gamma_H\}$ of the policy rules in equations (8.1), (8.4), (8.5), (8.6), (8.7), (8.10), (8.11), and (8.12) that minimize the loss function,[21] where all autoregressive parameters are restricted to the (0,1) interval and the policy parameters are unconstrained.

Table 8.2 shows the optimization results for three possible weights for the credit gap in the loss function, considering all policy instruments operating simultaneously. For each weight, we proceed with two types of optimization: one in which we do not constrain the support of the policy parameters and another in which we constrain the reaction of monetary policy to the credit gap to the nonnegative support. Constraining the set of possible solutions for optimal simple rules is common in the literature.[22]

In the constrained solution, we find that, in general, increasing the weight of the credit gap in the loss function increases the volatility of inflation and of the interest rate in the optimal solution, but reduces the volatility of credit and output. The relative magnitude of the former is substantially higher than the latter, implying that increasing the importance attributed to the financial cycle in monetary policy comes with an important cost in terms of the inflation target. In addition, the optimized constrained rules require a very aggressive response of monetary policy to inflation. As the weight of the credit gap in the loss function increases, so does the optimal monetary policy reaction to the output gap, which

---

[20]The volume of housing loans is not very sensitive to its corresponding risk-weight factor. The reason for this is that this market is heavily regulated with respect to both interest rates and funding sources.

[21]We use the Optimal Simple Rule routine in Dynare, which is based on Sims' minimization algorithm. The results that we report here are obtained after testing different initial points and comparing the value of the objective function obtained in each of these trials.

We find the optimal rules given all sources of disturbance estimated in the model of Carvalho and Castro (2015). The rule obtained from the setup that we adopt can be more easily compared with actual rules estimated with all shocks activated.

[22]Schmitt-Grohé and Uribe (2007) is such an example. They constrain the optimal parameter search to a particular set of so called "realistic" values.

TABLE 8.2

Optimal Simple Rules: Comparing Constrained and Unconstrained Optima at Different Credit Gap Weights in the Loss Function

Rules	Reaction Parameters of the Rules	Credit Gap Weight = 0.001		Credit Gap Weight = 0.01		Credit Gap Weight = 0.5	
		Unconstrained Optimum	Constrained Optimum	Unconstrained Optimum	Constrained Optimum	Unconstrained Optimum	Constrained Optimum
Monetary Policy	Coefficient of reaction to inflation	4.44	4.41	4.04	4.04	1.81	4.39
	Coefficient of reaction to output	0.90	0.89	1.72	0.85	2.69	5.95
	Coefficient of reaction to total credit gap	−0.06	0.00	−0.11	0.00	−0.35	0.75
Risk-Weight Factors (RWFs)	Autoregressive coefficient	0.93	0.93	0.93	0.94	0.91	0.93
	RWF of consumer loans: Reaction to consumer credit	0.10	0.12	0.09	0.09	0.27	0.33
	RWF of consumer loans: Autoregressive coefficient	0.99	0.99	0.99	0.99	0.84	0.96
	RWF of commercial loans: Reaction to commercial credit	0.83	0.84	0.84	0.84	−0.93	0.00
	RWF of commercial loans: Autoregressive coefficient	0.29	0.30	0.31	0.31	0.56	0.56
	RWF of housing loans: Reaction to housing credit	0.63	0.62	0.61	0.61	0.49	0.49
	RWF of housing loans: Autoregressive coefficient	0.98	0.98	0.98	0.97	0.00	0.00

(continued)

TABLE 8.2 *(continued)*

Optimal Simple Rules: Comparing Constrained and Unconstrained Optima at Different Credit Gap Weights in the Loss Function

Rules		Reaction Parameters of the Rules	Credit Gap Weight = 0.001		Credit Gap Weight = 0.01		Credit Gap Weight = 0.5	
			Unconstrained Optimum	Constrained Optimum	Unconstrained Optimum	Constrained Optimum	Unconstrained Optimum	Constrained Optimum
Reserve Requirements (RRs)		RR on time deposits:	20.96	20.96	20.96	20.96	20.91	21.07
		Reaction to total credit gap	0.03	0.02	0.00	0.00	0.67	0.98
		RR on time deposits: Autoregressive coefficient						
		RR on demand deposits:	5.02	5.02	5.02	5.02	5.02	5.16
		Reaction to total credit gap	0.00	0.00	0.00	0.00	0.76	0.84
		RR on demand deposits: Autoregressive coefficient						
		RR on savings deposits:	10.97	10.96	10.96	10.96	10.87	11.26
		Reaction to total credit gap	0.89	0.95	0.90	0.91	0.27	0.48
		RR on savings deposits: Autoregressive coefficient						
Countercyclical Capital Buffer (CCB)		Autoregressive coefficient	0.46	0.45	0.44	0.44	0.46	0.48
		Reaction to total credit gap	3.11	3.11	3.11	3.11	3.10	10.21
		Value of the objective function	0.00107	0.00108	0.00189	0.00194	0.00404	0.00462
		Variation coefficient	0.013	0.013	0.015	0.015	0.025	0.024
		Inflation	0.013		0.015	0.015	0.025	0.024
		Interest rate	0.012	0.012	0.014	0.014	0.023	0.024
		Output	0.057	0.056	0.052	0.050	0.047	0.038
		Credit-to-GDP	0.075	0.076	0.069	0.070	0.046	0.054

is an indirect channel to affect borrowers' incentives to get loans. Only with very large weights of the credit gap is it optimal for monetary policy to react to the credit gap within the constrained solutions. For low values of the weight associated with the credit gap, the constrained solutions achieve losses that are very close to the unconstrained solutions, suggesting some flatness in this region of constrained objective function. With respect to unconstrained solutions, in all of them the optimal reaction of monetary policy to the credit gap is found to be negative, somehow counterbalanced by an increase in the reaction to output. Although this result is not unprecedented in the literature (Faia and Monacelli 2007),[23] it is unlikely that the monetary policymaker will implement such a response. In addition, as mentioned earlier, the gains from adopting these policy combinations are only relevant when the weight of the credit gap in the loss function is very high. Hence, we shall restrict our analysis to the solutions where the monetary policy reaction to the credit gap is nonnegative.

In Brazil, changes in minimum capital requirement ratios have to be authorized by the National Monetary Council (CMN), which is composed of not only the Central Bank of Brazil's governor, but also the Minister of Finance and the Minister of Budget and Planning. With the implementation of Basel III, the countercyclical capital buffer can be set by the central bank, but needs to be announced 12 months in advance of its implementation. This constraint does not exist for reserve requirements or risk-weight factors. Hence, timely policy reactions to imbalances in the financial system are easier to be implemented through alternative policy instruments than with minimum capital requirements or even the countercyclical buffer.

Given the fact that a number of macroprudential instruments are available to the Brazilian central bank and can be more easily and immediately changed than capital requirements, we investigate whether optimal simple rules that make up only subsets of the available macroprudential tools can perform as well as the entire optimal set of macroprudential policy rules that react to the credit gap.

The following subsets are analyzed: (1) monetary policy with all macroprudential instruments; (2) monetary policy and the countercyclical capital buffer; (3) monetary policy, risk-weight factors, and reserve requirements; (4) monetary policy, the countercyclical capital buffer, and risk-weight factors; (5) monetary policy and risk-weight factors; (6) monetary policy and reserve requirements; and (7) all of the former combinations except for monetary policy.

Table 8.3 shows the optimum for each subset of optimal policy rules that include monetary policy. In most optimized combinations, the solution is pushed towards a very aggressive response of monetary policy to inflation and to output. The most important result in this exercise is that the subset of policies that includes monetary policy, risk-weight factors, and reserve requirements achieves almost the same loss as that obtained from the complete set of rules.

---

[23]Faia and Monacelli (2007) find, in a model with agency costs and nominal frictions, that monetary policy should react to increases in the asset price by lowering the nominal interest rate.

However, the optimal responses of monetary policy to inflation and output obtained in this exercise are very far from the values usually obtained in Taylor rule estimations using actual data. Hence, we proceed with a search for optimal simple rules that take these traditional parameters of the monetary policy as given, setting them according to the mode of the posterior distribution of the parameters estimated in Carvalho and Castro (2015). In other words, we seek to find simple and optimal macroprudential rules (reserve requirements, risk-weight factors, and countercyclical capital buffers) that can react to the credit gap, also allowing for the reaction coefficient of monetary policy to the credit gap to be obtained optimally.

Table 8.4 shows the results of this exercise. For the constrained optimal simple rules, we find that some subsets of macroprudential policy can perform almost as well as the complete set. The following subsets yield losses that are merely about 2 percent higher than the one with the complete set: (1) reserve requirements and the countercyclical capital buffer; (2) monetary policy reaction to the credit gap together with reserve requirements; and (3) monetary policy reaction to the credit gap together with risk-weight factors and reserve requirements. The combination of monetary policy, reserve requirements, and risk-weight factors reacting together to the credit gap requires a milder countercyclical response of each instrument. If only reserve requirements are allowed to help monetary policy react to the financial cycle, the optimal response of each of these instruments to the credit gap becomes very aggressive. Instead, if the countercyclical capital buffer is used together with reserve requirements and monetary policy, the latter loses its importance to directly target the credit cycle.

Table 8.5 shows the subsets of optimal simple macroprudential rules obtained when we do not include the possibility that monetary policy reacts to the credit gap. In this case, most subsets achieve very similar losses. However, the loss is the highest when only risk-weight factors are allowed to react to the credit gap.

Reserve requirements and risk-weight factors have actually been used on a number of occasions for macroprudential purposes in Brazil, especially after the financial crisis, and some of them countercyclically. Our results corroborate the perception that the direction of these policies can be used to help correct the buildup of risks in the Brazilian financial system with an efficiency to minimize the volatility of targeted macroeconomic variables similar to that of the combination with countercyclical capital. In addition, the other macroprudential instruments are easier to implement and have targeted impact on specific variables.

IMPULSE RESPONSES UNDER DIFFERENT RULES

Next, we compare the dynamic responses of the model under four different combinations of policy rules. In the first ("Benchmark"), the policy rules do not react to credit, and the model is exactly the one estimated in Carvalho and Castro (2015). The second combination is composed of optimal simple rules for the countercyclical capital buffer, reserve requirements, risk-weight factors, and monetary policy (all parameters in the augmented Taylor rule are included in the

TABLE 8.3

Optimal Simple Rules: Comparing Constrained Optima Using Different Subsets of Policy Rules for a Loss Function Credit-Gap Weight of 0.001

Rules	Reaction Parameters of the Rules	Complete Set: Monetary Policy & CCB & RR & RWF[1]	Monetary Policy & CC & RWF	Monetary Policy & CC	Monetary Policy & CC & RR	Monetary Policy & RWF & RR	Monetary Policy & RWF	Monetary Policy & RR
Monetary Policy	Coefficient of reaction to inflation	4.41	2.86	4.40	4.87	5.42	6.73	6.73
	Coefficient of reaction to output	0.89	0.40	0.88	1.63	1.30	0.42	1.15
	Coefficient of reaction to total credit gap	0.00	1.00	0.00	0.10	0.01	0.00	0.08
	Autoregressive coefficient	0.93	0.90	0.93	0.95	0.95	0.94	0.95
Risk-Weight Factors (RWFs)	Reaction to consumer	0.12	1.24			1.20	1.51	
	RWF of consumer loans: Autoregressive coefficient	0.99	0.97			0.92	0.96	
	RWF of commercial loans: Reaction to commercial credit	0.84	0.90			0.56	7.64	
	RWF of commercial loans: Autoregressive coefficient	0.30	0.96			0.93	0.72	
	RWF of housing loans: Reaction to housing credit	0.62	0.22			0.07	0.18	
	RWF of housing loans: Autoregressive coefficient	0.98	0.95			0.98	0.89	

(continued)

TABLE 8.3 (continued)

Optimal Simple Rules: Comparing Constrained Optima Using Different Subsets of Policy Rules for a Loss Function Credit-Gap Weight of 0.001

Rules	Reaction Parameters of the Rules	Complete Set: Monetary Policy & CCB & RR & RWF[1]	Monetary Policy & CC & RWF	Monetary Policy & CC	Monetary Policy & CC & RR	Monetary Policy & RWF & RR	Monetary Policy & RWF	Monetary Policy & RR
Reserve Requirements (RRs)	Reaction to total credit gap	20.96			16.49	7.38		22.01
	RR on time deposits:							
	Autoregressive coefficient	0.02			0.99	0.99		0.00
	RR on demand deposits:							
	Reaction to total credit gap	5.02			1.34	0.64		0.21
	RR on demand deposits:							
	Autoregressive coefficient	0.00			0.45	0.89		0.94
	RR on savings deposits:							
	Reaction to total credit gap	10.96			7.80	3.42		33.83
	RR on savings deposits:							
	Autoregressive coefficient	0.95			0.99	0.00		0.99
Countercyclical Capital Buffer (CCB)	Autoregressive coefficient	0.45	0.50	0.00	0.51			
	Reaction to total credit gap	3.11	0.16	13.76	0.29			
	Objective	0.00108	0.00149	0.00126	0.00114	0.00108	0.00140	0.00116
	Variation coefficient	0.013	0.013	0.013	0.014	0.013	0.011	0.012
	Inflation							
	Interest rate	0.012	0.013	0.012	0.013	0.012	0.012	0.012
	Output	0.056	0.062	0.061	0.055	0.055	0.064	0.062
	Credit-to-GDP	0.076	0.147	0.104	0.076	0.081	0.143	0.082

TABLE 8.4

Optimal Simple Rules: Comparing Constrained Optima Using Different Subsets of Policy Rules for a Loss Function Credit-Gap Weight of 0.001 and for a Given Monetary Policy Reaction to Inflation and Output

Rules	Reaction Parameters of the Rules	Monetary Policy & RR & RWF & CCB	Monetary Policy & RWF & CCB	Monetary Policy & RWF & RR	Monetary Policy & RR & CCB	Monetary Policy & RR	Monetary Policy & RWF
Monetary Policy	Coefficient of reaction to total credit gap	0.00	0.00	0.01	0.00	0.20	0.00
Risk-Weight Factors (RWFs)	RWF of consumer loans:	0.65	2.32	0.39			8.06
	Reaction to consumer credit						
	RWF of consumer loans: Autoregressive coefficient	0.96	0.93	0.99			0.80
	RWF of commercial loans: Reaction to commercial credit	0.30	3.73	0.23			16.75
	RWF of commercial loans: Autoregressive coefficient	0.68	0.99	0.73			0.90
	RWF of housing loans: Reaction to housing credit	0.07	0.26	0.04			90.30
	RWF of housing loans: Autoregressive coefficient	0.71	0.95	0.99			0.13
Reserve Requirements (RRs)	RR on time deposits:	4.39		2.35	17.42	66.32	
	Reaction to total credit gap						
	RR on time deposits:	0.98		0.73		0.94	
	Autoregressive coefficient						
	RR on demand deposits:	0.36		0.18		0.26	
	Reaction to total credit gap						
	RR on demand deposits:	0.85		0.73		0.87	
	Autoregressive coefficient						
	RR on savings deposits:	1.99		1.11		1.66	
	Reaction to total credit gap						
	RR on savings deposits:	0.12		0.73		0.59	
	Autoregressive coefficient						
Countercyclical Capital Buffer (CCB)	CCB:	0.50	0.50		0.50		
	Autoregressive coefficient						
	CCB:	0.11	0.29		0.05		
	Reaction to total credit gap						
	Objective	0.00138	0.00167	0.00141	0.00141	0.00141	0.00152

(continued)

TABLE 8.4 (continued)

Optimal Simple Rules: Comparing Constrained Optima Using Different Subsets of Policy Rules for a Loss Function Credit-Gap Weight of 0.001 and for a Given Monetary Policy Reaction to Inflation and Output

Rules	Reaction Parameters of the Rules	Monetary Policy & RR & RWF & CCB	Monetary Policy & RWF & CCB	Monetary Policy & RWF & RR	Monetary Policy & RR & CCB	Monetary Policy & RR	Monetary Policy & RWF
	Variation coefficient						
	Inflation	0.015	0.015	0.015	0.015	0.015	0.015
	Interest rate	0.015	0.015	0.015	0.015	0.015	0.015
	Output	0.060	0.064	0.061	0.062	0.063	0.061
	Credit-to-GDP	0.087	0.142	0.092	0.081	0.080	0.122

Note: In this exercise, monetary policy reaction to inflation and output is set according to the model estimated in Carvalho and Castro (2015), that is, $\rho = 0.829$, $\gamma_\pi = 1.961$, and $\gamma_y = 0.185$.

TABLE 8.5

Optimal Simple Rules: Comparing Constrained Optima of Subsets of Policy Rules for a Given Monetary Policy Rule and a Loss Function Credit-Gap Weight of 0.001

Rules	Reaction Parameters of the Rules	RR & RWF & CCB	RWF & CCB	RWF & RR	RR & CCB	RR	RWF
Risk-Weight Factors (RWFs)	RWF of consumer loans: Reaction to consumer credit	0.11	0.17	0.12			3.31
	RWF of consumer loans: Autoregressive coefficient	0.99	0.99	0.99			0.91
	RWF of commercial loans: Reaction to commercial credit	0.73	−0.04	0.38			5.28
	RWF of commercial loans: Autoregressive coefficient	0.71	0.99	0.85			0.99
	RWF of housing loans: Reaction to housing credit	0.37	0.15	0.03			0.36
	RWF of housing loans: Autoregressive coefficient	0.99	0.99	0.99			0.95
Reserve Requirements (RRs)	RR on time deposits: Reaction to total credit gap	5.23		2.68	20.68	17.42	
	RR on time deposits: Autoregressive coefficient	0.98		0.99	0.96	0.94	
	RR on demand deposits: Reaction to total credit gap	0.52		0.27	2.03	0.26	
	RR on demand deposits: Autoregressive coefficient	0.84		0.88	0.45	0.60	
	RR on savings deposits: Reaction to total credit gap	2.64		1.33	10.11	1.64	
	RR on savings deposits: Autoregressive coefficient	0.38		0.89	0.33	0.49	
Countercyclical Capital Buffer (CCB)	Autoregressive coefficient	0.50	0.50		0.51		
	Reaction to total credit gap	0.05	25.58		0.23		
	Objective	0.00136	0.00136	0.00138	0.00140	0.00141	0.00167
Variation coefficient	Inflation	0.015	0.015	0.015	0.015	0.015	0.015
	Interest rate	0.015	0.015	0.015	0.015	0.015	0.015
	Output	0.059	0.060	0.059	0.062	0.062	0.064
	Credit-to-GDP	0.085	0.084	0.089	0.080	0.081	0.141

Note: In this exercise, we set the monetary policy parameters according to the model estimated in Carvalho and Castro (2015), that is, $\rho = 0.829$, $\gamma_\pi = 1.961$, $\gamma_y = 0.185$, and $\chi = 0$.

optimization but are constrained to the nonnegative support, and the autoregressive parameters are constrained to the 0–1 interval). The third combination refers to optimal simple rules for the countercyclical capital buffer, risk-weight factors, and reserve requirements, taking all monetary policy parameters as given and set at the mode of the posterior estimated in Carvalho and Castro (2015). The last combination is composed of optimal simple rules for risk-weight factors and reserve requirements, also taking all monetary policy parameters as given, and set at the mode of the posterior estimated in Carvalho and Castro (2015). As mentioned earlier, the complete set of optimal simple rules that includes monetary policy requires a very aggressive response to inflation.

Figures 8.6 and 8.7 focus on exogenous shocks originating in the banking sector. In Figure 8.6, the model is perturbed by a negative shock to bank capital, which is close in meaning to what Gertler, Kiyotaki, and Queralto (2012) refer to as a "crisis shock." This shock simulates, for instance, the impact of a drop in bank capital due to losses that negatively affect banks' net worth. In Figure 8.7, the model is shocked with a drop in banks' preference for liquidity, which simulates a situation in which banks reduce their risk aversion and try to increase their exposure to the credit risk. This would result in a relaxation in credit origination conditions. For both shocks, the responses under countercyclical macroprudential policy rules are strikingly different from those obtained from the benchmark model. The optimal policies sharply reduce the volatility of total credit, and the dynamics of the main economic variables under subsets of active policy rules are very close to the complete set of active rules. The main difference stands in the banks' decisions concerning balance sheet locations and dividend distribution. For the bank capital shock, the subsets of optimal policies usually generate stronger responses in bank variables. With respect to the shock on bank liquidity preferences, since the complete policy combination requires a very strong response of reserve requirements to credit conditions, bank liquidity is more severely affected than in the case of subsets of optimal policy rules. Dividend distribution is also more strongly impacted in the case of the complete set.

The monetary policy shock makes it more clear how aggressive the complete set of optimal simple rules is in terms of its impact on the real economy (Figure 8.8). To stabilize credit under a monetary policy shock, the complete set of optimal simple rules requires a more sluggish response of interest rates, substantially affecting output, consumption, labor market conditions, and housing investment. The subset of optimal policies does almost as well as the complete set in stabilizing credit, but it also has the potential to stabilize real economy variables. In fact, the subsets of optimal simple rules improve the stabilization of the real economy compared to the benchmark model, a feature that cannot be observed in the complete set.

Figures 8.9 to 8.12 compare the model dynamics after external shocks. In the estimated benchmark model, a drop in world output has a recessionary impact on the domestic economy, with a significant reduction in investment and consumption. An increase in foreign direct investment inflows has an expansionary impact on domestic credit, but the impact on inflation and output is contractionary

Figure 8.6. Comparing Combinations of Optimal Simple Macroprudential and Monetary Policy Rules: Negative Shock to Bank Capital—10 Percent Drop on Impact

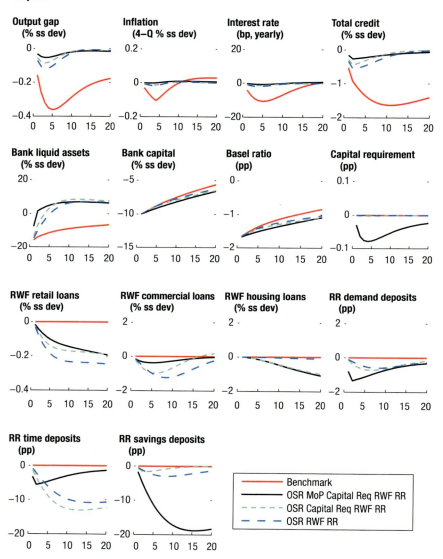

Note: bp = basis points; CapitalReq = capital requirements; MoP = monetary policy; OSR = optimal simple rules; pp = percentage points; RR = reserve requirements; RWF = risk-weight factors; ss dev = % change from the steady trend.

Figure 8.7. Comparing Combinations of Optimal Simple Macroprudential and Monetary Policy Rules: Bank Liquidity Preference Shock—65 Percent Drop on Impact

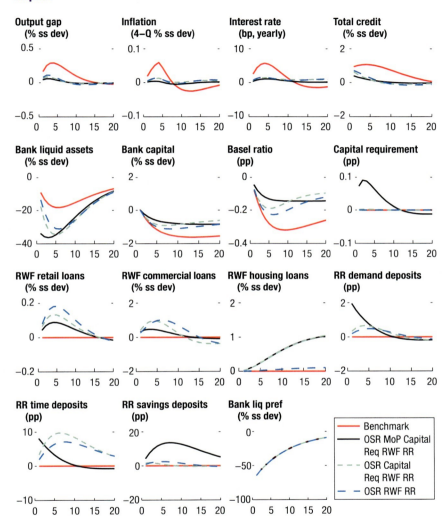

Note: bp = basis points; CapitalReq = capital requirements; MoP = monetary policy; OSR = optimal simple rules; pp = percentage points; RR = reserve requirements; RWF = risk-weight factors; ss dev = % change from the steady trend.

Figure 8.8. Comparing Combinations of Optimal Simple Macroprudential and Monetary Policy Rules: Monetary Policy Shock—100 Basis Point Increase on Impact

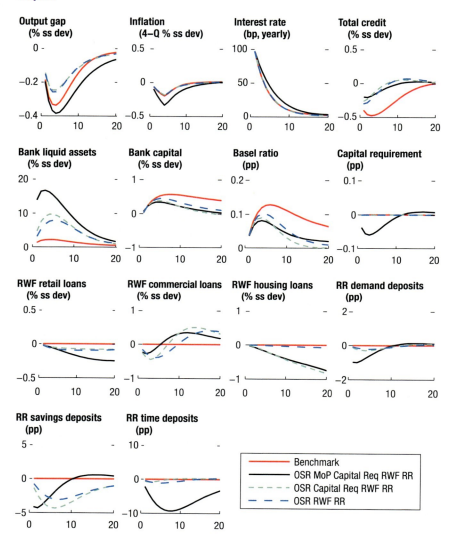

Note: bp = basis points; CapitalReq = capital requirements; MoP = monetary policy; OSR = optimal simple rules; pp = percentage points; RR = reserve requirements; RWF = risk-weight factors; ss dev = % change from the steady trend

Figure 8.9. Comparing Combinations of Optimal Simple Macroprudential and Monetary Policy Rules: Shock to World Output—1 Percent Drop

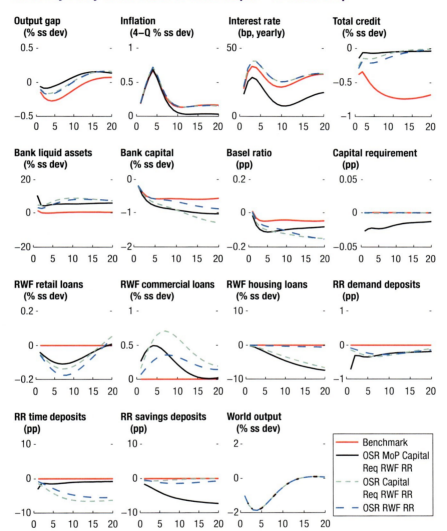

Note: bp = basis points; CapitalReq = capital requirements; MoP = monetary policy; OSR = optimal simple rules; pp = percentage points; RR = reserve requirements; RWF = risk-weight factors; ss dev = % change from the steady trend.

Figure 8.10. Comparing Combinations of Optimal Simple Macroprudential and Monetary Policy Rules: Shock to Foreign Direct Investment Flows—1 Percentage Point Increase

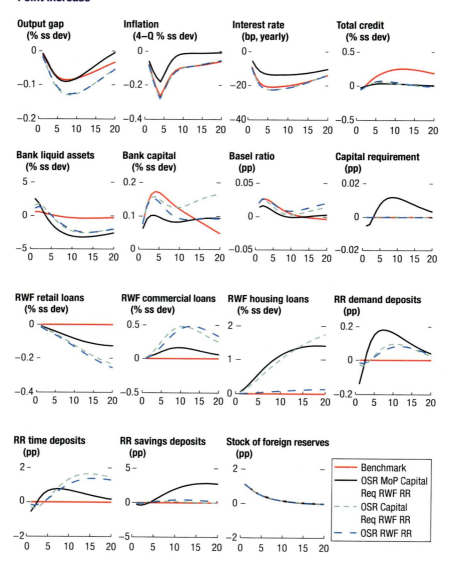

Note: bp = basis points; CapitalReq = capital requirements; MoP = monetary policy; OSR = optimal simple rules; pp = percentage points; RR = reserve requirements; RWF = risk-weight factors; ss dev = % change from the steady trend.

Figure 8.11. Comparing Combinations of Optimal Simple Macroprudential and Monetary Policy Rules: Shock to Foreign Interest Rates—100 Basis Point Drop

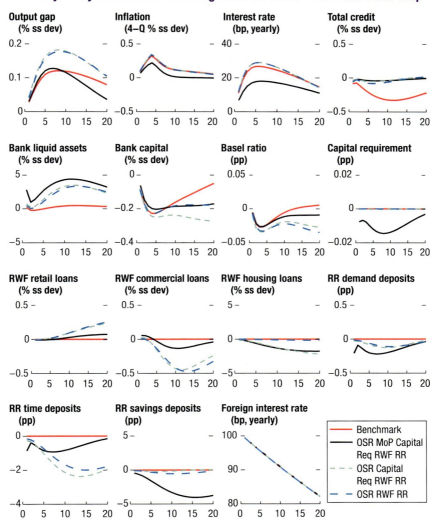

Note: bp = basis points; CapitalReq = capital requirements; MoP = monetary policy; OSR = optimal simple rules; pp = percentage points; RR = reserve requirements; RWF = risk-weight factors; ss dev = % change from the steady trend.

Figure 8.12. Comparing Combinations of Optimal Simple Macroprudential and Monetary Policy Rules: Shock to Export Prices—20 Percent Increase

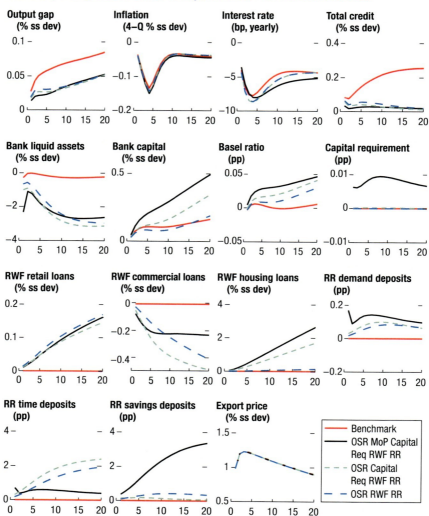

Note: bp = basis points; CapitalReq = capital requirements; MoP = monetary policy; OSR = optimal simple rules; pp = percentage points; RR = reserve requirements; RWF = risk-weight factors; ss dev = % change from the steady trend.

given the appreciation of the domestic currency. An increase in the world interest rate leads to a depreciation of the exchange rate, which calls for a response of monetary policy. A commodity price boom, which in the model is represented by a shock to export prices,[24] has an expansionary impact on credit, through the increase in available income and a surge in investment. In all cases, the optimal simple rules stabilize credit, and the impact of each subset of rules on real economy variables depends on the credit segment that is most significantly affected by each policy combination. The main difference in the dynamic responses of the model to different subsets of optimal policies occurs for banks' balance sheet variables, given that each subset requires a different reaction from each macroprudential instrument, affecting banks' incentives distinctly.

In the benchmark model of Carvalho and Castro (2015), macroprudential policy instruments that do not react to economic or financial cycles are more effective in stabilizing the credit-to-GDP ratio when shocks originate in the financial system. In fact, each instrument will have a potential niche where its impact is more pronounced. In general, macroprudential policies have a greater impact on financial variables, whereas monetary policy has a stronger effect on real variables, except for the case of housing loans, which are strongly influenced by monetary policy. Capital requirements have a strong impact on capital investment given the sensitivity of the value of capital to available funding from bank loans. Risk-weight factors have a substantial impact on actual capital adequacy ratios. Reserve requirements have the most important impact on bank liquidity.

THE IMPACT OF MACROPRUDENTIAL POLICY ANNOUNCEMENTS ON INFLATION EXPECTATIONS

A strand in the literature advocates that monetary policy can exacerbate risks to financial stability. In the case of Brazil, very few studies have investigated this risk-taking channel. Tavares, Montes, and Guillén (2013) study the impact of monetary policy on bank risk perception, associating the stance of monetary policy with lending spreads and on insurance engaged by borrowers against credit default. They find that contractionary monetary policy induces banks to use more insurance (the reverse is true in the case of expansionary monetary policy). The same is observed for reserve requirements, which also affect the risk-taking behavior of banks through insurance. Montes and Peixoto (2012) also find a positive relation between bank risk perception and the stance of monetary policy in Brazil.

To the best of our knowledge, the reverse channel has not been explored, especially for Brazil. Macroprudential policy announcements can have an impact on variables that are targeted by the monetary authority, and, depending on the coordination of business and financial cycles, macroprudential policy announcements can have an impact on the anchoring of inflation expectations.

---

[24] The export sector is modeled in accordance with a commodity-based economy.

According to the IMF (2013), monetary and macroprudential policies were complementary in Brazil during the postcrisis period. Both were used countercyclically, leaning against the business and the financial cycle, which were synchronized during the period analyzed. In more recent times, however, this synchronization has been challenged, and while monetary policy became more contractionary given inflationary pressures, some macroprudential measures were implemented with the purpose of easing credit conditions in specific segments.

To investigate whether macroprudential policy announcements had a significant impact on the anchoring of inflation expectations in Brazil, we select events when macroprudential policy was changed by explicitly targeting credit-related variables and assess their impact on the gap of inflation expectations from the inflation target.[25] Table 8.6 lists the events that classify under this category.

To assess the impact of the events on inflation expectations in Brazil, we use a panel of 12-month-ahead private inflation forecasts, surveyed on a daily basis by the Central Bank of Brazil's Investor Relations Office from 2011 to 2014. To control for other factors influencing inflation expectations, we follow Carvalho and Minella (2012) by estimating an expectations-formation-type rule. The rule is further augmented to account for the events under investigation here and includes the addition of dummy controls for the week of monetary policy meetings (and the preceding week) and for times when the consensus forecast was above the upper bound of the inflation target.[26] The estimated equation is:

$$\hat{\pi}_{i,t}^{e,12m} = \alpha + \beta_1 \hat{\pi}_{i,t-5}^{e,12m} + \beta_2 \hat{\pi}_{median,t-5}^{e,12m} + \beta_3 Std_{t-5}^{e,12m} + \beta_4 \Delta_{20} FX_{t-3}$$
$$+ \beta_5 \Delta_{20} Embi_{t-3} + \beta_6 \Delta_{20} Selic_{t-3} + \beta_7 (\pi_{t-3} - \pi_{t-4})$$
$$+ \beta_8 D_{copom,t} + \beta_9 D_{median,t} + \sum_i \beta_{10,i} D_{event,i,t} + u_{i,t}, \qquad (8.13)$$

where t corresponds to each day in the sample, and the variables are described as follows:

- $\hat{\pi}_{i,t}^{e,12m}$ is the gap between the 12-month-ahead inflation forecast for each participant i and the center of the inflation target band;
- $\hat{\pi}_{median,t}^{e,12m}$ is the gap between the median of 12-month-ahead inflation forecasts and the center of the inflation target band;
- $Std_t^{e,12m}$ is the standard deviation of 12-month-ahead inflation forecasts surveyed on a daily basis by the Central Bank of Brazil's Investor Relations Office;
- $\Delta_{20} FX_t$ is the change in the BRL/US$ daily quote over the past 20 days;
- $\Delta_{20} Embi_t$ is the change in JP Morgan's EMBI Brazil over the past 20 days;
- $\Delta_{20} Selic_t$ is the change in the annualized monetary policy (SELIC) rate over the past 20 days;

---

[25] We use the upper bound of the inflation target interval and not the midpoint target.

[26] The dummy for times when inflation expectations exceeded the upper inflation target controls for possible regime changes in the dynamics of inflation expectations.

TABLE 8.6

Macroprudential Policy Events

Event Number	Event Window	Event Description	Authors' Interpretation of the Expected Impact on Credit	Current Nominal Policy Interest Rate Cycle	Time Span since Last Change in Policy Direction	Previous Nominal Policy Interest Rate Cycle
1	19-aug-2014 to 22-aug-2014	Reduces RWF of long-term retail credit operations (Circular 3714)	Increase	Stability	4 months	Increase
2	24-jul-2014 to 28-jul-2014	Changes the compliance terms of reserve requirements on time deposits by introducing optional compliance with credit origination. Increases the set of institutions that can partially comply with reserve requirements on demand deposits with credit origination related to a specific development program (Circular 3712)	Increase			
3	23-jun-2014 to 25-jun-2014	Changes the calculation of risk-weight factors for retail loans (Circular 3711)	Increase	Stability	3 months	Increase
		Postpones the implementation of a stricter mandatory allocation of funds to rural credit (Resolução 4336) and gives more flexibility to compliance with mandatory rural credit originations (Resolução 4348)	Increase	Stability	2 months	Increase
4	30-sep-2013 to 2-oct-2013	Increases the maximum value of real estate authorized to be financed with lower interest rates. Sets loan-to-value caps on housing loans (Resolução 4271)	Ambiguous	Increase	5 months	Stability
5	9-aug-2013 to 13-aug-2013	Sets risk-weight factors on rural credit inversely related to lending rates (Resolução 4259)	Increase	Increase	4 months	Stability
		Changes the time window for computing the incidence base of mandatory allocation of demand deposits on microcredit originations (Resolução 4242)	Neutral			

(continued)

TABLE 8.6 (continued)

Macroprudential Policy Events

Event Number	Event Window	Event Description	Authors' Interpretation of the Expected Impact on Credit	Current Nominal Policy Interest Rate Cycle	Time Span since Last Change in Policy Direction	Previous Nominal Policy Interest Rate Cycle
6	2-jul-2013 to 4-jul-2013	Speeds up the schedule for normalization of the remuneration of reserve requirements on time deposits (the previous regulation reduced the remuneration of required reserves on time deposits if banks did not purchase credit portfolios of small financial institutions) (Circular 3660)	Reduction	Increase	3 months	Stability
7	19-jun-2013 to 21-jun-2013	Changes several regulatory pieces concerning mandatory rural credit origination (Resoluções 4233, 4234 and 4235)	Neutral	Increase	2 months	Stability
8	28-feb-2013 to 4-mar-2013	Implements Basle 3	Neutral	Stability	4 months	Reduction
9	27-dec-2012 to 2-jan-2013	Changes the compliance terms of reserve requirements on demand deposits by introducing optional compliance with credit origination, with a potential impact of R$15 billion in new credit origination (Circular 3622)	Increase	Stability	2 months	Reduction
10	14-sep-2012 to 17-sep-2012	Cancels additional reserve requirements on time deposits. Reduces the reserve requirement ratio on time deposits (Circular 3609)	Increase	Reduction	12 months	Increase
11	23-aug-2012 to 27-aug-2012	Changes required allocation of funds to rural loans, giving incentives for credit originations at low lending rates (Resolução 4127). Adds flexibility to the requirements for issuing long-term bank instruments (Letra Financeira) (Resolução 4123)	Increase	Reduction	11 months	Increase
12	28-jun-2012 to 2-jul-2012	Increases the set of institutions allowed to obtain export credit (Circular 3604). Increases mandatory allocation of demand deposits on rural credit (Resolução 4096) and reduces additional resere requirements on demand deposits (Circular 3603)	Increase	Reduction	9 months	Increase

(continued)

TABLE 8.6 *(continued)*

Macroprudential Policy Events

Event Number	Event Window	Event Description	Authors' Interpretation of the Expected Impact on Credit	Current Nominal Policy Interest Rate Cycle	Time Span since Last Change in Policy Direction	Previous Nominal Policy Interest Rate Cycle
13	21-may-2012 to 23-may-2012	Increase the set of credit operations allowed to be used as compliance with resere requirements on time deposits (Circular 3594). Requires the registry of collateral on housing and vehicle loans in authorized asset exchange systems.	Increase	Reduction	8 months	Increase
14	10-feb-2012 to 14-feb-2012	Increases the set of financial institutions allowed to partly comply with traditional and additional reserve requirements on time deposits with purchases of credit portfolios from other institutions and other operations. Increases the set of institutions exempted from these reserve requirements (Circular 3576)	Increase	Reduction	5 months	Increase

- $D_{copom,t}$ takes the value 1 on the days included in the following interval: the Friday immediately preceding a monetary policy meeting and the Monday immediately following it. For all other days, it takes the value 0;
- $D_{median,t}$ takes the value 1 on the days when the median of 12-month-ahead inflation forecasts are above the upper bound of the inflation target. For all other days, it takes the value 0;
- $D_{event,i,t}$ takes the value 1 in the event of window days according to Table 8.2. For all other days, it takes the value 0.

We perform a fixed effects panel regression applying a covariance matrix that is robust to heteroscedasticity, autocorrelation with moving average (MA)–type errors, and cross-sectionally dependent errors[27]. Since forecasts are made for 12 months ahead, the MA structure duly considers this time span. Table 8.7 shows the regression results, where "Forecast Gap" corresponds to the variable $\pi^{e,12m}_{i,t}$ in equation (8.13), "Median Gap" corresponds to the variable $\tilde{\pi}^{e,12m}_{median,t}$, and "Panel std" corresponds to the variable $Std^{e,12m}_t$.

We find that on six different occasions, macroprudential policy announcements had an impact on the gap between inflation expectations and the inflation target. Event numbers 1, 4, 5, and 9 contributed to increase the gap. Event number 1 was not particularly intended to increase credit, but the movement was in the direction of relaxing credit constraints. In event number 4, while the increase in the maximum value of the real estate that could be financed with more favorable rates would contribute to expanding credit, the implementation of a loan-to-value cap could have the opposite effect on credit. In any case, market participants seem to have interpreted it as inflationary. Event number 9 was specifically intended to stimulate credit origination through changes in the way banks could comply with reserve requirements on demand deposits. Event numbers 8 and 12 contributed to reducing the gap between inflation expectations and the inflation target. Event number 8 corresponded to the announcement of the implementation of Basel III. Event number 12 did not have an intention of reducing credit. Hence, the negative sign obtained in the estimation seems at odds with the intention of the event.

An alternative specification was tested, including shorter lags of the controlling variables, and event numbers 4, 5 and 9 remained significant,[28] suggesting that these events had an important impact on the anchoring of inflation expectations.

To test whether the cycle of monetary policy matters for the impact of macroprudential announcements on inflation expectations, we perform the same regression, except that, instead of using individual events, we separate those that would likely have an expansionary impact on credit into two groups: Group A is composed of events that happened when the cycle of monetary policy was

---

[27] The routine is implemented in Stata through the "xtivreg2" command, which applies the covariance matrix estimator of Driscoll and Kraay (1998).

[28] Since the panel used in the estimation is highly unbalanced, changing the lag structure of the regressors can have important implications for the number of observations actually used in the estimation.

TABLE 8.7

Panel Regression Results: Single Events

Forecast Gap	Robust Coeff.	Std. Err.	z	P > z	[95% Conf. Interval]	Forecast Gap
Forecast gap (−20)	0.657	0.012	53.90	0.000***	0.633	0.681
Median gap (−20)	0.109	0.082	1.32	0.187	−0.053	0.270
Panel std (−5)	0.458	0.247	1.86	0.064*	−0.026	0.942
Δ FX (−5)	0.496	0.214	2.31	0.021**	0.076	0.916
Δ π (−5)	0.876	0.120	7.29	0.000***	0.640	1.112
Δ Embi (−5)	0.109	0.129	0.85	0.398	−0.144	0.362
Δ R (−5)	0.577	0.453	1.27	0.203	−0.311	1.464
Dummy: COPOM week	−0.004	0.018	−0.20	0.839	−0.038	0.031
Dummy: Median above target	0.250	0.081	3.10	0.002***	0.092	0.408
Dummy: event 1	0.212	0.027	7.84	0.000***	0.159	0.265
Dummy: event 2	−0.032	0.038	−0.86	0.392	−0.106	0.042
Dummy: event 3	0.005	0.043	0.12	0.908	−0.078	0.088
Dummy: event 4	0.177	0.068	2.60	0.009***	0.043	0.311
Dummy: event 5	0.203	0.048	4.24	0.000***	0.109	0.298
Dummy: event 6	−0.039	0.046	−0.85	0.395	−0.129	0.051
Dummy: event 7	−0.040	0.047	−0.84	0.399	−0.133	0.053
Dummy: event 8	−0.253	0.037	−6.77	0.000***	−0.326	−0.180
Dummy: event 9	0.226	0.044	5.10	0.000***	0.139	0.313
Dummy: event 10	−0.000	0.026	−0.01	0.994	−0.051	0.051
Dummy: event 11	0.053	0.036	1.46	0.144	−0.018	0.123
Dummy: event 12	−0.150	0.016	−9.14	0.000***	−0.182	−0.118
Dummy: event 13	−0.033	0.033	−0.99	0.324	−0.098	0.032
Dummy: event 14	0.025	0.040	0.61	0.544	−0.055	0.104

Total (centered) SS = 18,196.85
Total (uncentered) SS = 18,196.85
Residual SS = 5,006.06
Number of observations = 68,722
Number of groups = 138
$F(23,1020) = 7,659.44$
Prob > F = 0.0000
Centered R^2 = 0.725
Uncentered R^2 = 0.725
Root MSE = 0.27

Note: Fixed-effects estimation. Statistics robust to heteroskedasticity and time clustering and kernel-robust to common correlated disturbances (Driscoll and Kraay 1998). Kernel = Bartlett; bandwidth = 242 days. SS = steady state.
*$p < .05$; **$p < .01$; ***$p < .001$.

contractionary, and group B is composed of events that happened in expansionary monetary policy cycles. Our monetary policy cycle classification is described below. If the change in the policy rate that immediately preceded the event was in the direction of increasing it, the monetary policy stance was considered to be contractionary. If the policy rate was stable, but the previous cycle had an increase in interest rates, the monetary policy stance was also considered to be contractionary. If the change was to reduce policy rates or if the current cycle was one of stable rates immediately following a reduction cycle, the monetary policy stance was considered to be expansionary. Hence, group A is composed of event numbers 1, 2, 3, 4, and 5, and group B is composed of event numbers 9, 10, 11, 12,

TABLE 8.8

Panel Regression Results: Grouped Events

Event group A: events expected to increase credit when the monetary policy stance was contractionary
Event group B: events expected to increase credit when the monetary policy stance was expansionary

Forecast Gap	Robust Coefficient	Standard Error	z	P > z	[95% Confidence Interval]	
Forecast gap (−20)	0.657	0.012	53.140	0.000***	0.633	0.681
Median gap (−20)	0.105	0.081	1.30	0.192	−0.053	0.263
Panel std (−5)	0.433	0.243	1.78	0.074*	−0.043	0.910
ΔFX (−5)	0.503	0.211	2.39	0.017**	0.090	0.916
$\Delta \pi$ (−5)	0.876	0.120	7.30	0.000***	0.641	1.112
Δ Embi (−5)	0.097	0.129	0.76	0.450	−0.155	0.350
ΔR (−5)	0.656	0.437	1.50	0.134	−0.201	1.513
Dummy: COPOM week	−0.003	0.018	−0.15	0.877	−0.037	0.032
Dummy: Median above target	0.252	0.080	3.17	0.002***	0.096	0.409
Dummy: events group A	0.121	0.054	2.22	0.026**	0.014	0.227
Dummy: events group B	0.015	0.036	0.41	0.683	−0.055	0.084
Dummy: event 7	−0.041	0.047	−0.87	0.382	−0.132	0.051
Dummy: event 8	−0.251	0.038	−6.63	0.000***	−0.326	−0.177

Total (centered) SS = 18,196.85
Total (uncentered) SS = 18,196.85
Residual SS = 5,030.21
Number of observations = 68,722
Number of groups = 38
$F(13,1018) = 1,748.76$
Prob > F = 0.0000
Centered R^2 = 0.72
Uncentered R^2 = 0.72
Root MSE = 0.27

Note: Fixed-effects estimation. Statistics robust to heteroskedasticity and time clustering and kernel-robust to common correlated disturbances (Driscoll and Kraay 1998). Kernel = Bartlett; bandwidth = 242 days. SS: steady state.
*$p < .05$; **$p < .01$; ***$p < .001$.

13, and 14. Event number 7 was not included in either of these groups, since the expected impact would be either neutral or of a reduction in credit. They were treated separately in the estimation.

Table 8.8 shows the estimation results. We find a significantly positive coefficient for the events in group A, but the coefficient for group B is not significant. The strict interpretation of this result is that macroprudential policy announcements that are interpreted to increase credit in moments when monetary policy is contractionary have unwanted effects on the anchoring of inflation expectations. This certainly creates challenges for monetary policy conduct and for central bank communication.

CONCLUSIONS

This chapter has discussed the interaction between monetary and macroprudential policy in Brazil from both normative and positive perspectives. From the normative perspective, we used an estimated DSGE model built to reproduce Brazilian particularities to investigate optimal combinations of simple and implementable macroprudential and monetary policy rules that react to the financial cycle. We find combinations of reserve requirements, risk-weight factors, and monetary policy that can achieve good results in terms of the central bank's loss function. The results are very close to those of a more comprehensive optimal combination of macroprudential policy, which includes the countercyclical capital buffer together with all other macroprudential policy instruments considered in this study. This chapter has argued that the smaller sets of optimal policy rules are also easier to implement in Brazil. Reserve requirements and risk-weight factors have actually been used on a number of occasions for macroprudential purposes in Brazil, especially after the financial crisis, and some of them countercyclically. Our results corroborate the perception that the direction of these policies can be used to help correct the buildup of risks in the Brazilian financial system with an efficiency similar to the combination with countercyclical capital.

From the positive perspective, we investigate whether recent macroprudential policy announcements that targeted credit variables had important spillover effects on the inflation target pursued by monetary policy in Brazil. To this end, we used a rich survey panel of private inflation forecasts collected by the Central Bank of Brazil's Investor Relations Office on a daily basis and investigated the impact of announcements of macroprudential policy changes on inflation forecasts. We find that some events increased the gap between inflation forecasts and inflation targets. When we group the events that were expected to increase credit into two different sets, one when monetary policy was contractionary and the other when monetary policy was expansionary, we find that the former had a positive and significant impact on inflation expectations, while the latter did not have a significant effect. This can be interpreted as evidence that when macroprudential policy announcements are desynchronized from monetary policy, the anchoring of inflation expectations can be challenged. This stresses the importance of improving communication of the central bank's policy intentions.

This chapter has also presented an overview of the macroprudential policy challenges in Brazil since the global financial crisis and offered a glimpse at a few important future challenges. Financial deepening, foreign capital flows, and the impact of fiscal policy on the credit cycle have been particularly relevant challenges that warrant further analysis. Financial deepening has resulted from financial inclusion, following technological improvements in the financial system, income distribution policies, public banks' credit origination policies, and a long period of macroeconomic stability. Household indebtedness increased substantially and credit accelerated, but several risk-mitigating measures have been put in place to strengthen the resilience of the financial system, in addition to a tight supervisory and regulatory policy stance.

However, since a substantial part of the risk inherent to the financial deepening process has been taken by public banks, and on some occasions transferred to the National Treasury, the impact of the fiscal policy stance on the Brazilian credit cycle should be constantly monitored and anticipated.

REFERENCES

Afanasieff, T., F. Carvalho, E. Castro, R. Coelho, and J. Gregório. 2015. "Implementing Loan-to-Value Ratios: The Case of Auto Loans in Brazil (2010–11)." Working Paper 380, Central Bank of Brazil, Brasilia.

Agénor, P., and L. Silva. 2013. "Inflation Targeting and Financial Stability: A Perspective from the Developing World." Working Paper 324, Central Bank of Brazil, Brasilia.

Angeloni, I., and E. Faia. 2013. "Capital Regulation and Monetary Policy with Fragile Banks." *Journal of Monetary Economics* 60(3): 311–24.

Benigno, G., H. Chen, C. Otrok, A. Rebucci, and E. Young. 2011. "Monetary and Macroprudential Policies: An Integrated Analysis." Paper prepared for the IMF Twelfth Jacques Polak Annual Research Conference, Washington, DC, November 10–11.

Bernanke, B., and M. Gertler. 2001. "Should Central Banks Respond to Movements in Asset Prices?" *American Economic Review* 91(2): 253–57.

Brzoza-Brzezina, M., and M. Kolasa. 2013. "Bayesian Evaluation of DSGE Models with Financial Frictions." *Journal of Money, Credit and Banking* 45(8): 1451–76.

Carvalho, F., and C. Azevedo. 2008. "The Incidence of Reserve Requirements in Brazil: Do Bank Stockholders Share the Burden?" *Journal of Applied Economics* 11(1): 61–90.

Carvalho, F., and M. Castro. 2015. "Foreign Capital Flows, Credit Growth and Macroprudential Policy in a DSGE Model with Traditional and Matter-of-Fact Financial Frictions." Working Paper 387, Central Bank of Brazil, Brasilia.

Carvalho, F., and A. Minella. 2012. "Survey Forecasts in Brazil: A Prismatic Assessment of Epidemiology, Performance, and Determinants." *Journal of International Money and Finance* 31(6): 1371–91.

Cesa-Bianchi, A., and A. Rebucci. 2015. "Does Easing Monetary Policy Increase Financial Instability?" IMF Working Paper 15/139, International Monetary Fund, Washington, DC.

Cúrdia, V., and M. Woodford. 2010. "Credit Frictions and Optimal Monetary Policy." *Journal of Money, Credit and Banking* 42: 3–35.

De Fiore, F., and O. Tristani. 2013. "Optimal Monetary Policy in a Model of the Credit Channel." *Economic Journal, Royal Economic Society* 123(571): 906–31.

Drehman, M., and K. Tsatsaronis. 2014. "The Credit-to-GDP Gap and Countercyclical Capital Buffers: Questions and Answers." *BIS Quarterly Review* (March).

Driscoll, J., and A. C. Kraay. 1998. "Consistent Covariance Matrix Estimation with Spatially Dependent Data." *Review of Economics and Statistics* 80: 549–60.

Faia, E., and T. Monacelli. 2007. "Optimal Interest Rate Rules, Asset Prices, and Credit Frictions." *Journal of Economic Dynamics and Control* 31(10): 3228–54.

Fendoğlu, S. 2014. "Optimal Monetary Policy Rules, Financial Amplification, and Uncertain Business Cycles." *Journal of Economic Dynamics & Control* 46: 271–305.

Gertler, M., N. Kiyotaki, and A. Queralto. 2012. "Financial Crises, Bank Risk Exposure and Government Financial Policy." *Journal of Monetary Economics* 59: S17–S34.

Gilchrist, S., and J. Leahy. 2002. "Monetary Policy and Asset Prices." *Journal of Monetary Economics* 49: 75–97.

Iacoviello, M. 2005. "House Prices, Borrowing Constraints and Monetary Policy in the Business Cycle." *American Economic Review* 95(3): 739–64.

———, and S. Neri. 2010. "Housing Market Spillovers: Evidence from an Estimated DSGE Model." *American Economy Journal: Macroeconomics* 2(2): 126–64.

International Monetary Fund (IMF). 2013. "The Interaction of Monetary and Macroprudential Policies." January 29. Policy Paper, Washington, DC. http://www.imf.org/external/np/pp/eng/2013/012913.pdf.

Jácome, L. I., E. Nier, and P. Imam. 2012. "Building Blocks for Effective Macroprudential Policies in Latin America: Institutional Considerations." IMF Working Paper 12/183, International Monetary Fund, Washington, DC.

Kannan, P., P. Rabanal, and A. Scott. 2012. "Monetary and Macroprudential Policy Rules in a Model with House Price Booms." *B.E. Journal of Macroeconomics* 12(1), Article 16.

Lambertini, L., C. Mendicino, and M. Punzi. 2013. "Leaning against Boom-Bust Cycles in Credit and Housing Prices." *Journal of Economic Dynamics and Control* 37: 1500–22.

Martins, B., and R. Schechtman. 2013. "Loan Pricing Following a Macro Prudential Within-Sector Capital Measure." Working Paper 323, Central Bank of Brazil, Brasilia.

Montes, G., and G. Peixoto. 2012. "Risk-Taking Channel, Bank Lending Channel and the 'Paradox of Credibility': Evidence for Brazil." Encontro Nacional de Economia–ANPEC.

Ponticelli, J., and L. Alencar. 2013. "Celeridade do Sistema Judiciário e Créditos Bancários para as Indústrias de Transformação." Working Paper 327, Central Bank of Brazil, Brasilia.

Reinhart, C., and K. Rogoff. 2011. "From Financial Crash to Debt Crisis." *American Economic Review* 101: 1676–706.

Sahay, R., M. Čihák, P. N'Diaye, A. Barajas, R. Bi, D. Ayala, Y. Gao, A. Kyobe, L. Nguyen, C. Saborowski, K. Svirydzenka, and S. Yousefi. 2015. "Rethinking Financial Deepening: Stability and Growth in Emerging Markets." IMF Staff Discussion Note 15/08, International Monetary Fund, Washington, DC.

Schmitt-Grohé, S., and M. Uribe. 2007. "Optimal Simple and Implementable Monetary and Fiscal Rules." *Journal of Monetary Economics* 54: 1702–25.

Silva, L., and R. Harris. 2012. "Sailing through the Global Financial Storm: Brazil's Recent Experience with Monetary and Macroprudential Policies to Lean against the Financial Cycle and Deal with Systemic Risks." Working Paper 290, Central Bank of Brazil, Brasilia.

Silva, L., A. Sales, and W. Gaglianone. 2012. "Financial Stability in Brazil." Working Paper 289, Central Bank of Brazil, Brasilia.

Tavares, D., G. Montes, and O. Guillén. 2013. "Transmissão da Política Monetária pelos Canais de Tomada de Risco e de Crédito: uma análise considerando os seguros contratados pelos bancos e o spread de crédito no Brasil." Working Paper 308, Central Bank of Brazil, Brasilia.

Taylor, A. 2015. "Credit, Financial Stability, and the Macroeconomy." NBER Working Paper 21039, National Bureau of Economic Research, Cambridge, Massachusetts.

Végh, C., and G. Vuletin. 2013. "The Road to Redemption: Policy Response to Crises in Latin America." Paper prepared for the IMF 14th Jacques Polak Annual Research Conference, Washington, DC, November 7–8.

CHAPTER 9

De-dollarization of Credit in Peru: The Role of Conditional Reserve Requirements

PAUL CASTILLO, HUGO VEGA, ENRIQUE SERRANO, AND CARLOS BURGA, CENTRAL RESERVE BANK OF PERU

This chapter documents and evaluates the use of conditional reserve requirements in Peru to reduce credit dollarization. The empirical analysis uses the counterfactual test proposed by Pesaran and Smith (2012) and shows that both the high reserve requirements, used countercyclically since 2010, and the de-dollarization program put in place by the Central Reserve Bank of Peru (BCRP) since 2013 had statistically significant effects on reducing dollar lending by banks in Peru. The chapter also discusses the impact on banks' balance sheets of the complementary tools created as part of the de-dollarization program to inject domestic currency liquidity.

Peru is a successful market-driven case of de-dollarization, which reflects both macroeconomic stability and prudential policies. Since the adoption of inflation targeting in 2002, inflation has averaged 2.7 percent and core inflation reached 2.1 percent, one of the lowest levels in Latin America for the period 2001–15. During the same period, loan dollarization declined steadily from levels close to 80 percent to less than 30 percent.

During 2011 and 2012, the low levels of international interest rates and the appreciation of the domestic currency in Peru that followed the U.S. Federal Reserve's quantitative-easing policies generated a rebound in the expansion of dollar credits, slowing the decline in credit dollarization. In this context, in 2013, the BCRP initiated a more ambitious program of credit de-dollarization that combined a set of contingent reserve requirements[1] and a new set of instruments

---

The authors would like to thank Eugenio Cerutti, Luis Jácome, Yan Carrière-Swallow, and the participants at the 20th Annual Meeting of the Latin American and Caribbean Economics Association in Santa Cruz, Bolivia, for useful comments and suggestions.

[1]Within the de-dollarization program, additional reserve requirements are activated when bank dollar lending exceeds certain levels set by the BCRP. Separate levels for two categories of banks' dollar lending were set. First, in February 2013, the BCRP set the limits for mortgage and automobile credits, and then in September 2013, it established the limits for total credit in dollar loans, excluding loans for trade. The limits were set as a fraction of the stock of dollar loans at the beginning of the program, and they are adjusted as banks comply with reducing credit dollarization.

aimed at providing the liquidity in domestic currency and the currency hedge that the conversion of dollar loans into sol loans required.

Following the implementation of these measures, credit dollarization decreased from 38 percent to 28 percent in 2015, and the stock of dollar loans declined by 15 percent on average for the banking system. However, a proper evaluation of the empirical impact of the de-dollarization program requires distinguishing its effects from those associated with changes in the determinants of credit dollarization, such as changes in exchange rate risk. In order to accomplish this task, we use the counterfactual test developed by Pesaran and Smith (2012), a methodology that allows us to generate an unbiased estimator of the impact of policy changes in order to statistically assess the impact on credit dollarization of the de-dollarization program and the use of countercyclical reserve requirements since 2010. We also discuss the impact on bank balance sheets of the complementary tools created as part of the de-dollarization program to inject domestic currency liquidity.

Our empirical results show that the de-dollarization program had a statistically significant effect on the degree of dollarization of bank credit in 2015. In particular, two-thirds of the reduction of credit dollarization in 2015 was explained by the de-dollarization program and one-third by other factors, such as exchange rate volatility. Moreover, the results show that the countercyclical use of reserve requirements since 2010 had a significant effect on dollar loan growth rates, but the impact on de-dollarization was not statistically significant. As both domestic and foreign currency reserve requirements have been raised in tandem since 2010, both credit in domestic and in foreign currency slowed simultaneously, making the impact on credit dollarization less clear. Also, the increase in capital requirements for dollar loans had a negative impact on mortgage and automobile loans, although its impact was not statistically significant according to the test of Pesaran and Smith (2012).

This chapter is related to a growing literature that studies the impact of regulatory tools on credit conditions and systemic risks. Garcia-Escribano (2010) used vector autoregressive models to assess the impact of prudential tools such as reserve requirements and higher capital requirements on the de-dollarization of credit for a selected set of Latin American countries. Armas, Castillo, and Vega (2014) tested the impact of reserve requirements on credit conditions for Peru using the Pesaran and Smith (2012) methodology. Vargas and Cardozo (2012) performed a similar evaluation for Colombia.

Another branch of the literature related to this chapter has linked monetary policy with systemic risks. For advanced economies, Borio and Zhu (2008) have highlighted the relevance of the risk-taking channel. This channel is further strengthened by regulatory standards that increase risk-weighted capital in response to a fall in default risks created by the appreciation of collateral values.[2]

---

[2]Ioannidou, Ongena, and Peydró (2009), Jiménez and others (2009), and Maddaloni and Peydró (2011) find empirical evidence supporting this channel using loan-level data. However, using more aggregate data, Merrouche and Nier (2010) and Dell'Ariccia and others (2012) find less conclusive empirical evidence in favor of this channel.

In addition, monetary policy affects borrowers' balance sheets by altering their income flows and loan repayment capacity. Thus, an increase in the policy rate may exacerbate default risks for borrowers by inducing higher leverage and lower income flows. The fall in asset prices in response to higher interest rates further reinforces the impact of monetary policy on default risks.[3]

The next section of this chapter explains the use of reserve requirements by the BCRP and capital requirements by the Superintendence of Banks, Insurance Companies and Pension Funds (SBS) to reduce credit dollarization in Peru. The chapter then discusses the rationale and main features of the de-dollarization program and quantifies the effectiveness of reserve requirements in foreign currency in reducing financial dollarization by employing a counterfactual test following Pesaran and Smith (2012). The final section presents some concluding remarks.

DE-DOLLARIZATION AND PRUDENTIAL POLICIES

De-dollarization is a fundamental strategy of prudential policies aimed at preserving financial stability in Peru. Since financial stability is not explicitly assigned to any particular institution, each regulatory body uses its own instruments to achieve this objective. The SBS is in charge of supervising and regulating financial institutions to guarantee their individual solvency conditions. Its toolbox includes capital requirements, provisioning, and limits to banks' operations. For its part, the BCRP has as its main objective to maintain price stability, although it has a mandate to regulate the credit and payment systems. The BCRP is also the lender of last resort, which makes financial stability an integral part of the monetary policy design.

Unlike that of other inflation targeters, the inflation-targeting regime implemented in Peru factored in the impact of financial dollarization on the transmission mechanism of monetary policy and on financial stability. The adoption of a target of 2 percent with a tolerance range of 1 to 3 percent for headline inflation aims to generate strong incentives for local agents to de-dollarize their assets and liabilities. This, along with the active use of additional monetary tools, is part of the BCRP's efforts to limit financial risks created by financial dollarization.[4] Reserve requirements and a precautionary accumulation of international reserves are employed to limit liquidity and solvency risks associated with exchange rate

---

[3]Consistent with this channel, Allen and Gale (2000), Goodhart, Tsomocos, and Vardoulakis (2009), and Illing (2007) find an increase in the probability of a financial crisis after monetary policy tightening. On the other hand, Sengupta (2010) shows that an increase in the interest rate in the United States after 2004 increased the debt service burden on adjustable rate mortgages, which increased the defaults of Alt-A mortgages loans in 2006.

[4]Although Peru has attained inflation rates below 5 percent since 1997, dollarization ratios remained above 50 percent until 2010. See Winkelried and Castillo (2010) and Rappoport (2009) for explanations of the persistence of financial dollarization.

fluctuations, and foreign exchange market intervention is used to limit exchange rate volatility.

Besides delivering low and stable inflation, the current monetary policy framework has also contributed to providing an effective response to the global financial crisis by limiting its spillover effects on the domestic financial system. The Asian and Russian crises had a severe impact on the Peruvian banking system, with bank credit collapsing in Peru and several banks falling into bankruptcy in 1999 and 2000. In contrast, during the global financial crisis, domestic banks continued to provide credit to the private sector at an even faster pace than in 2008, and no banks went bankrupt in Peru.

Liquidity and credit risks induced by exchange rate fluctuations are among the most relevant risks facing the Peruvian economy. Liquidity risks are associated with the central bank's inability to print dollars, which significantly reduces its ability to act as lender of last resort. Credit risk is associated with the existence of currency mismatches that increase the default probability of agents borrowing in dollars. The cash flows of those agents do not increase with the value of the dollar. A common feature of these two additional sources of financial vulnerability is that both create negative externalities that justify policy intervention. They can also trigger potential nonlinear dynamics with undesirable consequences for financial stability, which justifies the use of precautionary policy measures.

The existence of a currency mismatch on the balance sheet of domestic agents generates an externality to the financial system because agents either do not properly internalize the foreign-currency-induced risk or engage in moral hazard behavior. Even nontradable firms that set prices in foreign currency do not realize that the nature of the mismatch is real. In other words, a negative shock to the economy that depreciates the real exchange rate increases the real debt of nontradable firms by reducing the net present value of cash in dollars.

The complementary instruments used by the BCRP generate incentives to reduce credit dollarization and, thus, reduce the exposure of banks' assets to the credit risk associated with currency mismatches, as well as the spillovers and externalities for financial stability that dollarization generates. These instruments aim to (1) help banks to internalize dollarization risks; (2) prevent the impact of shocks from spreading across the economy; and (3) enhance the financial system's capacity to absorb shocks.

These objectives are achieved by (1) increasing the level of international liquidity in the financial system; (2) raising the cost of intermediation in dollars to curb excessive credit growth; and (3) reducing exchange rate volatility to prevent negative balance sheet effects.[5] Table 9.1 summarizes the main financial risks that each prudential instrument is tailored to mitigate, as well as the instruments

---

[5]See Rossini, Quispe, and Rodriguez (2011) for a detailed discussion about the BCRP foreign exchange intervention strategy.

TABLE 9.1

Use of Macroprudential Policy Instruments

Instrument/Objective	Liquidity Risk	Excessive Credit Growth	Mismatch
Reserve requirements on foreign currency deposit	Higher than reserve requirements on domestic deposits given that central bank cannot act as lender of last resort	Reserve requirements on foreign currency deposits are hiked during episodes of capital inflows	Additional reserve requirements conditional on the evolution of credit in foreign currency to curb mismatches on private agents' balance sheets
Reserve requirements on domestic currency deposits		Reserve requirements on domestic currency deposits are hiked during episodes of capital inflows	
Reserve requirements on short-term liabilities	Excessive reliance on short-term liabilities generates liquidity risk for banks		Reserve requirements on short-term liabilities provide banks with incentives to fund their activities with more stable funding (match maturity)
Capital requirements		Cyclical capital requirements	High capital requirements on foreign currency loans
Provision requirements		Cyclical provisions	

used by the SBS, such as capital requirements and higher provisioning, which have been designed to reduce credit risk and limit currency mismatches.

Although a formal macroprudential committee is not in place in Peru, the SBS, BCRP, and Ministry of Economy and Finance (MEF) have held periodic meetings since 2008 to analyze potential sources of systemic risk and coordinate policies to mitigate them. Several of the macroprudential policies implemented by each entity since 2008 have been closely coordinated within this committee.[6] However, a key difference between the instruments used by the SBS and the BCRP is the scope of the systemic risks they aim to mitigate. The BCRP's instruments target mainly liquidity risks, both in domestic and foreign currency and excessive credit growth, whereas SBS instruments focus mainly on strengthening the financial system's capacity to absorb potential losses.

In addition, reserve requirements are used to limit the spillover effects of capital flows on domestic monetary conditions, particularly after the quantitative expansionary policies put in place by the U.S. Federal Reserve. The use of the aforementioned monetary instruments by the BCRP is discussed below.

---

[6]For a detailed description and analysis of the macroprudential policies implemented in Peru, see Choy and Chang (2014).

Reserve Requirements

Reserve requirements in dollars are calibrated to increase the cost of lending and curb credit growth, or to increase the cost of using short-term external funding to expand domestic credit. In addition, since 2008 the BCRP has used reserve requirements in a more cyclical fashion by raising their average and marginal levels during periods of capital flow surges and reducing them during capital reversal episodes.[7] By increasing reserve requirements in foreign currency during periods of intense capital inflows, the BCRP reduces banks' incentives to lend in dollars. At the same time, it creates a foreign currency buffer to reduce banks' vulnerability to capital flow reversals.

The 2007–09 global financial crisis put the inflation target cum financial risk control to the test. Inflation was running above target during the first half of 2008. High inflation called for higher domestic policy interest rates and a widening spread vis-à-vis foreign interest rates. In turn, higher interest rate spreads against the U.S. federal funds rate induced more carry trades and short-term capital inflows in the run-up to the crisis. Elevated bank liquidity levels originated by capital inflows hindered the conduct of monetary policy and intensified appreciation pressures. In this context, in addition to raising the reference rate (from 4.5 percent in July 2007 to 6.5 percent in August 2008) in response to inflationary pressures, the BCRP increased reserve requirements on domestic and foreign currency deposits to ensure an orderly expansion of liquidity and credit. The BCRP also accumulated a significant amount of international reserves, mainly through foreign exchange intervention sterilized with fiscal savings.[8]

In September 2008, the BCRP responded immediately to the turbulence caused by the collapse of Lehman Brothers by injecting liquidity up to 9.3 percent of GDP through a wide range of instruments. These included the reduction of reserve requirements to end-2007 levels, foreign exchange sales of US$6.8 billion during September 2008–February 2009, and the provision of liquidity through repo operations and currency swaps.

These measures cushioned the domestic financial system from the impact of the crisis and facilitated a swift and sustained recovery of credit and growth starting in the second half of 2009. Even during the most acute period of the crisis (October 2008–March 2009), access to credit was preserved, and nonperforming bank loans remained low.

The global financial crisis provided policymakers worldwide with an important lesson: monetary policy can—and must—take financial stability concerns into account to a greater extent. During the crisis, central banks in advanced economies made innovative policy moves, including explicit guidance to steer

---

[7]See Perez-Forero and Vega (2014) for estimations of the quantitative effects of reserve requirements in Peru.

[8]See Rossini, Quispe, and Rodriguez (2012) for a detailed discussion on the interactions between monetary and fiscal policy in Peru.

Figure 9.1. Peru: Reserve Requirement in Domestic and Foreign Currency
(Percentage of total deposits)

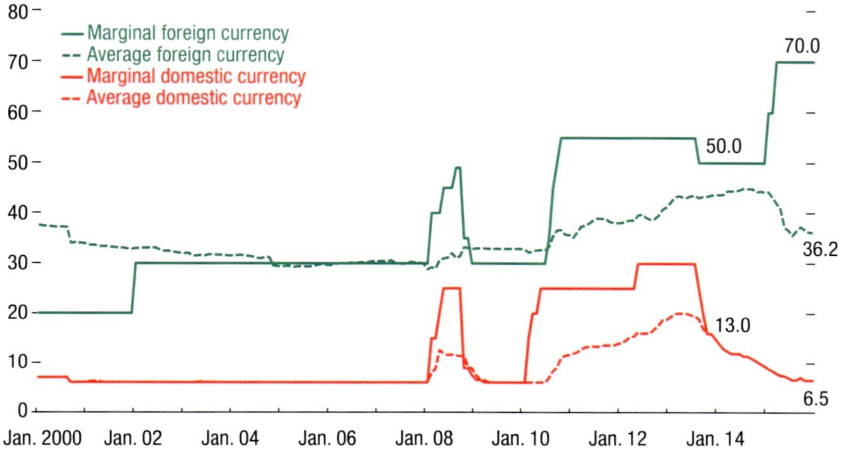

[Line chart showing marginal foreign currency, average foreign currency, marginal domestic currency, and average domestic currency from Jan. 2000 to beyond Jan. 2014. End values: Marginal foreign currency 70.0; Average foreign currency 36.2; Marginal domestic currency 13.0; Average domestic currency 6.5.]

Source: Central Reserve Bank of Peru.

expectations for future interest rates, and quantitative easing. These policies spilled over into emerging market economies, which had to face unprecedented capital inflows. Under these circumstances, monetary policy in Peru had to maneuver to sail against the wind and apply a sort of quantitative tightening (Armas, Castillo, and Vega 2014). This implied raising reserve requirements, as described in Figure 9.1.

The surges in capital flows that followed the implementation of quantitative easing by the U.S. Federal Reserve had a significant impact on monetary and credit conditions in Peru. This required a more active use of complementary policy instruments such as reserve requirements. As shown in Figure 9.1, the BCRP increased not only the marginal reserve requirement rate several times, but also the average rate, which has a stronger impact on banks' intermediation costs in foreign currency, thereby limiting credit expansion in foreign currency and contributing to reducing credit dollarization.

Measures Adopted by the SBS

The SBS has also used its policy instruments to induce banks to internalize the risks associated with financial dollarization. In November 2012, the SBS increased capital requirements for dollar lending by raising the risk weight for dollar credit from 102.5 to 108 percent. Also, since 2013, the SBS has established larger capital requirements for mortgage loans in dollars when the loan-to-value (LTV) ratio is above 80 percent.

Figure 9.2. Evolution of Credit Dollarization in Peru
(Percent)

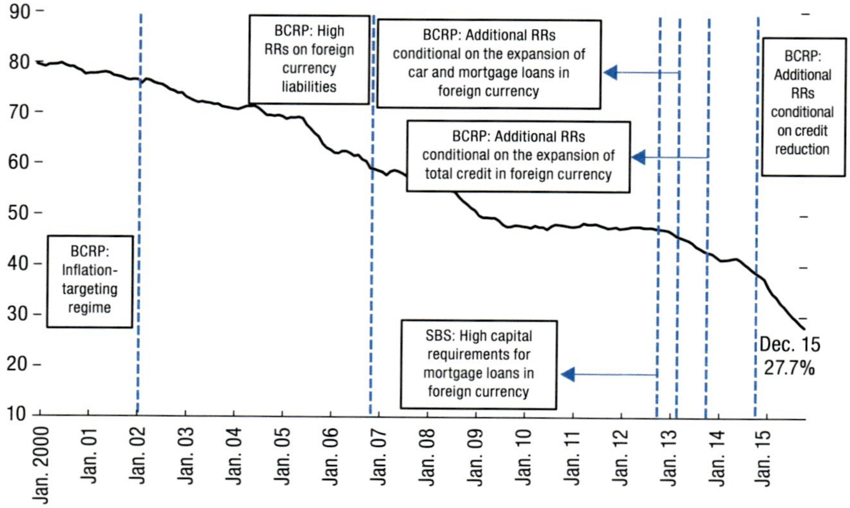

[Chart showing credit dollarization declining from about 80% in Jan. 2000 to 27.7% in Dec. 15, with the following annotations:
- BCRP: Inflation-targeting regime (around 2002)
- BCRP: High RRs on foreign currency liabilities
- BCRP: Additional RRs conditional on the expansion of car and mortgage loans in foreign currency
- BCRP: Additional RRs conditional on the expansion of total credit in foreign currency
- SBS: High capital requirements for mortgage loans in foreign currency
- BCRP: Additional RRs conditional on credit reduction
- Dec. 15: 27.7%]

Source: Central Reserve Bank of Peru.
Note: BCRP = Central Reserve Bank of Peru; RR = reserve requirement; SBS = Superintendence of Banks, Insurance Companies and Pension Funds.

Higher capital requirements for loans that have greater credit risk associated with the fluctuations of the exchange rate induce banks to increase lending rates for these types of credits, reducing demand for them. Figure 9.2 illustrates the evolution of credit dollarization and highlights the implementation of the three most important prudential policies adopted in Peru to foster the de-dollarization of credit. These are the countercyclical adjustment of the reserve requirement in dollars by the BCRP, the increase in capital requirements set by the SBS, and the BCRP's de-dollarization program.

As the figure illustrates, credit dollarization started to decline persistently after the adoption of the inflation-targeting regime in 2002. A slowdown in the decreasing trend in de-dollarization is observed from 2010 to 2012, associated with the increase in the demand for dollar loans in response to very low international interest rates and expected appreciation of the local currency. During this period, the BCRP increased the average and marginal reserve requirements several times to reverse the impact of external financial conditions on credit dollarization. The most significant change in the de-dollarization trend is observed in 2015, after the BCRP adjusted its de-dollarization program. As can be seen in Figure 9.2, the downward trend in credit dollarization started accelerating in 2013 and did so with more intensity during 2015. This period coincides with the application of the BCRP's de-dollarization program and also with the increase in expected depreciation of the exchange rate, which increases the expected cost of borrowing in dollars.

Figure 9.3. Dollarization Ratio of Mortgages and Automobile Loans
(Percent)

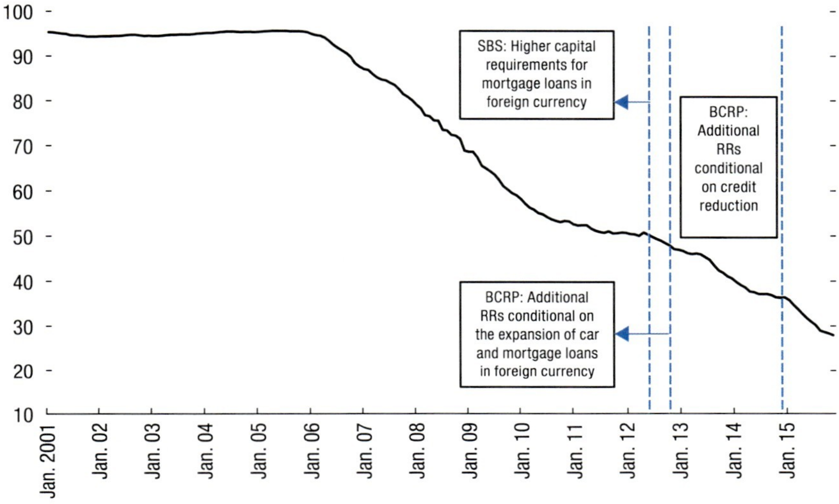

Annotations on chart:
- SBS: Higher capital requirements for mortgage loans in foreign currency
- BCRP: Additional RRs conditional on the expansion of car and mortgage loans in foreign currency
- BCRP: Additional RRs conditional on credit reduction

Source: Central Reserve Bank of Peru.
Note: BCRP = Central Reserve Bank of Peru; RR = reserve requirement; SBS = Superintendence of Banks, Insurance Companies and Pension Funds.

For the case of dollar-denominated mortgages and automobile loans (Figure 9.3), the clearest change in the de-dollarization trend occurs around the date the SBS increased capital requirements for dollar lending. This trend was reinforced in 2013 with the adoption of the de-dollarization program by the BCRP that year.

Later in the chapter we will test the impact of these three prudential policies using the Pesaran and Smith (2012) counterfactual test.

THE DE-DOLLARIZATION PROGRAM, 2013–16

In 2013, the BCRP implemented additional reserve requirements to induce a more rapid reduction in credit dollarization. Financial institutions with dollar-denominated-loan growth rates above certain thresholds established by the BCRP were subject to these requirements. Reducing financial vulnerabilities in a timely manner is crucial to maintain financial stability and effectively implement monetary policy, particularly under the current external conditions of high volatility in financial markets. In dollarized economies, the need to limit the risks attached to the considerable influence of foreign currency liquidity shocks and unexpected large exchange rate movements on liquidity conditions and credit spreads is crucial for the stability of the financial system.

This section discusses the rationality of these measures and the details of their application and presents some evidence that the de-dollarization program has been effective in achieving its main objective of reducing currency mismatches associated with financial dollarization.

Main Features of the Program

As a permanent feature, the BCRP has set higher reserve requirements for deposits in foreign currency compared to those in domestic currency. This difference increases the cost of financial intermediation in foreign currency, thereby reducing the incentives for financial dollarization.

In March 2013, the de-dollarization program started with the establishment of additional reserve requirements on foreign currency liabilities tied to the evolution of mortgage and vehicle loans denominated in foreign currency. The stock of these loans as of February 2013 was set as a reference point, and growth rates of 10 and 20 percent above it made the offending financial institution subject to the additional requirements. These were set at 0.75 percentage point for banks exceeding the first threshold, and 1.5 percentage points for those exceeding the second threshold.

In October 2013, a similar additional reserve requirement was established linked to a broader definition of credit, including all loans to the private sector denominated in foreign currency except those extended for international trade purposes. In this case, additional reserve requirements increased by 1.5 percentage points when total outstanding credit in foreign currency (excluding credit for trade operations) exceeded the reference stock—which was set to its September 2013 level—by 5 percent; by 3 percentage points when this definition of foreign total credit exceeded the reference balance by 10 percent; and by 5 percentage points when it exceeded the reference balance by 15 percent.

In December 2014, the BCRP modified the previous framework of additional reserve requirements defined in terms of threshold levels for the expansion of dollar-denominated loans. The new setup required reductions in dollar-denominated loans. Under the new rules governing the additional reserve requirements in foreign currency, banks were given until June 2015 to reduce their stock of total credit in foreign currency (excluding foreign trade operations as well as operations with terms longer than four years and amounts over US$10 million) to at least 95 percent of their September 2013 levels. Otherwise, banks faced additional requirements on their total liabilities in foreign currency proportional to the gap between their current stock and the desired balance. This measure became more demanding in December 2015, when banks had to reduce their balances of dollar-denominated loans to at least 90 percent of the September 2013 balance.

A similar set of rules applied for car and mortgage loans denominated in foreign currency. In this case, by June 2015 banks had to reduce their stock for this type of credit to at least 90 percent of the balance as of February 2013. For December 2015, the requirement was for banks to reduce their stock of dollar-denominated car and mortgage loans to 85 percent of the balance as of February 2013. With these measures, the BCRP aimed to reduce potential risks

Figure 9.4. Bank Credit in Foreign Currency Excluding Trade Loans
(Billions of U.S. dollars; September 2013 = 100 percent)

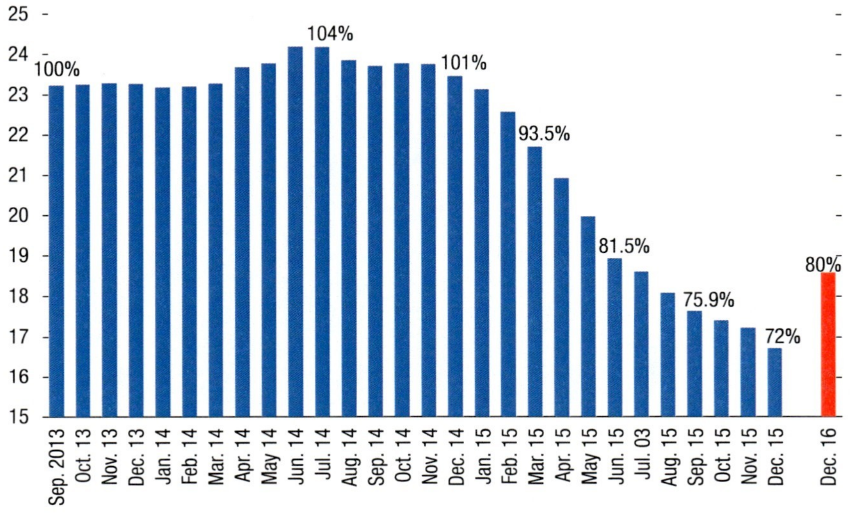

Source: Central Reserve Bank of Peru.

in the financial system by providing incentives for banks to reduce their balances of credit in foreign currency, without discouraging foreign trade operations and focusing on credit sectors that are more vulnerable due to their high dollarization level.[9]

As of July 2015, the reduction in total credit in foreign currency (excluding credit for trade operations) was significant, with levels below the threshold established by the BCRP for December 2015. By December 2015, total credit in foreign currency had fallen even more, going beyond the objectives of the program. At the level of individual banks, all achieved the reductions in total foreign currency credit set by the BCRP (Figure 9.4).

The reduction in the degree of dollarization of mortgage and car loans in foreign currency was even larger (Figure 9.5). Thus, as of July 2015, aggregate mortgage and vehicle credit was equivalent to 76.4 percent of the February 2013 balance—lower than the level required by the BCRP for December 2015. By December 2015, this figure had fallen even further to 68.1 percent.

Consequently, aggregate dollarization levels for bank lending dropped from 44 to 32 percent from December 2014 to December 2015 (Table 9.2). The reduction of dollarization was widespread across different credit market segments.

---

[9]In February 2013, dollarization of mortgage and car loans was 47.7 and 79.6 percent, respectively.

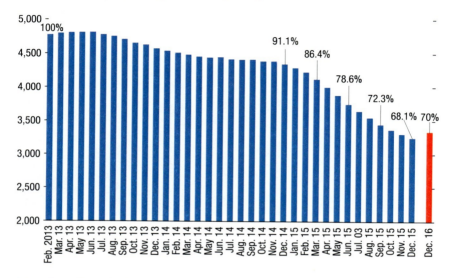

Figure 9.5. Banks' Car and Mortgage Loans in Foreign Currency
(Millions of U.S. dollars; February 2013 = 100 percent)

Source: Central Reserve Bank of Peru.

Given the program's success, and in order to consolidate the gains already obtained, in December 2015 further objectives were set for 2016. Total credit denominated in foreign currency, excluding foreign trade loans, was required to decrease at least to a level equivalent to 80 percent of the September 2013 stock, while mortgage and car loans denominated in foreign currency had to be brought down to 70 percent of the stock observed in February 2013.

TABLE 9.2

Ratio of Dollarization of Credit to the Private Sector (Percent)			
	Dec. 2010	Dec. 2014	Dec. 2015
Credit to firms	55.9	48.5	38.7
Corporation and large firms	69.4	59.9	46.4
Medium firms	67.4	59.3	47.5
Small firms	19.3	11.5	8.5
Household credit	**26.5**	**20.0**	**15.9**
Consumer loans	10.8	9.5	7.8
Car loans	64.0	68.9	44.9
Credit cards	7.2	6.6	6.4
Rest	8.4	5.9	5.8
Mortgage loans	52.2	33.9	26.8
Total	**46.1**	**38.3**	**30.5**
Dollarization at constant exchange rate	*47.6*	*38.3*	*27.7*
Dollarization of private banks' credit	*50.4*	*43.7*	*32.8*

Complementary Instruments to Inject Liquidity in Sols to Support the De-dollarization of Credit

Turning to banks' balance sheets, the de-dollarization program had two important effects:

1. Banks that had their balance sheets matched by currency before the program ended up with a short position in dollars after substituting (converting) dollar-denominated loans already on their balance sheet for sol-denominated loans. This meant that banks needed a means to regain their neutral position with respect to the dollar.

2. Strong incentives to denominate all new loans in domestic currency meant that banks needed long-term funding sources in sols in order to avoid a currency mismatch on their balance sheets. These were particularly scarce given that private agents expected strong depreciation of the sol and thus preferred to save in dollars.

The first effect would imply more demand for dollar instruments. Banks would hedge their position purchasing dollars either in the spot or forward market, generating pressure on the exchange rate. Given the prudential objective of low foreign exchange volatility, the de-dollarization program would require a hedge instrument provided by the BCRP.

Repos for Credit Substitution

Repos for credit substitution support the conversion of loans in foreign currency into loans in domestic currency. In this operation, banks purchase dollars from the BCRP and simultaneously perform a currency repo using these same dollars as collateral: they constitute a restricted deposit at the BCRP. As a result, banks' customers obtain loans in sols, while the banks maintain the same amount of assets in dollars. The repo for credit substitution provides banks with a dollar-denominated asset (the restricted deposit in U.S. dollars that serves as collateral for the repo) and a sol-denominated liability (the repo itself). These cancel the effect of credit substitution—which increases assets in sols and decreases dollar assets—on banks' dollar exposure.

Figure 9.6 shows the effects of the repo for credit substitution on the balance sheet of the BCRP and a private bank. Steps 1 and 2 show the situation before and after the credit substitution takes place.

In our example, we assume substitution takes place in the same bank: a client calls the bank and asks for his or her dollar-denominated loan to be replaced by a sol-denominated loan. From the private bank's point of view, this is an accounting matter that results in a lower dollar book position with no funds exchanged. However, we could consider the possibility of a client taking a loan in sols at bank A and then using the funds to pay for his or her dollar-denominated loan in bank B. In this case, it would seem both banks suffer no change in their book position: bank A gives sols to the client and obtains an asset in sols, whereas bank B receives dollars and loses an asset denominated in dollars. This is not the case, because the

Figure 9.6. Repo for Credit Substitution

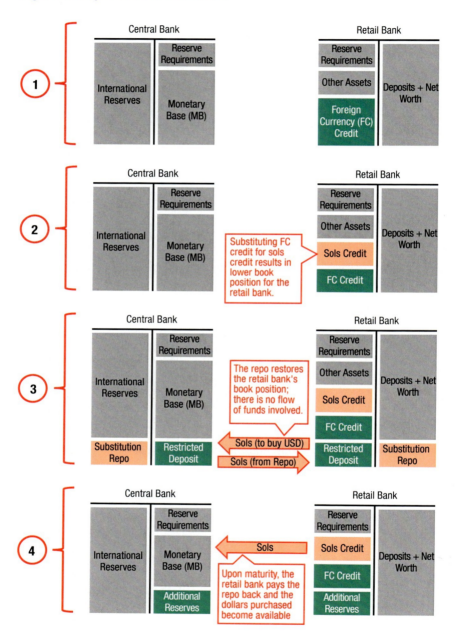

Source: Central Reserve Bank of Peru.

client must have purchased the dollars given to bank B from some other bank (which could be A, B, or a third party). The bank that sold the dollars in exchange for sols has lost book position.

Thus, the bank that loses book position needs to get it back. In step 3 of Figure 9.6, the bank buys dollars from the BCRP and uses them as collateral to borrow sols from the central bank. The dollars that the bank purchased become a restricted deposit at the BCRP. In this way, the retail bank regains its original foreign exchange position, but the foreign exchange position of the BCRP falls. The BCRP's international reserves are not affected, however.

Notice that the fall in the BCRP's foreign exchange position mirrors the increased foreign exchange position of the bank's client, who now has less outstanding loans in foreign currency. Thus, the operation allows the private sector to protect itself from depreciation at the expense of the BCRP's position.

When the substitution repo matures, the retail bank must pay the BCRP back (step 4 in Figure 9.6). This contracts the monetary base and makes the dollars the retail bank purchased available. In the figure, these dollars are shown as "Additional Reserves" at the BCRP, but the retail bank could choose to withdraw them.

In the external environment characterized by the strengthening of the dollar, the growth of domestic currency deposits diminished, thereby increasing banks' need for alternative sources of long-term liquidity in domestic currency. In this context, the BCRP implemented a new facility to inject liquidity in sols. This new facility reduces banks' required foreign currency reserves at the BCRP in order to use the liberated funds as collateral.

Repos for Credit Expansion

Repos for credit expansion were designed to support credit growth in domestic currency. Through this instrument, banks can use part of their reserve requirements in foreign currency (up to an amount equivalent to 10 percent of their total liabilities subject to these requirements, extended to 20 percent in December 2015) to make currency repos with the BCRP, obtaining long-term funding in domestic currency.

Figure 9.7 illustrates the workings behind the repos for credit expansion. Consider the case of a financial institution that uses a fraction of its dollar-denominated reserve requirements to obtain a repo for credit expansion (step 2 of Figure 9.7). When a private bank obtains one of these repos from the central bank, its foreign currency reserve requirement is reduced, and the dollars liberated are used to constitute a restricted deposit at the BCRP, serving as collateral for the repo. In exchange, it receives the equivalent amount in domestic currency, which constitutes an expansion of the monetary base for the central bank. The private bank uses the funds to expand credit in domestic currency. Note that the private bank's foreign exchange position does not change, and for the central bank the level of international reserves and the foreign exchange position are not affected either.

These new types of repo operations have been instrumental in facilitating a smooth reduction in credit dollarization, particularly during 2015, when

Figure 9.7. Repo for Credit Expansion

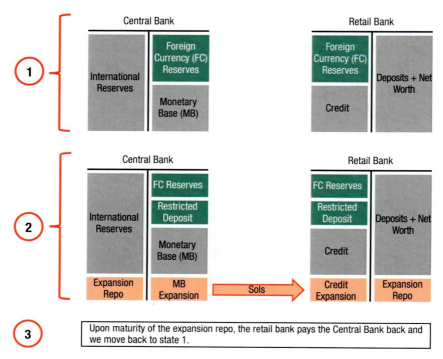

Source: Central Reserve Bank of Peru.

banks faced a shortage of domestic currency funding as depositors increased their preference for saving in dollar-denominated deposits. In addition, banks faced an excess of liquidity in foreign currency, generated both by the substitution of dollar-denominated loans for sol-denominated loans and by the increase in dollar deposits. The repos for credit substitution and for credit expansion contributed to swapping the excess of banks' funding in foreign currency into more funding in domestic currency, which allowed them to rapidly expand credit in domestic currency without creating pressures on domestic interest rates. Figure 9.8 illustrates the dynamics of these instruments. Bank credit expansion in 2015 was mostly financed by repo operations with the BCRP.

Looking forward, unwinding the instruments deployed by the BCRP in 2015 will require deposit dollarization to decrease as well, corresponding with credit dollarization. This will only be the case when depreciation expectations cease. However, this might not be enough. It is quite plausible that given the right conditions—for instance, an appreciation of the sol—credit dollarization could

Figure 9.8 Funding Sources of Bank Credit Expansion in Domestic Currency
(Millions of sols; annual flows)

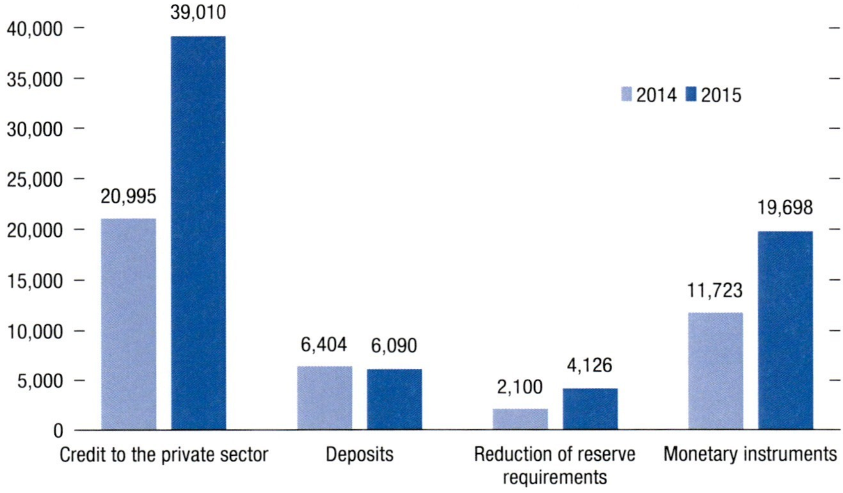

Category	2014	2015
Credit to the private sector	20,995	39,010
Deposits	6,404	6,090
Reduction of reserve requirements	2,100	4,126
Monetary instruments	11,723	19,698

Source: Central Reserve Bank of Peru.

increase again if the measures implemented by the BCRP in the last three years are phased out. A similar situation occurs with deposit dollarization: when the circumstances are adequate it will fall, but keeping it at low levels will probably require the central bank to implement backstops in the same spirit as the ones described here. Low inflation will provide incentives for private agents to de-dollarize deposits, but when the winds change again—particularly with regard to the exchange rate—policy will have to be in place to make sure dollarization does not rear its head again.

IMPACT OF RESERVE REQUIREMENTS ON CREDIT GROWTH RATE AND FINANCIAL DOLLARIZATION

This section empirically evaluates the effectiveness of reserve requirements in reducing financial dollarization by performing a counterfactual exercise following the methodology proposed by Pesaran and Smith (2012). We test the relevance of the cyclical use of marginal and average reserve requirements in foreign currency, and of the recent de-dollarization program launched in December 2014, for mitigating the growth of dollar-denominated loans and reducing the dollarization ratio.

The key assumption for our counterfactual policy exercise is that the policy instrument changes are due to an ad hoc change in the use of the instruments and not the result of a structural change. Following Pesaran and Smith (2012), the counterfactual values can be obtained as a conditional forecast generated by a reduced-form equation (static version) that assumes the policy was not in place:

$$y_t = \pi_1 x_t + \pi_2' w_t + v_{y,t}, \tag{9.1}$$

where y_t is the target or outcome variable, which is affected by a policy variable x_t and one or more control variables z_t. The methodology also allows us to consider a set of variables w_t affecting y_t or z_t, but invariant to changes in x_t and z_t. For small and open economies such as Peru, w_t includes commodity prices and U.S. interest rates, among other variables.

Under these assumptions, the counterfactual path y_t is defined as the difference of the impact of policy instruments considering the observed values and their counterfactual analogs. Let us define the set of expected values for the policy instruments and their counterfactual values as:

$$\Psi^1_{t+H} = \Psi_{t+H}(x^1) = \{x^1_{T+1}, x^1_{T+2}, \ldots, x^1_{T+H}\},$$

$$\Psi^0_{t+H} = \Psi_{t+H}(x^0) = \{x^0_{T+1}, x^0_{T+2}, \ldots, x^0_{T+H}\}.$$

However, the policy-reduced form presented in equation (9.1) is clearly misspecified for estimating the structural parameters of the model. Pesaran and Smith (2012) show that under the assumption that w_t, the parameters of the policy-reduced form (π_1, π_2'), and the errors $v_{y,t}$ are all invariant to policy interventions, the policy effect can be consistently estimated by:

$$d_{T+h} = \pi_1 \left(x^1_{T+h} - x^0_{T+h} \right). \tag{9.2}$$

It is clear that this result does not require the invariance of the structural parameters, but only that the parameters of the reduced form of the policy are invariant to policy intervention. In our policy evaluation, we use as the outcome variable the bank's dollarization of credit and the annual growth rate of dollar-denominated credit. As policy variables, we use both the average and marginal reserve requirement rates. In order to measure the effect of the de-dollarization program, we use a dummy variable that takes the value of 1 from January to December 2015 and 0 otherwise. Let us recall that under this program, banks were given six months to cut their dollar-denominated loans at least by 5 percent. Otherwise, they faced an additional reserve requirement starting in June 2015 that was proportional to the deviation of the balance of dollar-denominated loans and the level required by the BCRP.

As control variables that are time invariant to policy instruments, we use external variables such as the terms of trade, the federal funds rate, the 10-year U.S. Treasury yield, the U.S. unemployment rate, and an index of a basket of exchange rates for the main regional partners. For the dollarization ratio we consider regressions for both the change in the dollarization ratio and the level of this ratio. For the regressions that use variables in levels, we use the fully modified ordinary least square estimator to account for the effect of residual correlations on the t-statistics of the key policy variables. We also add lags for the endogenous variables to obtain well-behaved residuals for the case of the first-difference regressions.

We study the effects of the dollarization program both on the dollarization of total credit (excluding credit for trade operations) and on the dollarization of mortgage and car loans, which are the two types of credit targeted by the BCRP's de-dollarization program.

An additional dummy variable is included in the regression to account for the effect of the higher capital requirement established by the SBS for banks' foreign exchange exposure since November 2012. Table 9.3 presents the results of these reduced-form regressions. Monthly information is used for the period that spans from January 2004 to December 2015.

The estimators for both the impact of the average reserve requirement and the dummy variable capturing the effect of the de-dollarization program have the expected negative sign and are statistically significant in the regressions for the growth of dollar loans. In the case of the dollarization ratios, the de-dollarization program has a negative and significant effect on this indicator. The average reserve requirement also has a negative effect on the change in dollarization of total credit, but not in the case of the change in the dollarization of mortgage and car loans and deposits. The SBS's higher capital requirement also has a negative and significant effect on both the change and level of the dollarization of mortgage and automobile loans, but not for the aggregate level of dollarization or for deposits.

An interesting result in the regression for the level of dollarization is the negative and significant effect of the time trend variable, which we associate with the impact of the inflation-targeting regime and price stability on dollarization decisions. As Table 9.3 shows, the estimated impact is about −0.2 in the two cases of dollarization being analyzed, implying an average reduction in dollarization ratios of about 2.4 percentage points per year.

Next, we use the previous reduced forms to perform the counterfactual exercise and evaluate their statistical significance. The simple question we seek to answer in this case is what would have happened to the growth of dollar-denominated loans and the dollarization ratios if the BCRP had not increased, since 2010, both the average and marginal reserve requirement rates in foreign currency and if the de-dollarization program had not been established. In order to perform this test we measure the policy effectiveness as follows:[10]

$$\bar{d}_H = \hat{\pi}_1 \left[\frac{1}{H} \sum_{h=1}^{H} \left(x_{T+h} - x_{T+h}^0 \right) \right], \quad (9.3)$$

where the expression in brackets is a measure of the average size of the policy change. Following Pesaran and Smith (2012), the policy effectiveness test is then calculated as follows:

---

[10] In our model, the specification to be used includes two lags of dependent variables: $(1 - a_1 L)(1 - a_2 L) y_t = \pi_1 x_t + \pi_2 w_t + v_{j,t}$. This last expression will drive the next measure of the test: $\bar{d}_H = \hat{\pi}_1 \frac{1}{H} \sum_{j=1}^{H} \sum_{m=0}^{j-1} \left(\sum_{i=0}^{m} a_1^i a_2^{m-i} \left(x_{T+j-m} - x_{T+j-m}^0 \right) \right)$.

TABLE 9.3

Reduced-Form Models

	OLS Estimation	Long-Term Relationships (Fully modified estim.)[1]			Dollarization Coefficient			Dollarization Coefficient: Long-Term Relationship (Fully modified estim.)[1]	
					Total Credit		Mortgage-Auto Credit	Total Credit	Mortgage-Auto Credit
Dependent (growth rate of credit at):	12 months	12 months	In difference	In difference	In difference	In difference	In difference		
	M1	M2	M3		M4		M5	M6	M7
Explanatory:									
Constant	0.30	69.84*						99.46*	121.10*
	(0.85)	(0.00)						(0.00)	(0.00)
Banking Reserves Requirements Rate[2] (foreign currency)	−0.24*	−2.53*	−0.18**						
	(0.00)	(0.00)	(0.03)						
Banking Reserves Requirements Rate[3] (domestic currency)			0.18**						
			(0.01)						
Banking Reserves Requirements Rate[3] (foreign currency – domestic currency)					−0.14**			−0.17**	−0.86*
					(0.02)			(0.09)	(0.00)
SBS Program (started in November 2012) Higher Capital Requirement for FX Exposure							−0.28*		−1.71**
							(0.00)		(0.03)
De-dollarization Program (announced 2015)	−2.85**	−34.86*	−1.12*		−0.83*			−10.72*	−1.28
	(0.02)	(0.01)	(0.00)		(0.00)			(0.00)	(0.15)
Banking Marginal Reserves Requirements Rate[3] (domestic currency)									
Marginal Reserve Requirements Rate (foreign currency)	0.03	0.76*							
	(0.44)	(0.00)							
Exogenous Controls:									
Terms of Trade[4]	0.09*	0.19**	0.01				0.01	−1.80*	−0.21*
	(0.00)	(0.05)	(0.45)				(0.38)	(0.00)	(0.00)
U.S. Unemployment[5]					−1.80*		−0.51**		
					(0.00)		(0.01)		

(continued)

TABLE 9.3 (continued)

Reduced-Form Models

	OLS Estimation	Long-Term Relationships (Fully modified estim.)[1]	Dollarization Coefficient		Dollarization Coefficient: Long-Term Relationship (Fully modified estim.)[1]	
			Total Credit	Mortgage-Auto Credit	Total Credit	Mortgage-Auto Credit
Dependent (growth rate of credit at):						
FED Interest Rate	-0.09* (0.00)		-0.10* (0.00)		-0.93* (0.00)	1.69* (0.00)
Treasury Bill–10 Years (yield)		-5.35* (0.00)	0.11*** (0.06)	-0.09* (0.00)	-2.37* (0.00)	
Exchange Rate Basket (Main Regional Partners)[6]			-2.39*** (0.06)			
Trend Component					-0.24* (0.00)	-0.25* (0.00)
Inflation-Targeting Regimen Proxy				0.37* (0.00)		
Lags:						
Dollarization Coefficient Mortgage/Auto Credit in Differences; (lag2)						
12 Months (lag1)	1.19* (0.00)					
12 Months (lag1)	-0.30* (0.00)					
R-Squared	0.98	0.69	0.30	0.41	0.96	0.99
Durbin-Watson Stat	2.08		1.23	1.85		
Akaike info criterion	4.09		1.10	0.75		

Source: Authors' calculations.

Note: T-statistics probability in parentheses; * Significant at 1%, ** Significant at 5%, *** Significant at 10%. FED = U.S. Federal Reserve; FX = foreign exchange; OLS = ordinary least squares; SBS = Superintendence of Banks, Insurance Companies and Pension Funds.

[1] Phillips and Hansen (1990) methodology. In M6 SBS Program is modeled as deterministic. For M2, M6, and M7 de-dollarization program is modeled as deterministic, as well.

[2 3 4] M3 and M5 defined in difference. In 4 for M1, sixth lag is also put in, as well.

[5] M5 expressed in difference.

[6] M4 expressed in difference.

$$\varrho_H = \frac{\tilde{d}_H}{\hat{\sigma}_{v_r}} \sim^a N(0,1), \qquad (9.4)$$

where $\hat{\sigma}_{v_r}$ is the standard error of the policy reduced-form regression. We perform the counterfactual evaluation considering two periods to differentiate the impact of the increase in the average and marginal reserve requirements in foreign currency from those of the recent de-dollarization program. For the average and marginal reserve requirements in foreign currency, we restrict the sample until December 2014, whereas for the de-dollarization program we use the sample from January to December 2015. We also test the effect of the SBS's increase in capital requirements for foreign exchange exposure, and present the results in Table 9.4.

As Table 9.4 shows, the persistent increase in the average reserve requirement rate in foreign currency since July 2010 had a statistically significant effect on the annual growth rate of dollar-denominated loans. The counterfactual exercise considers 53 periods, from July 2010 to December 2014, and the counterfactual value used for the average and marginal rates is 33 percent, its corresponding value for July 2010. The average effect, depending on the model used, is a difference between 6 to 18 percentage points in the counterfactual path for the growth rate of dollar-denominated credit. In all the cases, the effect of higher reserve requirements is statistically significant.[11]

In the case of the de-dollarization program, we consider the period from January to December 2015 for the policy evaluation exercise. The policy effects on dollar-denominated credit growth are negative and statistically significant, as well as the effect on the dollarization ratio of total credit.[12] The impact of reserve requirements on the dollarization of mortgage and car loans is not significant, even though it has the expected sign. In the case of the SBS's higher capital requirements for foreign exchange exposure, we find that they have the expected sign, but the policy impact is not statistically significant.

In addition, to illustrate the effects of reserve requirements and the de-dollarization program on the dollarization ratios, Figure 9.9 shows both the observed path of credit dollarization and the counterfactual path for three models, M3, M4, and M6. The counterfactual estimated level of credit dollarization for December 2015 is on average 39 percent vis-à-vis the observed level of 32 percent. This difference of close to 7 percentage points in credit dollarization is explained by the impact of the de-dollarization program, which represents about two-thirds of the total reduction in the banks' credit dollarization ratio (12 percentage points, from 44 to 32 percent).

---

[11] See Perez-Forero and Vega (2015) for empirical evidence on the impact of reserve requirements on credit using a different methodology.

[12] Also, Garcia-Escribano (2010) finds that higher dollar reserve requirements have contributed, together with inflation targeting and the prudential regulatory measures taken by the SBS, to reduce credit dollarization.

TABLE 9.4

Policy Effectiveness Statistics

	Mean Effect	Policy-Effectiveness Statistics	p-Value	Expected Sign
Outcome: Growth Rate of Credit at:	**Banking Reserves Requirements Rate (Foreign Currency)[1]**			
12 Months (M1)	−14.29	−8.03	**0.00**	yes
12 Months (M2)	−18.78	−2.75	**0.01**	yes
	De-dollarization Program (Announced 2015)[2]			
12 Months (M1)	−11.22	−6.30	**0.00**	yes
12 Months (M2)	−27.60	−4.05	**0.00**	yes
Outcome: Dollarization Ratio of:	**Banking Reserves Requirements Rate (Foreign Currency)[1]**			
Total Credit (M3)	−0.04	−0.09	0.93	yes
Total Credit (M4)	−0.03	−0.07	0.94	yes
Total Credit (M6)	−1.26	−0.59	0.56	yes
	De-dollarization Program (Announced 2015)[2]			
Total Credit (M3)	−0.89	−2.11	**0.04**	yes
Total Credit (M4)	−0.66	−1.65	**0.10**	yes
Total Credit (M6)	−11.61	−5.40	**0.00**	yes
Mortgage-Auto Loans (M5)	0.00	0.00	1.00	yes
Mortgage-Auto Loans (M7)	−1.39	−1.31	0.19	yes
	SBS Program (Started in November 2012)[3]			
Mortgage-Auto Loans (M5)	−0.43	−1.34	0.18	yes
Mortgage-Auto Loans (M7)	−1.71	−1.62	0.11	yes

Source: Authors' calculations, following Pesaran and Smith (2012).
Note: SBS = Superintendence of Banks, Insurance Companies and Pension Funds.
[1] Sample period: July 2010–December 2015.
[2] Sample period: January 2015–December 2015.
[3] Sample period: November 2012–December 2015.

CONCLUSIONS

The experience of the Peruvian economy highlights the interaction between monetary and macroprudential policy. Particular characteristics specific to Latin American economies, such as currency mismatches and excessive leverage with foreign lenders, cause concerns for financial stability, as they may have an impact on the transmission mechanism of monetary policy through several channels.

In economies affected by financial dollarization, a large depreciation of the exchange rate can lead to higher default rates among firms with currency mismatches and affect borrowers' balance sheets by altering their income flows and loan repayment capacity. Thus, a large increase in the exchange rate may increase default risks of borrowers by inducing higher leverage and lower income flows. Therefore, additional prudential instruments that can limit the negative effect of the risk-taking channel, both ex ante and ex post, are central to effectively conduct monetary policy.

Figure 9.9. Counterfactual Effects of Reserve Requirements and the De-dollarization Program

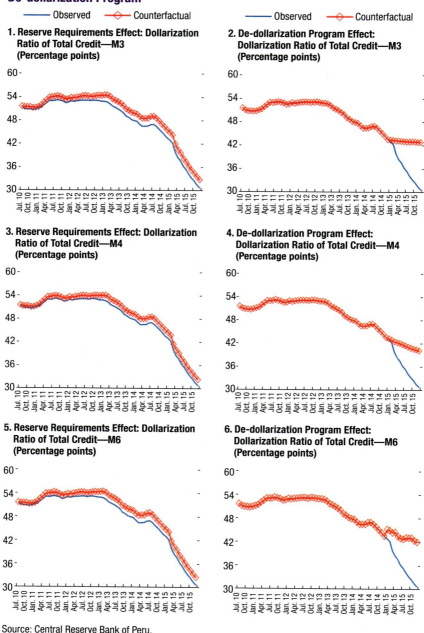

Source: Central Reserve Bank of Peru.

The BCRP and its peers in Latin America have used higher reserve requirements on foreign currency liabilities, liquidity management tools, and international reserve accumulation as tools to limit systemic risks, both ex ante and ex post. These tools have gained importance over the last decade, particularly given the current international context characterized by high uncertainty associated with the normalization of the U.S. Federal Reserve's monetary policy and volatility in the terms of trade of Latin American economies, particularly commodity exporters.

Peru's case illustrates that implementing these tools while preserving monetary stability is not only possible, but necessary. Furthermore, this chapter has provided empirical evidence that bolder measures to directly reduce vulnerabilities such as credit dollarization through the use of additional reserve requirements can significantly enhance financial stability, thereby creating space to allow traditional monetary policy to fulfill its role.

APPENDIX 9.1. ADDITIONAL FIGURES

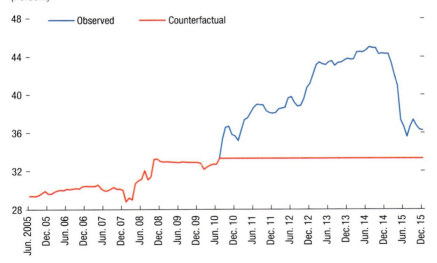

Appendix Figure 9.1.1. Bank Reserve Requirement Rates
(Percent)

Appendix Figure 9.1.2. Bank Marginal Reserve Requirements
(Percent)

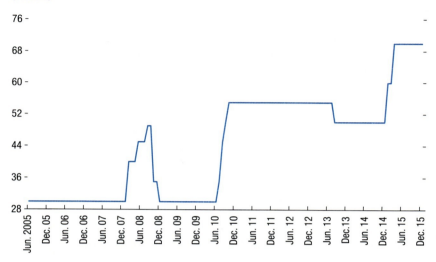

Appendix Figure 9.1.3. Terms of Trade
(Percent)

Appendix Figure 9.1.4. Annual Growth Rate of Credit: Foreign Currency
(Percent)

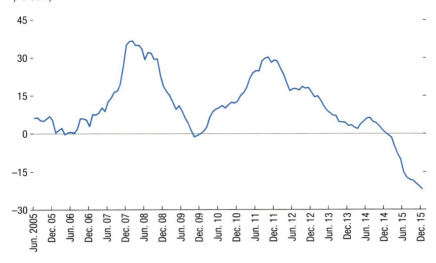

Appendix Figure 9.1.5. Dollarization Ratio: Total Credit
(Percent)

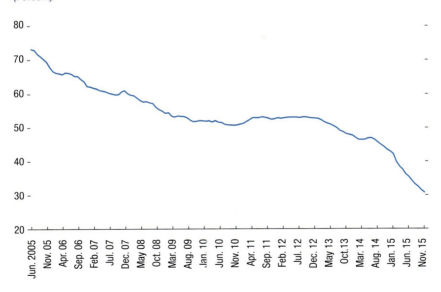

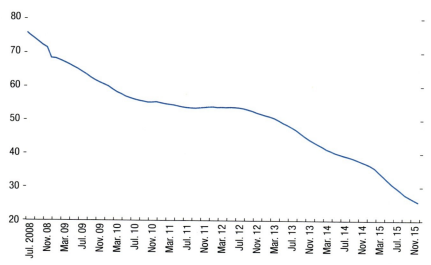

Appendix Figure 9.1.6. Dollarization Ratio: Mortgage and Auto Loans
(Percent)

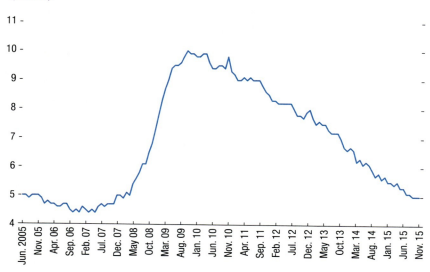

Appendix Figure 9.1.7. U.S. Unemployment Rate
(Percent)

Appendix Figure 9.1.8. U.S. Federal Reserve Interest Rate
(Percent)

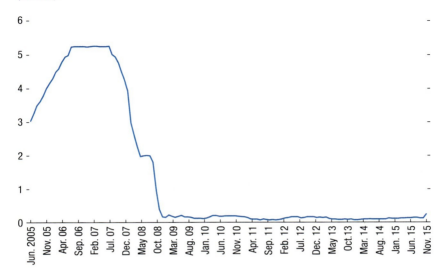

Appendix Figure 9.1.9. 10-Year Treasury Bills Yield
(Percent)

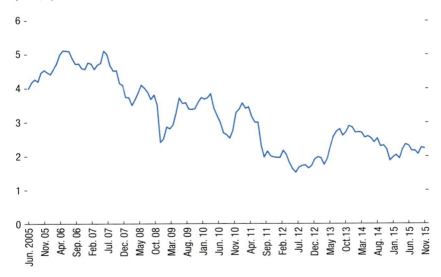

REFERENCES

Allen, F., and D. Gale. 2000. "Bubbles and Crises." *Economic Journal* 110(460): 236–55.
Armas, A., P. Castillo, and M. Vega. 2014. "Inflation-Targeting and Quantitative Tightening: Effects of Reserve Requirements in Peru." *Economía* 15(1): 133–75.
Avdjiev, S., M. Chui, and H. S. Shin. 2014. "Non-financial Corporations from Emerging Market Economies and Capital Flows." *Quarterly Review* (December). Bank for International Settlements, Basel.
Borio, C., and H. Zhu. 2008. "Capital Regulation, Risk-Taking and Monetary Policy: A Missing Link in the Transmission Mechanism?" BIS Working Paper 268, Bank for International Settlements, Basel.
Choy, M., and G. Chang. 2014. "Medidas macroprudenciales aplicadas en Perú." *Revista de Estudios Económicos* 27: 25–50.
Dell'Ariccia, G., D. Igan, L. Laeven, and H. Tong, with B. Bakker and J. Vandenbussche. 2012. "Policies for Macrofinancial Stability: How to Deal with Credit Booms." IMF Staff Discussion Note 12/06, International Monetary Fund, Washington, DC.
Garcia-Escribano, M. 2010. "Peru: Drivers of De-dollarization in Latin America?" IMF Working Paper 10/169, International Monetary Fund, Washington, DC.
Goodhart, C., D. P. Tsomocos, and A. P. Vardoulakis. 2009. "Foreclosures, Monetary Policy and Financial Stability." Conference Proceedings of the 10th International Academic Conference on Economic and Social Development, Moscow, April 7–9.
Illing, G. 2007. "Financial Stability and Monetary Policy—A Framework." CESifo Working Paper No. 1971, Munich.
Ioannidou, V. P., S. Ongena, and J.-L. Peydró. 2009. "Monetary Policy and Subprime Lending: A Tall Tale of Low Federal Funds Rates, Hazardous Loans and Reduced Loan Spreads." European Banking Center Discussion Paper 2009–045, Tilburg University, Tilburg, The Netherlands.
Jiménez, G., S. Ongena, J.-L. Peydró, and J. Saurina. 2009. "Hazardous Times for Monetary Policy: What Do Twenty-Three Million Bank Loans Say about the Effects of Monetary Policy on Credit Risk-Taking?" Working Paper 833, Banco de España, Madrid.
Maddaloni, A., and J.-L. Peydró. 2011. "Bank Risk-Taking, Securitization, Supervision and Low Interest Rates: Evidence from US and Euro Area Lending Standards." *Review of Financial Studies* 24: 2121–65.
Merrouche, O., and E. Nier. 2010. "What Caused the Global Financial Crisis? Evidence on the Drivers of Financial Imbalances 1999–2007." IMF Working Paper 10/265, International Monetary Fund, Washington, DC.
Pérez-Forero, F., and M. Vega. 2014. "The Dynamic Effects of Interest Rates and Reserve Requirements." Working Paper 2014-008, Central Reserve Bank of Peru, Lima.
———. 2015. "Asymmetric Exchange Rate Pass Through: Evidence from Peru." Working Paper 2015-011, Central Reserve Bank of Peru, Lima.
Pesaran, H., and R. Smith. 2012. "Counterfactual Analysis in Macroeconometrics: An Empirical Investigation into the Effects of Quantitative Easing." Cambridge University, Cambridge, United Kingdom. Unpublished.
Rappoport, V. 2009. "Persistence of Dollarization after Price Stabilization." *Journal of Monetary Economics* 56: 979–89.
Rossini, R., Z. Quispe, and D. Rodriguez. 2011. "Capital Flows, Monetary Policy and FOREX Interventions in Peru." Working Paper 2011-008, Central Reserve Bank of Peru, Lima.
———. 2012. "Fiscal Policy Considerations in the Design of Monetary Policy in Peru." Working Paper 2012-022, Central Reserve Bank of Peru, Lima.
Sengupta, R. 2010. "Alt-A: The Forgotten Segment of the Mortgage Market." *Federal Reserve Bank of St. Louis Review* 92(1): 55–71.

Vargas, H., and P. Cardozo. 2012. "The Use of Reserve Requirements in an Optimal Monetary Policy Framework." Borradores de Economía No. 716, Banco de la République, Bogotá.

Winkelried, D., and P. Castillo. 2010. "Dollarization Persistence and Individual Heterogeneity." *Journal of International Money and Finance* 29: 1596–618.

Index

A

Accountability, 5, 32, 44–45, 45n6
  in Atlantic model, 74
  with inflation targeting, 46
Argentina, 14n5, 15n7, 19n16
  exchange rate pass-through in, 102
  external shocks to, 14
  financial stability in, 43
  governing structure in, 17
  government financing in, 19, 23
  inflation in, 30, 50
  insurance companies in, 74n32
  international reserves in, 14, 23
  monetary policy development in, 35
  National Economic Council in, 19n14
  nationalization of banks in, 16
  reserve requirements in, 22n25
  short-term interest rate in, 92
Atlantic model, 15, 30
  accountability in, 74
Australia, 119
  expectations of inflation in, 55f
  inflation in, 54, 56
  nominal exchange rate in, 48f
Autonomy of monetary policy, 5–6, 29n37, 90–98, 98f
  determinants of, 96–98
  from external conditions, 3
  spillovers that impair, 94

B

Balance of payments, IMF and, 24
Banking crisis, in Brazil, 177–78
Basel III
  Brazil and, 174, 176, 177–78, 192
  Mexico and, 155n14
Benchmarks
  for currency depreciations, 101, 103f
  for financial shocks, 161, 161t
  for forward guidance, 136n4
  for inflation, 102
  in monetary policy, 148
  for price stability, 147

Bolivia, 15n7, 19n16
  dollarization in, 86
  international reserves in, 46
  short-term interest rate in, 92
Boom-bust cycles, risk of, 3
Brazil, 15
  banking crisis in, 177–78
  Basel III and, 174, 176, 177–78, 192
  capital flows in, 215
  countercyclical capital requirement in, 184
  Credit Bureau in, 180–81
  credit cycle in, 7
  Credit Default Law in, 181, 181n12
  credit-to-GDP gap shock in, 207
  database monitoring in, 182
  Deposit Guarantee Fund in, 181
  Derivatives exposure registry (CED), 181
  exchange rate in, 47f, 60f
  exchange rate intervention in, 68
  exchange rate pass-through in, 102
  financial crisis of 2008 and, 178, 178n10
  financial deepening in, 180–81
  financial stability in, 43
  Financial Stability Committee (COMEF), 183
  governing structure in, 43n4, 177n8
  household indebtedness in, 7, 178, 179f
  housing loans in, 186n18, 189n20
  independence of central bank in, 19, 43n2, 47f
  inflation in, 24, 25f, 29f, 30, 47f, 176–77
  inflation targeting in, 46, 47f, 56
  insurance companies in, 74n32
  IRFs in, 193, 199, 200f, 201f, 202f, 203f, 204f, 205f, 206f, 207
  liquidity in, 178
  macroprudential policy in, 173–215, 200f, 201f, 202f, 203f, 204f, 205f,

206*f*
monetary policy in, 28*n*36, 173–215, 200*f*, 201*f*, 202*f*, 203*f*, 204*f*, 205*f*, 206*f*
money supply in, 24, 25*f*
National Monetary Council in, 183*n*15, 184, 192
optimal policy in, 185–93, 190*t*–191*t*
regional presence of banks in, 180, 180*f*
reserve requirements in, 176, 186, 188
risk-weighted assets in, 72, 188–89, 207
short-term interest rate in, 92
social mobility in, 180, 181*f*
state-owned bank in, 15*n*6
See also Brazil, Chile, Colombia, Mexico, and Peru
Brazil, Chile, Colombia, Mexico, and Peru (LA5), 27–28
exchange rate intervention in, 68*n*28
exchange rate pass-through in, 101
global integration of, 90
in Great Recession, 31
inflation targeting in, 47–48, 49*t*
international reserves in, 63
Bretton Woods Agreement, 11, 15
demise of, 19, 24
devaluations and, 24
exchange rate and, 24
monetary policy in, 24
temporary suspension of, 16
Brussels International Financial Conference, 13

C

Canada, 119
inflation in, 56
nominal exchange rate in, 48*f*
Capital flows, 2, 25–26, 70, 84
in Brazil, 215
dollarization and, 25
exchange rate and, 26, 32, 57
financial crisis of 2008 and, 27–28, 58, 224
foreign exchange and, 28
IMF and, 86
increases in, 84
inflation and, 32

interest rate and, 21, 25
macroprudential policy and, 28
monetary policy and, 12, 84–86
in Peru, 49
reserve requirements and, 49, 223*t*
spillovers from, 223
taxation of outflows, 184
Central bank independence, 18–20, 21*f*, 47*f*
Cukierman index of, 20
in Brazil, 43*n*2
in inflation targeting, 44, 46
measuring, 45, 45*nn*6–8
for price stability, 43–44
reform and, 45*t*
Central banks. *See specific topics*
Chicago Board Options Exchange Volatility Index (VIX), 92, 93, 117, 119
Chile, 14n5, 15*n*7, 19, 19*n*18
assets of central bank in, 23*f*
discount rate in, 21*n*23
economic development in, 15
exchange rate in, 47*f*, 60*f*
exchange rate intervention in, 66*f*, 68
financial stability in, 73
fiscal deficit financing in, 19
gold standard in, 13*n*3, 22
governing structure in, 17
government financing in, 18*n*13, 23
independence of central bank in, 19, 47*f*
inflation in, 24, 25*f*, 47*f*, 54
inflation targeting in, 46, 47*f*
liquidity in, 63
long-term interest rate in, 110*n*1, 112, 113, 123
monetary policy in, 16
monetary policy development in, 35
in monetary policy golden age, 38
money supply in, 24, 25*f*
price stability in, 43
reform in, 43
reserve requirements in, 19*n*14
short-term interest rate in, 92
See also Brazil, Chile, Colombia, Mexico, and Peru
China, 32, 174
Christiano-Fitzgerald filtered business cycle, 117, 126

Colombia, 15nn7–8, 19n16, 19n18, 29f
  economic development in, 15
  exchange rate in, 47f, 60f
  gold standard in, 22
  governing structure in, 17
  government financing in, 18n13
  independence of central bank in, 47f
  inflation in, 47f
  inflation targeting in, 46, 47f
  monetary policy development in, 35
  in monetary policy golden age, 38
  price stability in, 43
  reserve requirements in, 28n36, 220
  See also Brazil, Chile, Colombia, Mexico, and Peru
Commercial banks, liquidity in, 13–14
Consumer Price Index (CPI), 90
  for U.S. term premium, 117, 126–27
COPOM. *See* Monetary Policy Committee
Costa Rica, 15, 19n16
  financial stability in, 43
  in monetary policy golden age, 38
  reserve requirements in, 22n25
  short-term interest rate in, 92
Countercyclical capital requirement, 15, 22, 42, 148
  in Brazil, 184
  external shocks and, 84
  in Peru, 7–8
Coverage ratio rule, 148, 164
  in Mexico, 155n14
CPI. *See* Consumer Price Index
Credit cycle, in Brazil, 7
Credit Default Law, in Brazil, 181, 181n12
Credit spread, 151–52
  financial shock with, 161, 162f
  macroprudential policy and, 165–69, 167t
  monetary policy and, 165
  policy rate on, 165
Credit-to-GDP gap, 155n14, 161, 163f
  in Brazil, 187–88, 207
  loss function and, 192, 194t–195t
Cuba, 15

D

De-dollarization. *See* Dollarization
Depreciation. *See* Exchange rate

Devaluations
  Bretton Woods Agreement and, 24
  of exchange rate, 24
  inflation and, 25n29, 30
  interest rate and, 25n29
Discount rate
  in Chile, 21n23
  loss of popularity with, 22
  in Mexico, 21n24
  as monetary policy, 21
  in monetary policy, 21
Dollar (U.S.)
  to gold, 11, 24
  petro, 25n30
  widespread use of, 101–2
Dollarization, 25, 86
  and de-dollarization, in Peru, 7–8, 219–20, 219n1, 226, 226f, 227f, 245f, 246f
  capital inflows and, 25
  exchange rate and, 220
  monetary policy autonomy and, 94
  prudential policy and, 221–27, 223f, 225f, 226f, 227f
  reserve requirements and, 228, 235–40, 238t–239t, 241t, 242f
Dollar swap lines, with Federal Reserve, 3n4
Dominican Republic, 15, 19n16, 43, 44t
Dynamic stochastic general equilibrium (DSGE), 173, 174, 185–86, 186f, 187f

E

Economic development, 31
  in Colombia, 15
  inflation targeting and, 88n2
  monetary policy for, 15–16, 19
Ecuador, 15n7, 19n16
  gold standard in, 13n3, 22
  governing structure in, 17
  monetary policy development in, 36
El Salvador, 14, 14n5, 15n7, 19n16
Employment, 31
  unemployment, in U.S., 246f
Exchange rate, 2, 23, 26, 41, 47f, 58–62, 60f, 86, 110, 119, 178,
  benchmarks for, 101, 103f
  Bretton Woods Agreement and, 24

capital flows and, 26, 28, 32, 57
de-dollarization and, 220
devaluations of, 24
fear of floating and, 46n9
flexibility of, 46, 58n18, 84–86, 87f, 96
following end of commodity super-cycle, 58-62
foreign exchange and, 222
gold standard and, 13n3
hedging markets and, 46
inflation and, 25n29, 26, 51, 53 110
inflation targeting and, 46, 57–69
interest rate and, 32, 91, 93n11
international reserves and, 46, 62–69, 64f
intervention in, 62–69, 66f, 66t, 68n28, 76
pegging, 84, 87f
price stability and, 90
spillovers and, 96
transparency in, 67, 69
U.S. term premium and, 124t–125t
volatility of, 48f, 65n21, 222
Exchange rate pass-through, 98–104, 101n20, 105f
estimates of, 105f
inflation and, 61, 102, 104f
inflation targeting and, 104, 104f
External shocks, 199
in Argentina, 14
countercyclical capital requirement and, 84
inflation and, 30
monetary policy after, 58–62, 84

F

FDI. *See* Foreign direct investment
Fear of floating, exchange rate and, 46n9
Federal Open Market Committee, 133
Federal Reserve, 32
dollar swap lines with, 3n4
interest rate of, 247f
long-term interest rate and, 96
monetary policy of, 94
Peru and, 219, 225
quantitative easing by, 111, 219, 225
Financial accelerator, 150, 175n5
Financial crisis of 2008, 1, 41

Brazil and, 178, 178n10
capital inflows and, 27–28, 58, 224
financial shock and, 27
forward guidance in, 131
macroeconomics and, 145–46
Peru and, 222
policy rate and, 1
Financial deepening, 6
in Brazil, 180–81
Financial shocks, 158–64, 162f, 163f, 168f
benchmarks for, 161, 161t
financial crisis of 2008 and, 27
Financial stability, 1, 31, 41–42, 69–75, 93
banking crises and, 71f
in Chile, 73
inflation and, 3, 6–7
inflation targeting and, 2, 145, 147n4
leaning against the wind and, 2
liquidity and, 173–74
macroprudential policy and, 145–69
in Mexico, 73
monetary policy and, 145–69, 147n5
in Peru, 222
reform and, 43
in Uruguay, 73
Financial Stability Board (FSB), 178
Foreign direct investment (FDI), 185
Foreign exchange intervention
empirical evidence on, 67–68, 76
instruments used for, 66
microstructure, 62–63
portfolio balance channel, 62
precautionary saving channel, 63
signaling channel, 62
Forward guidance, 6
benchmarks for, 136n4
defined, 131
Delphic, 132–33, 136nn5–6
in financial crisis of 2008, 131
interest rate and, 134–38, 134n2
in monetary policy, 131–39
Odyssean, 132–33
policy rate and, 132, 133
state-contingent, 134n1
transparency in, 133, 136
FSB. *See* Financial Stability Board

G

Genoa Conference, 13

Global financial crisis of 2008. *See* Financial crisis of 2008
Gold
  dollars to, 11, 24
  international reserves in, 21
Gold standard, 12–13, 12*n*2
  collapse of, 14
  currency issuance and, 18
  exchange rate and, 13*n*3
  in Great Depression, 22
  inflation and, 30
  in Mexico, 22
Governing structure, of central banks, 17–18
  in Brazil, 43*n*4, 177*n*8
  in monetary policy golden age, 38
Government financing
  in Argentina, 19, 23
  in Chile, 18*n*13, 23
  in Colombia, 18*n*13
  in Great Depression, 23
  inflation from, 30
  in Mexico, 18*n*13, 23, 23*n*26
  in Peru, 23
Government ownership of banks. *See* Nationalization (government ownership) of banks
Great Depression, 18, 31
  gold standard in, 22
  government financing in, 23
Great Recession, LA5 in, 31
Greenspan conundrum, 111
  U.S. term premium and, 109
Grove mission, 15*n*8
Guatemala, 15, 15*n*7, 19*n*16
  monetary policy development in, 36

H

Hedging markets, exchange rate and, 46
Heterodox economic programs, 26
Honduras, 15, 19*n*16
  in monetary policy golden age, 38
Household indebtedness, in Brazil, 7, 178, 179*f*
Housing loans, 175
  in Brazil, 186*n*18, 189*n*20
  in Peru, 229*n*9, 230*f*, 246*f*

I

IMF. *See* International Monetary Fund

Independence, central bank (*see* Central bank independence)
Inflation, 47*f*, 50*f*, 88, 155*n*14
  achievements and reversals in reducing, 42–51
  in Argentina, 30
  in Australia, 54, 56
  benchmarks for, 102
  in Brazil, 24, 25*f*, 29*f*, 30, 176–77
  in Canada, 56
  capital flows and, 32
  in Chile, 24, 25*f*, 29*f*, 54
  in Colombia, 29*f*
  Delphic forward guidance and, 136*n*6
  devaluations and, 25*n*29, 30
  exchange rate and, 25*n*29, 26, 51, 53, 101, 102, 103, 103*f*, 104*f*, 110
  expectations of, 54–56, 93, 97, 97*n*14
  external shocks and, 30, 58–62
  financial stability and, 3, 6–7
  gold standard and, 30
  from government financing, 30
  macroprudential policy on, 207–14, 209*t*–211*t*, 213*t*, 214*t*
  in Nicaragua, 30
  in Peru, 29*f*, 30, 221*n*4
  reduction of, 16, 88–89
  tolerance for, 15
  U.S. term premium and, 122
  volatility of, 4, 48*f*, 88, 89*f*
  See also Price stability
Inflation targeting, 41, 47*f*
  accountability with, 46
  central bank independence and, 44, 46
  economic development and, 88*n*2
  effectiveness of, 51–56, 88
  exchange rate and, 46, 57–69
  exchange rate pass-through and, 104, 104*f*
  expectations of inflation, 54–56, 55*f*, 57*f*
  financial stability and, 2, 145, 147*n*4
  framework used by Bank of England, 59
  in LA5, 47–48, 49*t*, 58
  loss function and, 147, 152
  in monetary policy, 4, 27, 28*f*, 54*n*15, 175
  in Peru, 219

price stability from, 146–47
reform and, 42–45, 44*t*
transparency with, 46, 49*t*, 65, 67
Insurance companies, 74*n*32
Interdependence, in monetary policy, 3
Interest rate
  capital inflows and, 21, 25
  devaluations and, 25*n*29
  exchange rate and, 91, 93*n*11
  exchange rate depreciation and, 32
  of Federal Reserve, 247*f*
  forward guidance and, 134–38, 134*n*2
  global financial integration and, 91, 91*f*
  liquidity and, 49*n*11
  long-term, 95–96, 95*f*
  loss function and, 134
  macroeconomics of, 6
  medium-term, 109
  money supply and, 21
  neutral real, 54
  nominal, 155*n*14, 193*n*23
  SELIC, 183*n*14, 184, 208
  short-term, 6, 90, 92, 92*n*7, 94, 95–96, 95*f*
  spillovers to, 95–96, 95*f*
  U.S. term premium and, 6, 109
  See also Long-term interest rate; Short-term interest rate
International Monetary Fund (IMF), 41*n*1, 68
  on Brazil, 183
  capital flows and, 86
  monetary approach to the balance of payments of, 24
  World Economic Outlook of, 51–52, 53*f*
International reserves, 7, 41
  in Argentina, 14, 23
  exchange rate and, 62–69, 64*f*
  foreign exchange and, 46, 62–69
  in gold, 21
  gross changes in, 64*f*
  in LA5, 63
Investment/saving curve (IS), 134
  macroeconomic block and, 151

K

Keynesian economics, 15
  See also New Keynesian model

L

LA5. *See* Brazil, Chile, Colombia, Mexico, and Peru
Leaning against the wind
  financial stability and, 2
  monetary policy, 146*n*3, 149, 158–59
Lehman Brothers, 3, 3*n*4, 173
Liquidity
  in Brazil, 178
  in Chile, 63
  in commercial banks, 13–14
  financial stability and, 173–74
  in Peru, 222
  petro dollars and, 25*n*30
  risk aversion and, 199
Loan-to-value (LTV), 186*n*18, 225
Local projection method (LPM), 99
Long-term interest rate
  in Chile, 110*n*1, 112, 113, 123
  Federal Reserve and, 96
  in Mexico, 112, 123
  spillovers to, 95–96, 95*f*
  in U.S. and selected countries, 112*f*
  U.S. term premium and, 109, 110–16, 114*t*, 115*t*, 126*f*
Loss function, 157, 186–87
  credit-to-GDP gap shock and, 192, 194*t*–195*t*
  inflation targeting and, 147, 152
  interest rate and, 134
  prudential policy and, 137
LPM. *See* Local projection method
LTV. *See* Loan-to-value

M

Macroprudential policy
  in Atlantic model, 72–74
  in Brazil, 173–215, 200*f*, 201*f*, 202*f*, 203*f*, 204*f*, 205*f*, 206*f*
  capital inflows and, 28
  interaction with dollarization, 221–23
  interaction with monetary policy, 75, 173–77
  credit spreads and, 165–69, 167*t*
  financial stability and, 145–69
  frameworks, 6–8, 72–75
  and inflation, 207–14, 209*t*–211*t*, 213*t*, 214*t*
  in Pacific model, 74

Mexico, 16, 19n18
  autonomy-impairing spillovers in, 94
  banking crises in, 26
  Basel III and, 155n14
  delinquency index in, 155n14
  discount rate in, 21n24
  exchange rate in, 47f, 60f
  foreign exchange intervention in, 68
  exchange rate pass-through in, 102
  financial stability in, 43, 73
  gold standard in, 22
  government financing in, 18n13, 23, 23n26
  independence of central bank in, 47f
  inflation in, 47f
  inflation targeting in, 46, 47f
  long-term interest rate in, 112, 123
  monetary policy development in, 37
  monetary policy golden age in, 38
  policy rate in, 49
  price stability in, 43
  reserve requirements in, 22, 22n25
  short-term interest rate in, 92
  See also Brazil, Chile, Colombia, Mexico, and Peru
Microprudential policies, 2n3
Monetary approach to the balance of payments, of IMF, 24
Monetary policy
  autonomy. *See* Autonomy of monetary policy
  in Brazil, 28n36, 173–215, 200f, 201f, 202f, 203f, 204f, 205f, 206f
  in Bretton Woods Agreement, 24
  capital flows and, 12
  in Chile, 16, 122
  coordination of, 2
  credit spreads and, 165
  developmental phase for, 23–26, 35–37
  discount rate in, 21
  early years of, 20–23
  for economic development, 15–16, 19
  evolving foundations of, 12–20
  after external shocks, 58–62, 84
  of Federal Reserve, 94, 109
  financial stability and, 145–69, 147n5
  forward guidance in, 131–39
  frameworks for, 6–8, 20–29, 22f
  global financial integration and, 83–106, 85f, 91f
  golden years of, 26–29, 38
  independence in, 5–6, 29n37, 90–98, 98f
  inflation targeting in, 4, 27, 28f, 54n15, 175
  leaning against the wind, 146n3, 149, 158–59
  prudential policy and, 139–41
  reserve requirements in, 22, 22n25
  risk-weighted assets and, 220–21
  short-term interest rate as, 111
  spillovers from, 3, 5–6, 90–98
  Taylor-type rules and, 93, 175
  transparency with, 47
Monetary Policy Committee (COPOM), 59, 183, 183n14
Money supply
  in Brazil, 24, 25f
  in Chile, 24, 25f
  interest rate and, 21
Mortgages. *See* Housing loans

N
National Economic Council, in Argentina, 19n14
Nationalization (government ownership) of banks, 15n6, 17, 17t
  in Argentina, 16
Neutral real interest rate, 54
New Keynesian model, 136n6, 152
  financial accelerators and, 175n5
New Zealand
  Delphic forward guidance in, 136n5
  nominal exchange rate in, 48f
  transparency in, 65
Nicaragua, 15, 19n16
  reserve requirements in, 22n25
Nominal exchange rate, 48f
Nominal interest rate, 155n14, 193n23

O
Output gap
  measurement of, 52
  revisions to, 51–52

P
Pacific model, 14
  macroprudential policy in, 74

Paraguay, 15, 19n16
  dollarization in, 86
Pegging, of exchange rate, 84, 87f
Peru, 15, 15n7, 19n18
  assets in, 23f
  autonomy-impairing spillovers in, 94
  capital flows in, 49
  car loans in, 229, 229n9, 230f, 246f
  countercyclical capital requirement in, 7–8
  de-dollarization in, 7–8, 219–43, 219n1, 221n4, 242f
  dollarization in, 7–8, 86, 219–20, 219n1, 226, 226f, 245f, 246f
  exchange rate depreciation in, 59
  exchange rate volatility in, 65n21
  Federal Reserve and, 219, 225
  financial crisis of 2008 and, 222
  financial stability in, 222
  gold standard in, 22
  government financing in, 23
  housing loans in, 229n9, 230f, 246f
  inflation in, 29f, 30, 221n4
  inflation targeting in, 46, 219
  insurance companies in, 74n32
  international reserves in, 46
  liquidity in, 222
  monetary policy development in, 37
  in monetary policy golden age, 38
  price stability in, 43
  prudential policy in, 219, 221–27, 223f, 225f, 226f, 227f
  repos for credit expansion in, 233–35, 234f, 235f
  repos for credit substitution in, 231–33, 232f
  reserve requirements in, 28n36, 49, 219–43, 219n1, 225f, 238t–239t, 241t
  risk-weighted assets in, 220–21
  short-term interest rate in, 92
  See also Brazil, Chile, Colombia, Mexico, and Peru
Petrodollars, liquidity and, 25n30
Phillips curve, 134, 140
  macroeconomic block and, 151
Policy rate, 27
  on credit spreads, 165
  financial crisis of 2008 and, 1
  forward guidance and, 132, 133
  inflation and, 53
  inflation targeting and, 148
  in Mexico, 49
Price stability, 3, 29–32, 88
  benchmarks for, 147
  exchange rate and, 90
  independence of central bank for, 43–44
  from inflation targeting, 146–47
  reform and, 43
Prudential policy
  de-dollarization and, 221–27, 223f, 225f, 226f, 227f
  loss function and, 137
  in monetary policy, 139–41
  in Peru, 219, 221–27, 223f, 225f, 226f, 227f
  risk aversion and, 138–40
  See also Macroprudential policy

Q
Quantitative easing
  in Brazil, 178
  by Federal Reserve, 111, 219, 225

R
Ramsey-type optimal policy analysis, 175n3
Real exchange rate, 151
Real Plan, 177
Reform
  financial stability and, 43
  independence of central bank and, 45t
  inflation targeting and, 42–45, 44t
  price stability and, 43
Repos for credit expansion, in Peru, 233–35, 234f, 235f
Repos for credit substitution, in Peru, 231–33, 232f
Reserve requirements
  in Brazil, 176, 186, 188
  capital flows and, 49
  capital inflows and, 223t
  in Chile, 19n14
  in Colombia, 28n36, 220
  de-dollarization and, 228, 235–40, 238t–239t, 241t, 242f
  in Mexico, 22, 22n25
  in monetary policy, 22, 22n25

in Peru, 28n36, 49, 219–43, 219n1, 225f, 238t–239t, 241t
Risk aversion, 6
  liquidity and, 199
  prudential policy and, 138–40
Risk-neutral state, 111, 113, 115t, 117
Risk-weighted assets, 7
  in Brazil, 72, 188–89, 207
  monetary policy and, 220–21
  in Peru, 220–21

S
Second World War, 15
SELIC interest rate, 183n14, 184, 208
Short-term interest rate, 6, 90, 92, 92n7, 94
  as indicator of monetary policy, 111
  spillovers to, 95–96, 95f
Social mobility, in Brazil, 180, 181f
Spillovers
  that impair monetary policy autonomy, 94
  from capital flows, 223
  exchange rate and, 96, 119
  to interest rates, 95–96, 95f, 122
  from macroeconomic policy, 174
  in monetary policy, 3, 5–6, 90–98, 118–26
State-owned banks. *See* Nationalization (government ownership) of banks

T
Tablita arrangements, 25, 25n29
Taper tantrum episode, 3, 5, 5n8, 65, 68
  U.S. term premium and, 109
Taylor-type monetary policy rule, 93, 148, 175, 187
Term premium, 109–29, 113f
  data for, 126–27
  empirical model for, 116
  estimation of, 127–29
  exchange rate and, 124t–125t
  impact on small and open economies from U.S. term premium, 116–25
  inflation and, 122
  for interest rate, 6
  long-term interest rate and, 109, 110–16, 114t, 115t, 126f

quantitative easing with, 111
  in small open economies, 112–16
Transparency, 45n6, 187
  in exchange rate, 67, 69
  in forward guidance, 133, 136
  with inflation targeting, 46, 49t, 65, 67
  with monetary policy, 47
  in New Zealand, 65

U
Unemployment, in U.S., 246f
United States (U.S.)
  long-term interest rate in, 112f
  monetary policy of, 109
  Treasury Bills of, 247f
  unemployment in, 246f
  See also Federal Reserve; U.S. term premium
Uruguay, 15, 19n16
  dollarization in, 86
  financial stability in, 73
  insurance companies in, 74n32
  in monetary policy golden age, 38
  short-term interest rate in, 92
  state-owned bank in, 15n6

V
Vector autoregressions (VAR), 91, 93
  for estimating spillovers, 92–93, 116–17
  interacted-panel (IPVAR), 96–97
  identified impulse-response functions, 109, 117, 118, 118t
  for U.S. term premium, 117
Venezuela, 14, 14n5, 15n7, 19n16
  banking crises in, 26
  financial stability in, 43
  inflation in, 50
  in monetary policy golden age, 38
  reserve requirements in, 22n25
VIX. *See* Chicago Board Options Exchange Volatility Index

W
World Economic Outlook, 51–52, 53f